SIDECAR
CHAMPIONS
SINCE 1923

Dedications

My sincere thanks and appreciation to the following 'Disciples' for their effort and commitment to *Sidecar Champions*:

Wolfgang Gruber
Steve Webster
Simon Birchall
Jan Barszczynski
Peter Beeton
Peter Greenfield
John & Richard Mushet
Lewis Ward
Steve & Angie Abbott
Roy Francis
Dick Greasley

A Special Appreciation
To my rock; my dear wife Susan.

SIDECAR
CHAMPIONS
SINCE 1923

MICK WALKER

First published in Great Britain in 2010 by The Derby Books Publishing Company Limited, 3 The Parker Centre, Derby, DE21 4SZ.

Paperback edition published in Great Britain in 2012 by The Derby Books Publishing Company Limited, 3 The Parker Centre, Derby, DE21 4SZ.

ISBN 978-1-78091-211-0

Printed and bound by Copytech (UK) Limited, Peterborough.

CONTENTS

Wolfgang Gruber at the 2007 Centennial TT at Ginger Hall.

Wolfgang Gruber (72) sold his first motorsport picture to England in 1956, which was of Enrico Lorenzetti for *Motor Cycle*, and started to cooperate with Mick Woollett in 1958 for *MCN*. From 1960, again with Mick Woollett, Gruber regularly covered GP races for *Motor Cycling* and *Motor Cycle*. He started his own product from 1968, a Grand Prix Racing Calendar, distributed through Motorbuch-Verlag Stuttgart, the biggest company in Germany in this field, which lasted until 1993. Three books were published from him, *Akrobaten auf drei Rädern*, *Das Risiko im Griff* and *Formel 750 – Die Klasse der Asse*.

Working for the British motorcycle press, numerous doors were open for the chance to take pictures of racing machines without fairings, showing every technical detail – a special part of his work over more than 50 years. Nowadays a freelance mostly for Oldtimer Markt in Germany, the Austrian from Salzburg has illustrated many motorcycle racing books, in a wide range of countries, from England to Japan.

PREFACE

Sidecar Champions Since 1923 is the ninth in a series which sets out to cover the world's leading motorcycle competitors. It is also the first to cover more than a single personality in one book. It has also been the most difficult project that I have undertaken during what is now over a quarter of a century of writing.

There are no less than 26 chapters, plus my usual trademark boxed-sections covering several other notable sidecar competitors. It was also a subject which I've wanted to cover for many, many years. Why? Well, I've always thought that the sidecar boys (and a few girls!) seemed to get a raw deal, both with the organisers and the press, when in actual fact the sidecar event was often the highlight of a days racing and were generally loved by spectators.

Having also acted as a passenger (in 1967) helped me appreciate the unique nature of sidecar racing from the inside, so to speak.

When the idea of *Sidecar Champions Since 1923* first began, I initially considered (briefly) choosing a single competitor. Almost immediately this grew to maybe half-a-dozen, then, ultimately, it had to include every world champion, plus a considerable number of other important names.

Due to the size of the task – and the huge enthusiasm the project received from both competitors and enthusiasts alike – several people gave of their time, energy and expertise in making this book possible.

I have credited them on the Dedications page, in which I have given them the title of 'disciples' – because this is exactly what they were to the cause. And *Sidecar Champions Since 1923* is the richer for their involvement.

Other kind people who helped in some way either with photographs or information, or both, include: Mick Boddice, Philip Wain, James Neil, Ian (Mose) Hutchison, Jonathan Hill, Chris Vincent, Jim Blanchard, Norman Nemeth, Roy Hanks, Ken Barker, the Birchall family (2009 champions), Stan Dibben, Caroline Skelton, Colin Washbourne, Steve Collins, Mick Potter, Colin Seeley, Roger Oliver, Andy Ward, Reg Everett, The Vintage Motorcycle Club, Eddie Wright, Peter Eames, Ernie Crust, Pat Hamblin, Vic Bates and Jimmy Mitchell.

Also to my good friends Rita and Ian Welsh for their continued support.

Finally, I must say that of all the 120-plus books that I have written, *Sidecar Champions Since 1923* has been the most demanding and complicated one I have ever undertaken. I hope that you, the reader, think all this effort has been worthwhile. As for myself, I certainly think this is the case, as it finally gives credit to a group of true champions.

Mick Walker
Wisbech, Cambridgeshire
July 2010

CHAPTER 1

DIXON, BROOKLANDS, THE TT AND OTHER EARLY SIDECAR RACING ACTIVITIES

How It All Began

Once the motorcycle had become firmly established, the next question was how could it carry more people? The earliest examples of the 'sidecar' arrived just after the turn of the 20th century, and by 1903 a couple of firms were already offering them for sale. Most sidecar bodies during these pioneering days were of wicker work construction, mainly in an attempt to keep weight to a bare minimum.

The War Machine

Then, as a war machine, the motorcycle – often with a sidecar attached – replaced the horse as not only an important means of communications and message dispatch, but with a sidecar a functional and highly mobile means of transport or a light assault vehicle as a gun carrier, during the so-called Great War of 1914–18.

Following the end of the conflict, there came an urgent need to provide motorized transport for the family. This meant that not only were there many specialised sidecar manufacturers, but also that several early motorcycle producers also offered their own branded sidecar – usually as a complete combination.

The Manufacturers

In Great Britain this latter group included the likes of Ariel, BSA, Chater-Lea, Douglas, Dunelt, Matchless, New Imperial, P & M (later known as Panther), Raleigh, Royal Enfield, Sunbeam and Triumph.

Of the many continental European manufacturers, the two most important names were without doubt both German – BMW and Steib. The Munich-based concern, who built its first motorcycle in 1923, was also a sidecar manufacturer for many, many years (until the late 1960s in fact), while Steib only made 'chairs'.

By the mid-1930s there were half a million motorcycles on British roads, of which no less than a quarter hauled sidecars, while by 1939 there were three sidecar combinations to every 10 solos. The third wheel had proved it was an important section of motorcycle sales and was here to stay.

A Norton sidecar outfit is helped into life in a combined motorcycle and car event, during the very early days of motorised sport.

Sidecars in Racing and Record Breaking

Racing and record breaking with sidecars began during the period immediately following the end of World War One. And manufacturers saw this as an ideal way of promoting their products.

Record breaking was particularly popular during the 1920s, with venues in several countries including Montlhéry (France) and Brooklands being by far the most popular.

As for machinery, the official FIM-sanctioned record breaking was first recorded in 1920, using motorcycles equipped with a third wheel. These included L. Parkhurst with a Harley-Davidson v-twin (at Daytona Beach, Florida), Daniel O'Donovan and H.H. Beach Norton-mounted (at Brooklands). The Harley-Davidson was 1000cc, the Norton 500cc.

Harry Reed DOT and Swallow sidecar runner-up in the 1924 Isle of Man Sidecar TT.

The first sidecar world records in the 350cc category were established in 1922 by Cyril Pullin at Brooklands, piloting a Douglas outfit. In fact, as we will see, Douglas was also a pioneer in sidecar racing.

A Douglas Victory

Although Brooklands racing and record breaking had been where the sidecar was first blooded in competitive action, the real prestige of this time was an Isle of Man TT victory. And the first Sidecar TT was staged in 1923.

Introduced, said the ACU (Auto Cycle Union), in response to 'popular demand' it attracted 14 entries, with no fewer than eight different marques

A wonderful period shot of 1925 TT sidecar competitors, including Les Parker (second left) and Freddie Dixon (second right).

Freddie Dixon

Frederick William (Freddie) Dixon was born in Stockton, Durham, on 21 April 1892 and left school, as was then the custom, at the tender age of 13. Dixon's motorcycling career began in 1901, and by 1911 he made his Isle of Man TT debut – on a Cleveland machine – but retired from the race.

The outbreak of war in 1914 interrupted many a young life, and Freddie Dixon was soon called up for military duties, joining the Army Service Corps, in its Motor Transport depot at Grove Park, London. Here he rapidly rose to the rank of Staff Sergeant. His time in the Army proved an important point in Dixon's early life, helped by the fact that he was responsible for the maintenance of a complete range of military vehicles.

Like many, the war changed Freddie, and upon leaving the military he was not content to simply be someone's employee; instead, after his demobilisation he set up his own motor vehicle firm in Middlesbrough (where he had moved to in his early years). He went on to build up a successful business, helped by his brother Frank who, although never a partner, was Freddie's manager for many years.

By 1920 Freddie was back in motorcycle competitive events, notably the Scottish Speed Championships (held over the sands at St Andrews) where he was victorious in the solo and sidecar events; but it was the following year, 1921, when his real success was to begin. Not only did he finish runner-up to Howard Davies (AJS) in the Isle of Man Senior TT (on a 500cc side-valve Indian single) but, more importantly for this book, had his first association with the Douglas firm; he being offered a works ride on one of the Bristol-built machines in that year's French Grand Prix.

But as the main text records, Freddie Dixon really hit the headlines in 1923. This was, of course, when he won the very first Sidecar TT with his famous banking sidecar hitched to a fore-and-aft flat twin Douglas, passengered by T.W. (Walter) Denny. He also finished third on an Indian in the Senior TT. Subsequently, Freddie rode Douglas machinery in the 1924 and 1925 Sidecar TTs, but retired on both occasions after setting the fastest

F.W DIXON "DOUCLAS"
WINNER OF THE SIDECAR T.T. RACE 1923

Freddie Dixon and passenger Walter Denny after the pair had won the first-ever Sidecar TT in 1923. The outfit comprised a 600cc overhead-valve horizontal twin-cylinder Douglas with an aluminium banking sidecar.

lap. He took another third in the Senior TT in 1924, this being his first solo TT on a Douglas.

Actually, he had led the race easily, setting in the process the first under 36-minute TT lap. Then a marshal stupidly threw an excess of sand onto some oil at Governor's Bridge and Freddie crashed, injuring a hand. Not long afterwards, he discovered his engine had oiled a plug, but his tool-rool had come adrift in the crash. So he was forced to complete the race on one cylinder; hence a third rather than victory.

It must be said that Freddie Dixon's main interest was in the mechanical side of racing, once saying: 'It was just a bit of luck that I could ride as well.'

And, of course, Dixon not only rode Douglas machines, but also became closely involved in the development of the firm's products.

Besides the Isle of Man, Dixon was also successful at many other venues – St Andrews, Saltburn and Brooklands to name but three. In 1927 he abandoned Douglas, riding HRD in the TT and Brough Superiors at Brooklands. And on the HRD he was to emerge victorious in that year's Junior TT.

When Cyril Pullin left Douglas in 1928, Freddie was persuaded to rejoin the firm as a development engineer. This also saw him riding for Douglas that year. As HRD had gone bankrupt, many offered the opinion that Dixon had no other option than a return to the Douglas fold.

The Douglas factory suffered a fire in early 1927 and thereafter could not compete in the TT that year; however, Dixon became heavily involved in developing new machines for the 1928 event, in both the Junior and Senior TTs (the sidecar race having been deleted from the programme). In the Junior event Dixon's machine was never in the hunt. And things did not get any better in the Senior, as Freddie crashed at the Gooseneck and retired.

Next, after 1928 Freddie Dixon quit two wheels for four and began a motor racing career, but this did not really begin seriously until 1932. He held a Riley agency at his Middlesbrough garage, and it was with this marque that he had his first real success in his new venture. He not only took part in racing events, but set a number of speed records with his Riley-based special; including lapping Brooklands at over 110mph (177km/h).

The year 1936 marked not only the virtual end of Dixon's Riley driving era, but also a move to a new home in Reigate, Surrey. One should also realise that in many ways, as with motorcycles, his car career was more as an engineer and inventor than simply a driver. And during the immediate pre- and post-World War Two periods, Freddie Dixon was involved in several engineering projects, even including four-wheel-drive experiments. Important names with which Freddie Dixon was involved during these years included Harry Ferguson, Rex McCandless and John Treen.

There was another side to Freddie Dixon, and that was his ever-growing love of alcohol. As David Mason says in his excellent biography, *Freddie Dixon The Man With The Heart Of A Lion*: 'It seems to have assumed an ever greater part of his life as he grew older, and is probably connected to his relatively early death.'

In October 1951 Dixon signalled his decreasing interest in the four-wheel world by advertising his remaining Riley stocks for sale.

Post-war Douglas debuted the T35, virtually the first new British motorcycle of the period. Unfortunately, this suffered a number of problems, notably frame failures and engine gremlins. And so, in 1950 Freddie Dixon was persuaded to make a return to Douglas to assist development, this work being done in his Reigate workshop. He was also involved in the Bristol company's return to racing, working in conjunction with Eddie Withers, an association which lasted until the 1954 Junior Clubman's TT.

He died suddenly (probably a heart attack) on 4 November 1956, aged 64.

Listing just some of Freddie Dixon's achievements is proof of just how great the man was.

Freddie Dixon transferred to four wheels at the end of the 1920s. He is seen here (left) in his car racing days, circa mid-1930s.

1. The only rider in history to win both a solo and sidecar TT.
2. The only TT winner who not only won the car Tourist Trophy, but also prepared the cars which won this legendary event.
3. The first to lap Brooklands with a sidecar at over 100mph (161km/h).
4. As a star hill-climber, speed trial expert, sand racer, Brooklands exponent and record breaker, to say nothing of his TT successes, he was the outstanding all-rounder of the 1920s.

   When the Dixon family collection of memorabilia was auctioned by Christies in February 1997, the sale raised over £50,000; proving in how high esteem Freddie Dixon is still held.

being represented. The Bristol-based Douglas factory was the most prominent with three machines, and Norton, Scott and Sunbeam came next with two outfits each. The race took place over three laps of the 37.73-mile (60.70km) Mountain course, a total distance of 113.19 miles (82.12km).

A Dixon Win

Freddie Dixon created history by becoming the first-ever Sidecar TT winner. He was using a 596cc Douglas flat-twin with a banking, aluminium-bodied sidecar, passengered by Walter Denny.

At this time, and for many years thereafter, the sidecar class, unlike the solo, had a capacity limit of 600cc, rather than 500cc.

Dixon and Denny beat off a strong challenge from Harry Langman, with a 596cc Scott twin-cylinder two-stroke. But Langman crashed, after setting the fastest lap at 54.69mph (87.99km/h), Dixon's winning average speed being 53.13mph (85.51km/h). Norton combinations driven by Graham Walker (father of Murray) and George Tucker were to finish second and third respectively.

The Banking Sidecar

Freddie Dixon's victory was, in part at least, due to his own ingenuity as he had produced an extremely cunning tilting sidecar chassis; this being controlled by his passenger. The chair could be raised on right-hand bends and lowered on left-hand ones. But it was Freddie Dixon's language when ACU officials decided that the device was dangerous and could only be used in rigid form which really created the biggest noise. But eventually, and prior to the race itself, the ACU relented. And as Dixon proved, his device was perfectly safe and he went on to show this in the best possible way, by winning the race.

The two other Douglas entries also finished, in fourth and sixth places (D.H. Davidson and F.T. Hatton respectively).

Freddie Dixon with his factory Douglas outfit at Ramsey Hairpin during the 1925 TT.

Fastest Lap but not the Winner

The following year, in the 1924 Sidecar TT, after again setting the fastest lap, Freddie Dixon was forced to retire. This let in George Tucker (Norton), with Harry Read (DOT) runner-up and A. Tinkler (Matador) third. However, there were only 10 entries.

The future looked much brighter for the 1925 TT, with entries up to 18 and no fewer than 11 manufacturers represented. Once again, Freddie Dixon set the fastest lap, at a new record speed of 57.18mph (92.00km/h). But once again luck was not to be on Dixon's side. Actually, it could well have been a Douglas one-two in this race, had not Freddie Dixon dropped out. His retirement left teammate Len Parker to take the victory, with a race average of 55.22mph (88.84km/h).

Although there was to be no more sidecar races at the TT until 1954, Freddie Dixon went into the record books in 1927 when, riding an HRD into the Junior (350cc) race, he became the only rider to win both solo and sidecar Isle of Man TT events.

Cyclecars

Before and immediately after World War One saw the era of cyclecars. Many of these were, in fact, partially developed motorcycles and were often powered by motorcycle engines, and were a direct rival to the sidecar.

W.G. McMinnies at the wheel of the Morgan three-wheeler with which he won the 1913 Cyclecar Grand Prix.

Undoubtedly the most numerous and successful were the Morgans. The basic frame conception had altered hardly at all since its first appearance in 1908 and, indeed, its 'two-in-front-and-one-behind' arrangement of wheels was employed both in racing and commercially marketed tricars of the era. There were a few exceptions – notably the Scott Sociable which featured a sidecar-type layout – but it was a comparatively long time before the 'one-in-front, two-behind' version achieved any popularity and, more importantly for this book, the two-front, one-rear layout was what the vast majority of cyclecars used in racing.

Holding firmly to their independent front-wheel suspension by vertical telescopic units, Morgan rang the changes of v-twin engines. Mostly they were JAP, both air- and water-cooled, side- or overhead-valve, but also at various times the Malvern-based firm used MAG, Anzani, Blackburne and Matchless motorcycle engines, before the fourth wheel was eventually added, 1100cc four-cylinder Ford car units were fitted. For many years sporting Morgans followed the style of the Grand Prix model which won the Cyclecar GP of 1914. It had its engine out in front of the radiator. The Aero with its all-metal, streamlined body followed and then the Super Aero.

The sports Morgans were great machines and the leading tuners of the day were to be seen tuning, fettling, adapting and experimenting and their record in the field of competition was outstanding. Many well-known names in the world of speed were associated with them. In particular were

Tom Bryant with the ex-Henry Laird 1098cc Morgan at the ACU International Road Race meeting at Thruxton in August 1951.

two Brooklands devotees who won races and set new speed records, Gwenda Stuart and Harold Beart (the latter no relation to the famous tuner Francis Beart).

Beart's Morgans were entirely hand-built and, with one of them at Brooklands during 1925 and 1926, Beart captured no less than 20 of 22 Class K (up to 1100cc cyclecars) records. His flying kilometre at 103.37mph (166.32km/h) was actually quicker than anything that had been achieved by any car under 1500cc.

For many years, up to the end of the 1940s, cyclecars and sidecars often competed against each other at circuits all around Great Britain. This led, in fact, to 'Three Wheeler' rather than 'Sidecar' races. But by the early 1950s the sidecar ruled supreme in the racing world, probably due to the introduction by the FIM of the World Championship series from the 1949 season, which besides 125, 250, 350 and 500cc solo categories also included the sidecar class.

Brooklands

Sidecars were an integral part of the legendary Brooklands circuit, which with the possible exception of the Isle of Man TT, was the premier British racing venue of the pre-World War Two era.

Conceived in 1906 by wealthy landowner Hugh Locke-King and his wife Dame Ethel, the Brooklands track on 30 acres of his estate – near Weybridge, Surrey – opened for racing (with cars) in July the following year. The design work for the circuit is credited to Royal Engineers Colonel Capel Holden (manufacturer of the Holden four-cylinder motorcycle) and it took a work force of some 2,000 craftsmen nine months to complete the project.

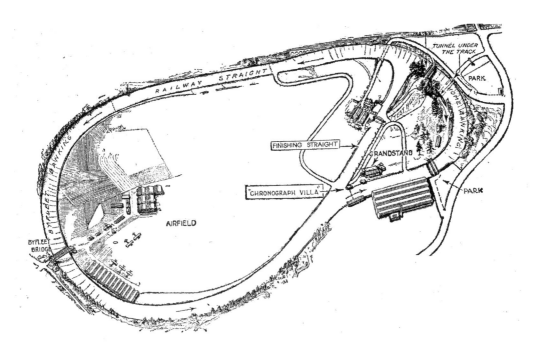

The 2.75-mile (4.42km) Brooklands track was a purpose-built racing complex and probably the first significant engineering project in Britain to be constructed in concrete.

The 2.75-mile (4.42km) track built at a cost of £150,000 (many, many millions in today's money) which came from the Locke-King coffers, was 100ft wide at all points and included two 30ft-high bankings, for it was the intention of Colonel Holden that a car of sufficient power would be capable of a 'hands off' lap at an unbelievable 120mph (193km/h). So steep was the banking that the builders and the subsequent maintenance gangs were unable to stand upright unaided on it, and had to be roped up the rim to carry out their tasks.

The circuit comprised the main Railway straight followed by the Byfleet banking, a shorter straight and then the higher radius Home and Members banking, the lap being conducted in an anti-clockwise direction. From a spectator's point of view this was a very good layout, for the whole of the circuit could be seen from any one vantage point.

So large was the complex that its infield contained an aerodrome, complete with landing strip and hangers. Steam technology helped in the building of this vast complex, with steam-powered shovels, drags and their own light gauge railway shifting some 350,000 cubic feet of soil and laying 200,000 tons of concrete. This purpose-built racing complex was probably the first significant civil engineering project in Britain to be constructed in concrete.

Concrete technology was in its infancy in 1907, and the finished track surface was very bumpy, nothing like the smooth surface of today's motorways. The first motorcycle racing activity was not until 1908, when two machines raced over a single lap, during a Brooklands Automobile

Racing club (BARC) car meeting. The winner, W.G. McMinnies on a 3.5hp single cylinder Triumph, averaged 58.8mph (94.6km/h) over the flying half mile. The first true open motorcycle race was held on Easter Monday of the same year, and this attracted an entry of 24 riders. So popular was this meeting that the BARC put on another the following month, but this time with a prize purse of 25 sovereigns. By 1911, lap speeds had risen to over 80mph (129km/h), and by the time war was declared in 1914 the record stood at 93.48mph (150.4km/h), set by Stewart St George on a 1000cc Indian v-twin. Brooklands was unique in that, unlike other venues, it was a flat out, full throttle blast from start to finish. Once motorcycle racing became popular in Great Britain the FIM imposed its rules and regulations and regulated the sport, but the Brooklands' race organisers remained aloof and drew up their own set of rules by which competitors had to abide. As the venue was a sheer speed-oriented event, non-existent front brakes, alcohol fuels, unorthodox riding positions and primitive streamlining abounded, and in fact were the norm at this unique venue.

Between the wars the Brooklands circuit was a thriving complex, with motorcycle manufacturers, tyre depots and fuel and oil distributors setting up business in the paddock, for the circuit had become a haven for motorcycle testing, tuning and record breaking. These activities came under the jurisdiction of the British Motor Cycle Racing Club (BMRCC) which was founded in 1909.

The 1920s were considered to be Brooklands' golden years, when there was much more racing and record-breaking activity for both motorcycles and cars. The venue, which could be hired by the hour, the day or even the week, had become so popular that the paddock housed a very thriving and active mini industrial estate. At all times there was so much noise and activity that it made life for the local residents somewhat unbearable. This was overcome in 1924, with the introduction of silencing regulations for both cars and motorcycles. Specific dimensions were given for the obligatory silencer, with its lozenge-shaped body and fishtail outlet. This unique shape was soon dubbed the 'Brooklands Can' or 'Brooklands Silencer'.

During the depression years of the early 1930s following the New York Wall Street financial crash, Brooklands was hit very hard, with a lack of motor vehicle sales and dwindling interest in motor racing activities (especially record breaking) taking its toll.

By mid-decade, the major oil companies pulled out and concentrated their money into the Isle of Man TT in an effort to gain better returns from advertising. In an effort to rekindle spectator interest, artificial circuits (taking in various parts of the outer circuit) were constructed and chicanes introduced. Long-distance handicap races gave way to shorter scratch events, but this was not enough to attract crowds back.

The last motorcycle race to be staged was the BMRCC meeting in August 1939. With the onset of World War Two all racing at Brooklands ceased, while the entire complex was utilised for the war effort. When the conflict finally ended, the track was sold off to aircraft manufacturers Vickers Armstrong who converted it into a large industrial estate, building factories on the concrete itself and damaging its structure in other places to gain access. Today some of the site has been restored to its former glory, with the paddock, clubhouse and the test hill splendidly refurbished, a testament to the efforts of the Brooklands Society.

The Isle of Man TT

The very first Isle of Man TT (Tourist Trophy) began on the morning of Tuesday 28 May 1907, run over 10 laps of a 15.8-mile (25.4km) course, and the machines (all solos) started and finished in St John's by Tynwald Hill.

This first course, called the Short Circuit, ran anti-clockwise to Ballacraine, along the present circuit by Glen Helen, up Creg Willey's Hill to Kirkmichael, where it U-turned left, following the coast road via the awkward Devil's elbow, to Peel and back to St John's.

First used in 1911, the 37.73-mile (60.70km) Mountain circuit is, to many, what the TT is all about. The start and pits were situated at Glencrutchery Road, high above the town of Douglas. But it was not until the 1920s that a tarmac surface was provided for its entire length; before this although the areas around Douglas were surfaced, much of the remainder was little more than what can best be described as dirt roads.

Soon after leaving the start, there is the slight rise of Brown's Hill, followed by the drop down to Quarter Bridge, a slow right-hander needing hard breaking, engagement of bottom gear and usually the use of the clutch. Bradden Bridge is the next landmark, a spectacular S-bend over the railway and river, then on to Union Mills three miles from the start. Winding and undulating, the course drops down to the Highlander and through bends at Greeba to Ballacraine – a sharp right-hander – some 7.25 miles (11.66km) from the start.

The course was then very much out in the country, with the road twisting and turning through the leafy tunnel of the Neb Valley, past Laurel Bank and Glen Helen, then up the 1:10 rise of Creg Willey's Hill to the heights of Cronk-y-Voddee. The descent of Baaragarroo before the 13th Milestone section is generally viewed as the fastest part of the course. It is followed by a tricky section ending with Westwood's Corner, a relatively fast left-hander. Soon competitors reach Kirkmichael (14.5 miles – 23.33km), with its relatively slow right-hander, followed by a trip through the narrow village street, after which there is a winding but fast stretch to Ballaugh – with the famous humpback bridge where wheels leave the ground. Left, right, left – the trio of Quarry Bends is taken in the region of 100mph (161km/h) on a modern machine or more, the bends leading on to the start of the famous mile-long Sulby Straight, with, at its end, an extremely sharp right-hand corner on Sulby Bridge (20 miles – 32km). Then comes hard acceleration up to and round the long, sweeping left-hander at Ginger Hall. Through the wooded Kerromoor and the foot of Glen Auldyn, the circuit winds its way on to the town of Ramsey, where competitors flick right-left through Parliament Square in the very heart of the town. Then comes the beginning of the long mountain climb, the road rising up May Hill to the testing Ramsey Hairpin (24.5 miles – 39.4km) and up again to Waterworks Corner and the Gooseneck.

Still climbing, competitors pass the Guthrie Memorial (erected in memory of the great Norton rider who suffered a fatal accident on the final lap of the 500cc German Grand Prix at the Sachsenring in 1937) before reaching East Mountain Gate (28.5 miles – 45.8km), where the long, gruelling ascent at last begins to flatten out. A further mile on leads to a quartet of gentle bends at the Veranda Section, followed by a bumpy crossing of the mountain railway tracks at the Bungalow. The highest point on the course is at Brandywell, a left-hand sweep beyond the Bungalow, and from there the road begins to fall gently, through the aptly-named Windy Corner, a medium fast right-hander and the long 33rd Milestone Bend.

Kate's Cottage, past Keppal Gate, marks the beginning of the flat-out, exhilarating sweep down to Creg-ny-Baa (34.5 miles – 55.5km). Still dropping, the course sweeps towards the left-hand Brandish Corner and down yet more to the fast right-hander at Hillberry.

With less than two miles to the finish, there follows the short climb to Creg-ny-Mona and the sharp right-hand turn at Signpost Corner. Bedstead Corner and the Nook follow in quick succession, and within a quarter of a mile it is a case of hard on the brakes for Governor's Bridge – an acute hairpin – which is the slowest corner on the course. The short detour through the Hollow was a link to earlier days when it formed part of the main hi-way. Once out of the hollow, competitors accelerate into Glencrutchery Road less than half a mile from the finish line and pit area.

In essence, the Mountain circuit remains the same as years gone by when the Sidecar event was run during the 1920s.

Finally, it should be explained that the Clypse circuit, employed from 1954 until 1959, was used for the newly reintroduced Sidecar event, details of which occur in several of the later chapters.

CHAPTER 2

JACKIE BEETON

Jack (more usually known as Jackie) Beeton was born in Louth, Lincolnshire, on 15 February 1915. His father William John Beeton became an engineer, but was originally from the Cambridge area and had been a driver before World War One. William had left home at only 11 years of age and subsequently moved to Lincolnshire. His wife Nellie was a native of Brigg, near Scunthorpe.

William opened a small garage, in Queens Street, Louth, during the mid-1920s; then during the Great Depression he was able to purchase Upgate Garage, also in Louth, in 1930.

After leaving Louth Grammar School, Jackie joined his father at Upgate Garage, the latter being mainly cars, but motorcycle repairs were also undertaken, and bought and sold.

A Competitive Debut

Jackie Beeton's competitive motorcycling career began at a young age of 16 in 1931, when he debuted on an Ariel overhead-valve two-fifty at a grass-track event held in Mill Lane, Louth, organised by Charles Wilkinson (of Cadwell Park fame). And for some 12 months he competed in solo events, including sand racing at Mablethorpe, on Lincolnshire's coast.

Sidecars

Then in late 1932 a 596cc Scott Flying Squirrel and sidecar were traded into Upgate Garage, when a customer purchased a car. This event was to change the course of Jackie Beeton's life. Soon the Scott was converted into a racing outfit. And so began the sidecar career of Jackie Beeton. At first this was restricted to grass, but later the Scott also took in some tarmac action.

The Mill Lane venue eventually became more residential, being within the town boundaries of Louth, and complaints over noise began to be made by the local population.

At this stage it is important to mention that Jackie's first passenger was local man Arthur Stephenson. And that besides the Scott, a six-hundred Douglas fore-and-aft horizontal twin was also used on the grass.

Cadwell Park

In 1934 Cadwell Park (then known as Cadwell Vale), between Horncastle and Louth, held its first motorcycle event as a grass-track on 24 June. This was the brainchild of Charles Wilkinson, who was the son of Manty Wilkinson, then owner of the Cadwell estate. In fact, many questioned Manty's decision to purchase Cadwell, because of its hilly nature and chalk. In fact, at first it had been used to grow mushrooms! The initial Cadwell events were entitled the Mountain Grass Track races.

The Coronation Day meeting of 1937 in the spring of that year had to be abandoned owing to heavy rain and the subsequent state of the course – which by that time exposed the chalk and was thus dirt rather than grass...

So prior to the next meeting on August Bank Holiday Monday that year the organising club (Louth and District) had to expand considerable time and money improving the track.

The starting straight (still in use today) had been laid in rough-surfaced concrete, while the Hairpin had been similarly treated, and the sections which had already been concreted were widened. The race winners that day included Tommy Woods (Velocette) in the 350, 500 and Unlimited solo events – and Jackie Beeton (Rudge) in the Sidecar class.

Jackie then purchased his first Norton (an overhead-cam 490cc single), and this was used from 1938, and was campaigned for the first time at the Cadwell Easter Monday meeting in April that year. In its race report dated 21 April 1938, *The Motor Cycle* said: 'The sidecar handicap presented a nice problem for the handicapper. J. Beeton one of the Louth "locals" had gone into Louth during the afternoon to fetch his Norton outfit, because the 499cc Rudge sidecar he had entered had packed up during the earlier race.' In the event Jackie emerged the winner, to make amends for the disappointment of his Rudge retirement.

Jackie Beeton is pictured here together with mother Vera and his Scott outfit at Cadwell Park in May 1935.

Bill Beevers

William (Bill) Beevers began racing on solos in 1931 at Post Hill, Leeds in his native Yorkshire. And he continued racing until 1960 when he was finally forced to hang up his leathers, as he had reached 55 years of age, and the FIM decided this was too old for World Championship-status events.

After a few attempts at scrambling, a Velocette gave way to an overhead camshaft Norton and on this latter machine he entered the Manx Grand Prix in 1934 but was destined to retire after crashing in thick fog on the mountain. At the time he was a locomotive stoker and spent the next six weeks in bed recovering from the disastrous crash. And with money tight, he turned the Norton into cash. But the following year he returned to the Isle of Man, to take part this time in the TT on another Norton in the Senior event. This time, however, he did finish the race – in 14th position.

In 1936 he not only returned to the TT, finishing 10th in the Senior, but also ventured over to Continental Europe, where he competed against such stars as Ted Mellors and Ginger Woods. Bill roamed the length and breadth of Europe, taking off much more time than his railway bosses could have wished.

The following year, he quit the railways to open his own motorcycle dealership in Sheffield for the repair and sale of motorcycles. By burning plenty of midnight oil Bill Beevers built up quite a successful little business, and one in which he still managed to compete in not only the TT, but abroad until the war started in early September 1939. In the 1939 TT he had come home 19th in the Junior on a Velocette and 27th in the Senior on a Norton. But at this stage he was still racing solos rather than sidecars.

After the war, Bill's name was to be seen in many a race programme, riding in every TT from 1947 to 1960 inclusive on solos and from 1954 in the sidecar event too. His sidecar TT results are as follows: 1954, 13th; 1955, retired; 1956, ninth; 1957, 14th; 1958, retired; 1959, retired; all these races being on Norton machinery. Then, in his final TT, on a newly acquired BMW Bill came home seventh.

Bill Beevers and passenger John Chisnall during the 1960 Isle of Man TT. The machinery is a BMW Rennsport with Watsonian sidecar.

During the 1959 Belgian Grand Prix, Bill Beevers (20) leads French champion Jo Rogliardo.

In fact, the 1960 season, which was to be Bill Beevers's swansong in international events, was to probably be his best ever. As we know in the TT he was seventh (despite losing three and a half minutes sorting out an oiled spark plug!), but results elsewhere were just as good: Belgian GP, eighth; Dutch TT, eighth; French GP, eighth; Czech GP, fifth; German GP, ninth; Spanish GP, ninth. Bill was also fifth in the British Championship race at Oulton Park (the one race for the British title, rather than a series as it is today). And he was also a member of the official BMW team in the TT.

After the FIM's axe had descended, Bill sold his BMW Rennsport outfit to Harold (Harry) Scholes, a garage owner from Rochdale. The latter was sadly to be fatally injured on the BMW outfit at Brands Hatch in August 1962.

However, even though he had been banned from international events, Bill Beevers was to be seen competing nearer home for much of the early 1960s, particularly at Cadwell Park. In these races, having sold his original BMW he built another one, using an ex-Florian Camathias engine, a Pip Harris frame (Bill Beevers never used a kneeler), Jackie Beeton tanks, braking adapted from a BMW Isetta micro-car and a pair of 33mm Dell'Orto carburettors with thin Gilera-type float chambers.

More Cadwell Improvements

More improvements were then made to the Lincolnshire course in time for the Whit Monday meeting in late May. This included the concreting of a long section of the track, and the removal of the competitors' enclosure to a point opposite the Manor House.

At the start of the sidecar handicap, over 12 laps Jackie Beeton set himself a tough proposition for, as the commentator so aptly put it: 'He seemed to be starting about a week behind everyone else!' However, after easily setting the fastest pace he stormed through the field to claim runner-up spot behind R. Wood (499cc Rudge) and in front of third-place man H.E. Caunt (998cc Harley-Davidson). Jackie had earlier won the sidecar scratch race from Wood and F. Dakin (490cc Norton).

Easter Monday 1938, Jackie Beeton and passenger at Donington Park. Note the two-piece leathers!

Good Friday 1939

For the Louth club's race meeting at Cadwell Park on Good Friday 1939, Jackie was entered on 490 and 596cc Nortons. The circuit had now been resurfaced throughout and a record entry had been received, including Jack Surtees (John's father) in the sidecar races on a 490cc Norton.

The Motor Cycle dated 13 April reported: 'Big Crowds at Cadwell' and: 'T.L. Wood (348 Velocette) and J. Beeton (490 Norton) Each Win Two Events at Louth Club's Meeting.'

Whit Monday 1939

As Morgan three-wheelers appeared for the first time at Cadwell, the 'sidecar' title gave way to 'passenger-machine', but it made no difference to Jackie Beeton – quite simply he dominated both the scratch and handicap races.

An additional meeting was staged at the beginning of July, which proved 'highly popular' (*The Motor Cycle)*, with thousands of spectators and a record entry (78), including several newcomers to the Lincolnshire Wolds course. But Jackie Beeton was beaten in the three-wheel scratch race for the first time in many meetings – as he had by now become master of the tricky Cadwell circuit; his conqueror being Ernie Walker (490cc Norton); the nine-lap final being run in heavy rain.

August Bank Holiday Monday 1939

Jackie made a quick return to winning form at the next Cadwell meeting, held on Bank Holiday Monday, 7 August 1939, and in doing so got the better of Walker.

The final meeting at Cadwell Park had been scheduled during mid-September; however, this never took place, even though posters had already been printed proclaiming 'Beeton v Surtees for the Cadwell Sidecar Championship'.

Besides Cadwell Park, Jackie Beeton had also, occasionally, competed during the late 1930s at Donington Park with his Norton outfit. His best position being a third place in 1938.

World War Two began on 1 September 1939 when Germany invaded Poland, with Britain (and France) declaring war on Germany two days later.

Being a qualified engineer, Jackie was required in wartime production, rather than fighting – this called Reserved Occupation. He worked at BSA – not on motorcycles, but the small arms side for the length of the war, together with an engineering role in the Post Office. His hobbies included swimming and shooting.

Getting Married

Jackie Beeton had got married to Vera during the summer of 1939. Their first child, John, being born on 23 June 1940, followed by another boy, Peter, on 24 June 1945.

Cadwell Park 1946

A crowd estimated to have been between 12–15,000 saw England's first post-war meeting at Cadwell Park on Good Friday 1946. Then three days later on Easter Monday came the second meeting at the popular

Cadwell Park 1946, Jackie Beeton cresting Cadwell's famous Mountain.

Lincolnshire venue. The 'Passenger' races at both were dominated by Eric Oliver, Jack Surtees and Ernie Walker, in that order. However, a notable absentee was Jackie Beeton.

Then in early June came Saturday and Monday meetings over the Whitsun period. Jackie's 490cc Norton suffered problems in the Saturday scratch. Then on the Monday he finished third behind Eric Oliver and C.E. Wichman (both with 596cc Nortons).

Next came the August Bank Holiday meeting at the beginning of the month. In this Jackie was third on his 490cc Norton outfit, behind the 596cc models of winner Jack Surtees and runner-up Eric Oliver. Towards the end of August came a Sunday meeting at Cadwell. The scratch race saw Oliver victorious from Jackie, with Surtees third and Len Taylor fourth. Again Jackie gave away over 100cc to the other three Norton men.

The curtain came down for the '46 season at Cadwell when the final meeting was staged at the end of September; the result this time was Oliver, Jackie Beeton, Taylor and Ernie Walker.

Shelsey Walsh Hillclimb

For many years before the war controversy had raged as to whether a motorcycle could match the times set by the fastest cars at the famous Shelsey Walsh Hillclimb. This was finally answered when the first post-war running of the climb took place in early October 1946. Irishman Ernie Lyons (498cc Triumph) proved quicker than the fastest car – an ERA driven by Raymond Mays, the acknowledged maestro of the Shelsey car brigade. Beside Lyons, other notable solo names included: Freddie Frith, Harold Daniell, Johnny Lockett and Bob Foster.

The sidecar entry was headed by Jackie Beeton and his 490cc Norton outfit, who, for the record, achieved the climb in 49.21 seconds on his run, the fastest sidecar performance of the day.

Ansty

Ansty, near Coventry, was a typical airfield circuit of the type which became popular during the immediate post-World War Two era. Organised by the Antelope MCC, itself a comparatively new club formed as a development from the wartime Home Guard motorcycle activities in 1944, its first meeting was staged at the beginning of November 1946 – a month after Shelsey Walsh – and was something of a gamble as the weather could well have been a problem. But as *The Motor Cycle* dated 7 November that year stated: 'The meeting was a noteworthy success', with some 140 entries and spectators in many thousands.

Among the riders competing were ones from France and Belgium, and all the British stars of the period – plus sidecar aces Eric Oliver and Jackie Beeton. These two dominated their races, as they were to do so for the rest of the 1940s at the Warwickshire venue, being joined later by Bill Boddice.

Cadwell Park 1947

The 1947 Cadwell Park season began with meetings on Good Friday and Easter Monday. At the Friday event Jackie Beeton scored his first post-war victory at his local circuit, when he won the Sidecar Handicap, from Eric Oliver, the position being reversed in the Scratch race. Then on Easter Monday Jackie finally won a post-war scratch race, not only this but he also beat none other than Eric Oliver. Then, in the Handicap event he also beat Oliver to register another victory – his third of the four sidecar events at the two-day Easter meetings. Jackie Beeton had done much to restore his 'King of Cadwell' crown! And he had achieved these victories with a 490cc engine, whereas Oliver's was 596cc.

At the 1947 Whit Monday Cadwell meeting Jackie showed that his Easter results were no fluke when he again beat Eric Oliver, with Jack Surtees (998cc Vincent) third. In the Handicap race he was forced to retire with plug trouble.

Then came a meeting in July, followed by two in August, with battle resuming between Jackie and his chief rival, Eric Oliver.

The last Cadwell meeting of 1947 came during the final days of September and a record attendance of over 20,000 saw Jackie Beeton crowned 'Sidecar Champion' after victory in the eight-lap sidecar Scratch final.

Brough and Scarborough

Beside his successes at Cadwell, Jackie also raced at Brough and Scarborough during this period.

Brough was situated to the west of Hull in East Yorkshire, organised by the Blackburn Welfare Motor Club the circuit was in essence an airfield belonging to the Blackburn Aircraft Company (later absorbed into BAC – British Aircraft Corporation). The first meeting was staged on Sunday 23 March 1947. But it was not until the second meeting, run at the end of June that year, when the Brough circuit really began to take off. Not only had the circuit been improved – and also much kinder weather – but Jackie marked his debut at the East Yorkshire venue with victories in both his races, the Scratch and Handicap sidecar events. The third and final meeting of the 1947 Brough season took place in early October. Not only were there record crowds, but also the debut at Brough of Eric Oliver. However, Jackie still emerged victorious at the end of the Scratch race, with *The Motor Cycle* dated 9 October commenting: 'J. Beeton (490cc Norton) and his passenger provided a splendid performance.'

Although the first race meeting at Oliver's Mount, Scarborough, took place in September 1946, it was not until the third meeting, some 12 months later, that the sidecar boys were accommodated. And even then Jackie Beeton was not among the results. Although the Lincolnshire star won his heat, he broke down in the final, the only consolation was setting the fastest lap – which as sidecars had not raced there before was also the lap record for the North Yorkshire costal venue. However, there was then to be a substantial lapse in sidecars coming back to Scarborough; this not being until 1954 – the same year as chairs returned to the Isle of Man TT since the 1920s.

Silverstone

In the summer of 1948 it was announced that, after many months of negotiation with the Air Ministry, the RAC (Royal Automobile Club) had obtained a lease to use the now redundant wartime airfield at Silverstone near Towcester, Northamptonshire. This was also the very first time that the RAC had taken the full financial responsibility for running a race circuit. The first meeting (for cars) took place in October 1948. Then in early 1949 came news that the RAC was to make Silverstone available for motorcycles, and the first and only bike meeting staged at the Northamptonshire circuit that year was held in October – no less an event than the legendary Hutchinson 100 – but this was for solos only.

When the next meeting was run, *Motor Cycling's* Silverstone Saturday on 22 April 1950, sidecars were at last included. And the distinction of the first victory on three wheels went to none other than Jackie Beeton, now armed with a 596cc Norton. Averaging almost 70mph (112.6km/h), Jackie finished ahead of many leading men – with Len Taylor runner-up and future world champion Cyril Smith third.

The remainder of the 1950s were to see several changes at Silverstone, notably in 1951 the RAC gave up its lease, handing the track over to the BRDC (British Racing Drivers' Club). The pits were moved from their original location at what was referred to as the farm, to the straight between Woodcote and Copse corners, thus introducing a club circuit leaving the Grand Prix course just before Becketts and utilising the central runway down to Woodcote.

For the remainder of the decade Silverstone held two major motorcycle meetings each year, the spring *Motor Cycling* Saturday event and the

John (Jack) Surtees Senior

John Norman Surtees (later known as Jack) 'Dad' to John Junior (world champion on two and four wheels), was born on 28 March 1901, the youngest of two brothers, but did not enjoy a particularly stable or happy childhood. This was because in the years prior to the outbreak of World War One his father had become involved in attempting to form union representation on one of Sainsbury's stores, the result being domestic problems, leading to his two sons being taken in by the Salvation Army. But not happy there, the two brothers ran away and joined the army. They both ended up in France early in the war and sadly the older of the two, Henry, was fatally injured when the ambulance he was driving was blown up.

John Surtees Senior had learned to drive while in the forces and emerged from the war unscathed, at least physically. But earning a living in 'Civvy Street' was not easy post-Armistice, so he remained in the army. He spent the next six years in Egypt and Palestine, driving the GOC (General Officer Commanding), the military man in charge of the combined civilian/military commission in various parts of the Middle East previously administered by the defeated Ottoman Empire.

After he left the army he found himself in an identical position to many former military personnel, jobless; however, this state of affairs was addressed when he became a bus driver. Yet, as John Junior recalls: 'His competitive nature and, I suppose, a bit of the inherent Surtees family cussedness meant he didn't stop there. He didn't like the way things were done, so he upped and left.' By this time, John Senior had met Dorothy Cynthia Gray, whom he married at Croydon, Surrey, in early 1933.

Shortly after the arrival of their first child (John, on 11 February 1934) John Senior opened a small motorcycle business in Tamworth Road, Croydon. Two years earlier he had had his first outing on a racing motorcycle, a B14 Excelsior-JAP, at Layhams Farm Mountain Mile grass track near West Wickham, Kent. And as John Junior describes: 'This had a one-in-three climb called Bob's Knob, with a hump near the bottom, a downhill S-bend and an acute hairpin leading to the bumpy straight.' Surtees Senior led on the first lap, then applied a shade too much throttle, which resulted in his looping the Excelsior-JAP. After that, with a sidecar attached, and his wife in the chair, he gained useful experience prior to the birth of the couple's first child. As John Junior says: 'But then I came along and perhaps spoilt it all!'

John Senior did not stop racing, and in fact he was to become probably the most successful sidecar exponent on the mountain grass tracks (hillside tracks in south-east England) prior to the outbreak of World War Two. At that time, during the late 1930s, there were very few permanent tarmacked circuits, though he did compete around the Campbell circuit at Brooklands, and at Alexandra Palace, Crystal Palace, Cadwell Park and Donington Park. By then the Excelsior-JAP had given way to a 596cc camshaft Norton.

All forms of motorcycle sport had to be forgotten when the war came along. John Surtees Senior was now 38 years of age, above the normal recruitment age, but was one of the first to volunteer and was accepted into the Royal Signals. This was thanks to a scheme devised by Graham Walker (former racer, editor of *Motor Cycling* and father of Murray) for recruiting some of the stars of road racing, grass track and trials into the Royal Signals in order to help with the training of DRs (Dispatch Riders) as well as establishing the servicing workshop facilities needed.

Surtees Senior was posted to Catterick in North Yorkshire and given responsibility for both the setting up of the workshops and for ensuring new recruits received a thorough grounding in their training to become Dispatch Riders. As he was to reveal to John Junior much later: 'It was necessary to try and train the lads to have a better than average chance before they were sent to the front.' Obviously the carnage of World War One and the loss of his brother in that conflict had influenced the way he felt about his task.

By the time John Surtees Senior was posted to Catterick, the family was living in a flat above another shop at Elmers End near Beckenham, Kent, to which the motorcycle business had been relocated. By this time John Junior had been joined by brother Norman and sister Dorothy. Since John Junior and Norman shared their father's two Christian names, John Senior became increasingly referred to as Jack.

The London bombing by the Germans prompted Jack to arrange for his family to join him in Yorkshire. Later in the war, they were to return south, while he remained at Catterick. And he would visit his wife and children whenever he could. The pressures of this hectic schedule of military and family life eventually caught up with him, and one winter's night he fell asleep and his motorcycle crashed down into a quarry. The result was a fractured femur and several other broken bones. This left Jack with one leg an inch or so shorter than the other, and thereafter he walked with a limp. By now it was early 1945 and the war was almost over. He was invalided out of the army. The combination of six years of war and the injuries Jack had sustained in the crash meant that the Surtees family's finances were in a poor state. Jack had also been in and out of hospital for many months, but finally in early 1946 he was able to concentrate on the resumption of his business. John remembers: 'Travelling around with him looking at various shops until he found one not very far from where Harold Daniell and Steve Lancefield were operating in Forrest Hill, south London.' With their help and that of other friends, Jack Surtees was able, slowly and by dint of sheer hard work, to earn enough money to support his family and eventually make a return to racing. In fact, a return came at the very first post-war race meeting at Cadwell Park, over Easter April 1946, the whole family having travelled north to Lincolnshire in a Ford V8 car with the outfit towed behind.

The remainder of the 1940s were spent running the business and racing either a 596cc Norton (not the one campaigned pre-war) or a 998cc Vincent v-twin. The latter marque was to play a major part in not only reshaping Jack's racing and business (he became a Vincent main dealer at the end of 1946) but also son John's early racing career.

As John told the author: 'Dad loved Vincents, and at times he would display what I can only describe as an over-abundance of enthusiasm for the marque.'

The big v-twin and Jack Surtees were to become a familiar sight at circuits throughout southern and eastern England of the remainder of the 1940s.

From the early 1950s, when his son's career was in its infancy, Jack slowly ran down his own racing to help his son. Not so much in a financial sense, but with his contacts, experience and considerable enthusiasm for the sport. Even when John Junior switched from bikes to cars at the end of 1960, his father (and mother) were still deeply involved. When one journalist asked recently: 'What sort of chap was your father?' John replied: 'Oh, dad was a wonderful character. He had a reasonable degree of temper, but a great heart. He would always be a sucker for someone's sob story. If he had a couple of shillings in his pocket and some kid came along he'd give them to him. He was a good dad and a good friend as well.'

Jack Surtees died in 1972, aged 71. He is buried, together with John's mother who died in 1998, at St Mary's Church, Tatsfield, a small village on the Kent-Surrey border.

Brands Hatch as it was in 1948, with Jack Surtees's HRD Vincent outfit; Jack is in the middle of the picture in shirt sleeves.

Jack Surtees in action, with passenger Frank Lilley at Crystal Palace in July 1938. The outfit is a 596cc overhead cam Norton.

Hall Bends, Cadwell, Jackie Beeton (18) first in the Handicap race, August 1951.

Hutchinson 100 later in the year. And Jackie Beeton's name was to feature regularly in the results at the famous Northamptonshire circuit during this period.

The Sidecar TT Returns

In June 1954 the Sidecar TT made a return after almost 30 years. However, this time it was to be staged over the much shorter, but still very demanding, Clypse course. Used from 1954 until 1959, the Clypse hosted not only the sidecars, but also the 125 and 250cc solo races. Like the Mountain circuit, the Clypse – measuring 10.79 miles (17.36km) – placed great emphasis on

Cadwell Park, August Monday 1953, now with a Featherbed Norton outfit, much more modern than the previous girder-fork models.

Silverstone April 1954. Left to right: Pip Harris, Jackie Beeton, Charlie Billingham (passenger) and John Shakespear (Charlie's best friend). The boy standing in front is Jackie's son Peter.

rider ability. The start and finish were still in Glencrutchery Road, Douglas, but then the vast majority was through new terrain, but competitors did emerge, occasionally, on sections of the Mountain course, particularly at the beginning and end of the lap.

Jackie Beeton's TT career spanned the entire Clypse period, taking in six years. And he did not return to race when the organisers axed the Clypse in favour of the longer Mountain lap, this beginning in 1960.

Additionally Jackie exclusively campaigned a 499cc Norton and was a finisher on all six occasions. Not only this but he put in some impressive performances, finishing third in 1958, behind the BMWs of Walter Schneider (the 1958 and 1959 world champion) and the Swiss star Florian Camathias. Besides this, he had two fourth places (1955 and 1957), a fifth (1956), a seventh (1954) and, finally, in 1959 a 15th.

Scarborough 1954
With sidecars returning to the TT in 1954, the organisers of the Scarborough meetings decided to follow suit. And the 'chairs' have remained a popular feature ever since at the North Yorkshire costal venue. The first outing for the sidecar class at Scarborough in 1954 was at the July Cock o' the North national meeting the month following the TT. Jackie and his passenger Charlie Billington finishing runner-up to Pip Harris/Henry Mikos; both with Norton outfits. However, there was no sidecar class at the September International Gold Cup meeting that year.

An Oliver's Mount Victory

Jackie Beeton scored his first Scarborough victory at the July 1955 Cock o' the North meeting, beating Fred Hanks, with Frank Taylor third. In addition, Jackie set a new sidecar lap record for the circuit with an average speed of 57.32mph (92.22km/h).

His next major success at Oliver's Mount came with a third place against the Continental stars in the September 1956 Gold Cup meeting. But, then for much of the remainder of the 1950s chairs only appeared occasionally in the Scarborough programme. But this all changed with the arrival of the 1960s.

First in September 1960 Jackie finished runner-up to no less a pairing than that year's world champions, Helmut Fath and Alfred Wohlgemuth (BMW).

Next time out at Scarborough, the June 1961 Cock o' the North national, he scored a victory on his recently acquired BMW Rennsport (the engine having been a joint purchase with fellow sidecar racer Pip Harris, from the Australian solo rider Jack Forrest).

Other British Mainland Circuits

Besides those already mentioned, Jackie Beeton regularly competed at certain other British mainland circuits, notably Snetterton and Oulton Park, both of which became operational during the mid-1950s onwards.

A Successful Continental Foray

Besides his visits to the Isle of Man and short-circuit meetings in Britain, Jackie Beeton made a habit of competing in the Dutch TT at Assen and also

Jackie Beeton's Austin Transporter in late 1958, with the late George Catlin in front.

1960, the first outing on the newly acquired 492cc BMW Rennsport twin.

the Belgian GP at Spa Francorchamps. In fact, as early as 1957 he had finished runner-up to that year's world champion Fritz Hillebrand at Assen. Then the following year in 1958 he had come fifth in Belgium. Next, in 1960 he bettered his Belgian performance with a fourth – this being one of his first big races after switching from Norton to BMW. In 1961 Jackie was third at Assen, behind the BMWs of world champion Max Deubel and Edgar Strub.

His final GP success came at the Belgian GP in July 1963 when he and passenger Eddie Bulgin came fourth behind the winner Fritz Scheidegger, Max Deubel and Georg Auerbacher.

Jackie's Finest Hour

In the author's view, Jackie's finest hour came at Silverstone in April 1962, the scene of the annual international Hutchinson 100 – the 30th in the series. I can still remember the excitement generated that day by Jackie and his passenger Eddie Bulgin as they closed in and passed first world champion Max Deubel and then, on lap 10, Florian Camathias to take the lead – a position they were to hold until the finish of the race. By then Jackie was truly a veteran of the sport, so his performance that cold spring day was even more fantastic.

This is what none other than Geoff Duke had to say in *Motor Cycle News* dated 11 April 1962: 'As for Jack Beeton – he was outstanding, and it's nice to see him gain such a deserved success against world-class opposition. His BMW was obviously spot on.'

A Repeat Performance at Snetterton

Anyone who thought that his Silverstone performance was a flash in the pan were proven wrong at Snetterton shortly afterwards when Jackie put in

Dutch TT at Assen, 30 June 1962 with BMW. Jackie (in great-coat), passenger, mechanic (in white overalls) and Pip Harris (back to camera, with cap).

another winning performance at the circuit's Easter international meeting. This time he beat all the top British sidecar men, including Chris Vincent, Bill Boddice, Pip Harris and Colin Seeley, in both Sidecar races, the 500cc and 1200cc events; he piloted his 492cc BMW in both outings at the Norfolk circuit.

Announcing His Retirement

Jackie Beeton announced his decision to retire at the international Cadwell Park meeting in mid-September 1963. This a week after he had competed in his final race at Snetterton on Sunday 8 September. Unfortunately, that day suffered from driving rain, a saturated track and appalling light to produce what *Motor Cycle News* described as 'nightmare conditions.'

And so came to an end a competitive motorcycle career which had begun well over three decades earlier. During this time, he had competed against the world's best and on occasions had beaten them all.

Race of the Year, Mallory Park, September 1962. Jackie (8) leading Florian Camathias (3) and the rest of the field.

CHAPTER 3

ERIC OLIVER

Eric Staines Oliver was born on 13 April 1911 in Crowborough, rural Sussex. And Eric was not only to become the very first World Sidecar Champion in 1949, but went on to win four in total, and also a total of 13 races counting towards Championship points. One also has to take into account that this was achieved in the days when there were a mere three rounds counting towards points each year! Eric also won the very first Isle of Man Sidecar TT when it was re-introduced in 1954, after a break of almost 30 years.

After Eric Oliver's death in March 1980, journalist Charlie Rous wrote the following in the April/May issue of *Classic Bike*, saying: 'This remarkable man, who so often achieved the "impossible" against riders who enjoyed more powerful machines – but lacked his implacable will to win and astonishing ability.' There is no doubt that Eric Oliver was a true superstar – before the term had even been coined.

Early Riding Experiences

As Eric was to reveal himself, in a series of articles published by *Motor Cycling* in September and October 1955: 'The first circuit I ever rode was small, private and rather slippery. It consisted of a chaff-scattered rectangle enclosing one of the haystacks on my father's farm at Crowborough, Sussex. I was about 15 at the time, and the proud owner of a small two-stroke of obscure make. I hadn't a licence but that didn't mater; so long as I confined myself to the *Circuit de la Ferme*, there was nothing the law could pin on me, except perhaps on the grounds of noise nuisance to the local residents.'

He continued: 'After a while, looking for fresh fields to "conquer", I promoted myself to open meadowland. There are worse ways than this of getting an early training. The knowledge that outsiders can't see you making a fool of yourself allows you to concentrate on the riding without developing stage-fright or self-consciousness. Soft surfaces, moreover, with their relatively poor traction, always make a better nursery than hard ones. For one thing, you are liable to fall off more easily and more often; and it does a beginner no harm to find out what it feels like to land on his ear. For another, grass quickly teaches you finesse in throttle control, which is something you're going to need – and, in fact, never stop learning – all your racing life.' As Eric himself later described: 'Of course, back in those far-off days, I had no idea that I should eventually develop into a sidecar specialist, but accuracy of throttle control is actually more vital to a sidecar driver than a soloist. The reason for this is that a chair outfit is taken through most of its corners in a deliberate slide, even on a road course, whereas a solo isn't.'

Grass-track Action

Eric Oliver's first competitive motorcycling came not on the road, but on the grass in the 1930 season.

Some years were spent taking part in local grass events at Ashford, Hastings and Wilmington and, as he was to reveal later, gave him the urge both to ride on a regular basis and build more competitive machinery.

Thus the first special emerged, essentially a modified AJS described below. With the AJS came regular victories at grass-track events in Kent and Sussex. It was 1935 when things began to improve and Eric moved to a higher level. At his first appearance on the Sydenham Flying Mile grass circuit he set a new four-lap record at over 51mph (82km/h); some 3mph (5km/h) quicker than the previous best. And it was this which first brought the name E.S. Oliver to the press and public attention.

In 1934 the first Oliver Special appeared, essentially a 1924 Big Port AJS. However, later Oliver Specials employed a 499cc JAP speedway engine housed in a modified Rudge Speedway frame. The definitive version which debuted in 1946 used Matchless teledraulic forks, a Norton gearbox, and speedway rims built onto Velocette hubs and brakes. Having served a traditional apprenticeship in motor engineering played an important role in his ability to construct his own machinery.

A Sidecar Introduction

Sidecars came into the frame during 1936. At the time, Eric was racing a KTT Mark IV Velocette and a B14 Excelsior-JAP. On small circuits the Excelsior was a handful, and Eric thought he would tame the beast with a sidecar. By the next year he was good enough to begin his memorable battle with Jack Surtees. During a post-war interview he said: 'I well remember my first meeting with a chair. The course was very small and the track anticlockwise. On the day in question, too, it was damp. When entering the left-hand turns, flat out in second gear, I found I had to use full right-hand lock, to the extent that the Norton's starboard [right] handlebar was digging into the tank. I knew a little about the all-important throttle control, but evidently not enough. On top of these hectic left-handers, the outfit over-slid violently, spun like a top and over turned.' He continued: 'What I hadn't realized was that you can't just *force* an outfit to follow the desired path by holding the tiller against the lock stop and keeping the throttle wound fully open. Once it starts to lose the arc of the corner and run wide, it can only be brought back under discipline by delicately paying-off a little of the surplus power; in other words, mixing some science with the brute force and so-and-so ignorance.'

Graduating to the Larger Tracks

But it was not until Eric Oliver graduated to the larger tracks such as Brands Hatch, Layman's Farm, Leatherhead, Farleigh Castle, Blackmore Vale and West Wilts that he began to appreciate 'the value of strategy and tactics.' Going on to say: 'For the sake of the psychological effect on the opposition, I found it was always well worth while to break the lap record, or, anyway, get as close to it as possible – during practice. Nothing like it for giving the other chaps an inferiority complex! At the drop of the starter's flag in the race itself, I would invariably go like fury, straining every nerve to get to the first corner first: "There he goes again – we'll never catch him". With a little imagination, you could almost hear them saying it.'

Brands Hatch

Eric, together with Jack Surtees (father of John) and Harry Ditchburn (father of 1970s Kawasaki works rider Barry), were three of the leading names in the pre-war days at Brands Hatch.

The origins of this now famous circuit, situated on the Kentish Downs to the south east of London, dates back to 1926, when a group of passing cyclists noticed what they saw as a natural bowl – at the time a mushroom field – beside the road. This belonged to Brands Hatch farm. After discussion with the farmer, agreement was reached to allow the cyclists to compete there. Motorcycles arrived in 1928, but the real signs of organisation came in 1932, when the Bermondsey, Owls, Sidcup and West Kent clubs joined forces to become the original Brands Hatch combines. Their first meeting – on the grass, as were all pre-war events – took place on 28 March that year. The natural amphitheatre was ideal for spectators. As speeds grew, the oval grass-track was extended to one mile (1.61km).

It is also worth while pointing out that Eric competed in the Brighton Speed Trials (along the promenade) during the mid-1930s.

A TT Debut

In June 1937 the name E.S. Oliver first graced a road race programme at no lesser an event than the Isle of Man TT. The machine used was a 499cc

Vincent HRD, an overhead-valve single, and in fact Eric was co-opted into the official factory works team on his own machine (joining Jack Williams and Chris Tattersall). The whole episode must be something of a record – the first event in someone's road racing career taking part in the Senior TT – and not only that, but as a member of a factory squad!

However, that was as good as it got, because, as author David Wright says in his book *Vincent The Complete Story* (Crowood): 'After the customary week of practice it was clear that none of the team would be a threat to the fast men like Freddie Frith, Stanley Woods and Jimmy Guthrie, but it was a disappointment that all three Vincent HRD runners retired from the race, due to a variety of problems.' Eric Oliver's retirement was due to a crash (caused by a fractured oil pipe, on the fifth lap).

Norton and Velocette
In the 1938 TT, Eric Oliver rode a 348cc Norton in both the Junior (number 20) and Senior (number 18) races. In the Junior he had the bad luck to break a primary chain at Ramsey on the last lap. While in the Senior Eric suffered a split fuel tank at the end of lap five.

For the 1939 TT, Eric switched to a new three-fifty Velocette KTT Mark VIII, with riding numbers 24 (Junior) and 25 (Senior). In the former event he came home 17th, averaging 76.24mph (122.67km/h); there were 35 finishers. Strangely, he also finished 17th in the Senior event a few days later, but with a higher average speed of 77.49mph (124.68km/h). At least he had finished a TT – two in fact!

Sidecar Racing
While Eric had used Vincent, Norton and Velocette machines in his solo road racing career, his sidecar grass-track activities had been aboard his home-built Oliver JAP 499cc specials. And although Eric said in a 1955 issue of *Motor Cycling*: 'Before the war, all of my road racing was on solos', the author has discovered that he did compete on the tarmac with a 499cc Oliver JAP Special at Crystal Palace in May 1938. But, in truth, the vast majority of his racing was on the grass during the 1930s.

Wartime
Then at the beginning of September 1939 came the outbreak of World War Two. Eric closed his business in Crowborough and worked in the inspection department of an engineering works. But in 1941 he managed to get released to join the Royal Air Force. His capabilities were soon recognised, resulting in his appointment as flight engineer with the rank of sergeant; in 1943 he

was commissioned and ultimately reached the rank of Flight Lieutenant. He did some one and a half operational tours of European bombing in Avro Lancasters. When one considers that the life expectancy of these crews was less than one tour, his comment to Harry Louis of *The Motor Cycle* in 1947 of his RAF experience as: 'Comparatively uneventful and good fun', gives a measure of his ability to cope under pressure.

When motorcycling was possible during the long years of conflict, he used his Mark IV Velocette in road trim.

Peacetime Returns

Finally demobbed in April 1946, it did not take Eric Oliver long to return to racing – on both two and three wheels and on grass and road. He also, at this time, had returned to running the small car and motorcycle business in his home town of Crowborough.

At the very beginning it was Brands Hatch on the grass and Cadwell Park, Lincolnshire, on the tarmac. After Army occupation during the war, grass-track racing returned to Brands Hatch with some epic team battles between Brands and Wingfield (a grass venue near Derby) and between England and Ireland.

Often Eric rode in 350, 500cc solo and sidecar races all on the same day. In between heats and finals, while he might be riding in a different race, his mechanics would be changing engines from one frame to another. Eric also featured in one of the greatest Brands occasions, the 1946 team race when the Northern Ireland team brought across the first McCandless spring-frame machines. Grass-track racing at Brands was exciting and rugged, with top speeds often reaching 90mph (144.81km/h). A major problem was dust – it making it nearly impossible for competitors to see. In fact, quite often Brands was more like a *dirt* track. And races were run anti-clockwise, not

Eric Oliver (second from the left) is seen here with other Brands Hatch grass track stars including Les Schweiso, Jock West and Harry Ditchburn, during 1946.

Eric Oliver with his 596cc Norton-engined sidecar outfit, Cadwell Park, 22 September 1946.

clockwise as is the case today. Finally, during the winter of 1949–50, a mile-long kidney-shaped tarmac circuit was laid down; the opening meeting taking place at Easter, April 1950.

Cadwell Park

The first post-war road race meeting on the British mainland took place at Cadwell Park on Good Friday, 25 April 1946, followed by another at the same venue three days later on Easter Monday, 28 April. In both cases the sidecar scratch winner was Eric Oliver (596cc Norton). Not only this, but on a KTT Velocette (loaned to him by Peter Goodman) finished runner-up in the 350cc solo races to Tommy Wood (Velocette) on the Friday and Les Graham (AJS) on Monday.

Later Eric described: 'During my earlier Cadwell attempts [starting in April 1946], the Norton outfit's lap speeds were somewhat restricted by the need to use the throttle gingerly on the steep Mountain climb, due to the tendency to flip over backwards like a steer in a wild West rodeo; but this difficulty was somewhat overcome by standing on the footrests and thrusting the head and shoulders forward into a position where the point of one's chin was somewhere above the front hub.'

Certainly, until Eric began racing on the Continent during 1948, Cadwell Park (road) and Brands Hatch (grass) were taken in on a regular basis.

As we have already seen with his wartime service Eric Oliver was capable of dealing with pressure. To ride in both solo and sidecar events, in the heats and finals, meant that he was frequently on the course in two or even three consecutive races. This was *hard* work for which a high standard of physical and mental fitness was required. Mid-week Eric would do: 'a spot of training' with Frank Osborne, one of his sidecar passengers (for southern events), while in the north the passenger was Les Nutt.

Post-war Solo TT Activities

As far as the Isle of Man TT was concerned, Eric Oliver competed in 1947, 1948 and 1949 on solo machines (there was no sidecar event until 1954). During this three-year period he used a mixture of Velocette and Norton machinery.

The first post-war TT race was the Junior, staged on Monday 9 June 1947. There were exactly 50 entries, of which E.S. Oliver (Velocette) was number 10. And for the first time he finished a TT in the top 10 – ninth, averaging over 70mph (113km/h) for the seven-lap 264.11 mile (424.95km) in 3 hours 37 minutes 5 seconds. But in the Senior four days later, he was to retire his Norton at the end of the second lap, when lying 12th.

The following year, in June 1948, Eric went one better and brought his Velocette home eighth. Still run over seven-laps, his time was 3 hours 25 minutes 58.8 seconds, a speed of 76.94mph (123.79km/h). Then, riding the same KTT Mark VIII Velocette, he finished 10th in the Senior event later the same week. An excellent result bearing in mind most of the other competitors were mounted on 500cc machines.

But from the 1949 season onwards Eric rode a solo Velocette in some Grand Prix and European International events to gain start and prize money to subsidise the travel and racing costs, before he then curtailed both his solo road racing and grass-track racing careers to concentrate upon sidecar racing.

1949 and the World Championship

As I began the 'Three Wheels' chapter in my book *The Manx Norton* third edition (published by Redline in 2005): 'Any story of Norton on three wheels is closely related to the four-times world champion, Eric Oliver.'

Denis (Jenks) Jenkinson with Eric Oliver's World Championship-winning Norton outfit, Belgian GP 1949. Jenks and Eric were the first pair to become sidecar world champions later that year.

Hans Haldemann

Hans Haldemann was one of the great Continental sidecar racers of the immediate post-World War Two era. During the late 1940s and early 1950s the Swiss star was often up near the front and in the World Championship series (which began in 1949). His best years were 1950 and 1953, when he, together with passenger J. Albisser, finished third in the title race on both occasions.

Born in 1916, Hans began racing in 1936 as a passenger to Alfred Kirsch, the pair using a 1000cc JAP-engined Swiss Universal machine. Then in 1937 Hans purchased his own JAP/Universal outfit on which he was to enjoy many successes until the war stopped play in Europe from September 1939 onwards.

Hans had first journeyed to Britain during 1938 with Alfred Kirsch when the pair took part in an international meeting at Donington Park, where they led the race until mechanical trouble caused their retirement.

After the war Hans began racing his own JAP/Universal, but soon found it uncompetitive and made a switch to an overhead-cam Norton outfit – plus a brand new three-fifty KTT Velocette for solo events.

Later still, the Velocette was joined by an ex-works two-fifty Moto Guzzi and also various Manx Nortons for the 500cc solo classes. So that from 1946 until he eventually retired during the late 1950s, he was a regular competitor, who appeared very prominently in the results in both sidecar and solo classes throughout Europe.

Of special interest was an ultra-low space frame outfit built by Hans for the 750cc sidecar class, popular in his homeland and Germany at the time. This featured a Haldemann-modified Norton single-cylinder engine with a displacement of around 700cc – and was extremely potent.

After he retired from motorcycle racing Hans had an occasional competitive event on four wheels, but he spent the vast majority of his time working at his motor business in Berne, where he lived with his wife, Hilda. Also during the early 1960s he would not only fly over to visit the Isle of Man TT, but was also involved in helping fellow Swiss sidecar racer Fritz Scheidegger.

When interviewed in 1961 Hans said that in comparing the sport then to his experiences of 10 years before: 'In the sidecar class the leading men are well ahead of the rest – there's nothing like the close competition we had in the old days, but of course this is partly due to the lack of interest shown by the manufacturers.'

The FIM World Championship series began in 1949, with 125, 250, 350 and 500cc solo, plus Sidecars (the latter with a maximum engine size of 600cc).

There were only three rounds in that first year of the world Sidecar Championship, against, for example, six rounds for the 500cc solo class. These races were in Switzerland (Berne), Belgium (Spa Francorchamps) and Italy (Monza).

The Swiss round came first on Sunday 3 July, and the 16-lap race distance was 72 miles (117km) over the Bremgarten circuit. There were no fewer than four Gilera entries, including Ercole Frigerio and Albino Milani. But even so, Eric and passenger Denis Jenkinson (who had joined him halfway through the previous season) won comfortably by almost a minute from Frigerio and the Swiss Champion Hans Haldemann (Norton). Seven days later came the Belgian GP and yet another victory.

Actually, the 1949 Championship was decided in Belgium where, although slowed by a leaking petrol pipe, Eric made it two wins in two races; and as both Haldemann and Frigerio had retired, the title was his. Piloting a four-cylinder Gilera outfit on home ground in Italy, Ercole Frigerio scored his first classic win of the new series, even though the English team set the fastest lap at 86.74mph (139.56km/h). Perhaps they might have won had not the need arisen for a plug change; in the end Oliver and Jenkinson finished fifth.

Record Breaking at Montlhéry

After the 1949 racing season was over, and in the very week of the London Show Norton, race boss Joe Craig led a team of riders to Montlhéry a few miles south of Paris. Here from the 25 to 28 October the team smashed 21 world records, which included both two- and three-wheel figures. The riders were Artie Bell, Geoff Duke and Eric Oliver. Besides Joe Craig, the back-up members included mechanics Charlie Edwards and Frank Sharratt. For

Norton's record-breaking squad, Montlhéry, October 1949. Left to right: Artie Bell (far left), Geoff Duke (seated on bike), team manager Joe Craig (in shirt and tie) and Eric Oliver. The others in the photograph are Norton mechanics and helpers.

about a week this small group had waited at Montlhéry for favourable weather conditions. Then on Tuesday 25 October, Eric Oliver wheeled his 596cc sidecar outfit onto the French circuit. He thundered off, intent on putting the one-hour sidecar record up to 100mph (it stood at 92mph, set by Frenchman Amort on a 574cc Gnome-et-Rhone back in 1934). Even though tyre problems ultimately sabotaged the attempt, he had shattered, during his attack on the hour, three other sidecar records: the 50-mile, 50-kilometre and 100-kilometre.

And far more was to come in both the solo classes (with Eric acting as the third rider) and on three wheels.

There were also a couple of other important developments that came out of the 1949 Montlhéry record attempts. To start with, the tyre wear experienced with Eric's outfit proved that considerable tyre development was needed. And also Geoff Duke noticed that Artie Bell's better-fitting leathers gave him added speed, which led to Duke commissioning a new one-piece set for the following season, a trend which continues to the present day.

The 1950 World Championship Series

The 1950 season saw the World Championship series hosted at the same three venues. The big change for Eric was a new passenger, the Italian Lorenzo Dobelli. The new pairing won all three rounds, each at record speed. Quite simply, no one could touch them, not even Frigerio and his four-cylinder Gilera. In all 16 victories were gained that year, as well as the Championship. After the racing season had ended Eric was once more headed to Montlhéry, where this time he managed to beat the problems which had beset him a year earlier, by establishing a new sidecar hour-record of 97.04mph (156.13km/h).

Role changes and More Rounds for 1951

For 1951 a new FIM ruling saw the engine size for World Championship sidecar events decreased from 600 to 500cc. At the same time the number of rounds was increased from three to five; the existing venues being joined by the Spanish GP (Montjuich Park, Barcelona) and the French GP (Albi).

Eric Oliver's Norton now used a 1950 works-type 499cc dohc engine mounted in a Featherbed frame. Previously he had employed an unsprung frame and girder type forks. The front forks, although, were now of the telescopic type and featured a leading axle, rather than central axle layout.

Any doubts about how the new outfit would handle were dispelled as soon as the first corner was reached at the season opener, the Spanish GP.

Eric's 1951 Norton outfit, a new FIM ruling that year meant that all sidecar machines were now of 500cc capacity instead of 600cc as previously. The Oliver Norton had a works type dohc engine in a Featherbed frame with leading-axle telescopic front forks.

The Oliver outfit lead the pack from the drop of the flag. After three laps he held a 40-second lead over his nearest challenger, Ercole Frigerio on the Gilera four. At the end of the 17-lap six-mile (101km) long race, the order remained unchanged, with Albino Milani on another Gilera third.

The Swiss GP

Next came the Swiss GP at Berne. When well in the lead, Eric had the misfortune to suffer a broken primary chain just before the start of the final lap. All he could do now was to wait until the crew who were second (Frigerio) had received the chequered flag and then push the outfit across the line to take fifth place. Before this misfortune *The Motor Cycle* had described the performance: 'Oliver was at his best. His superb, determined style seemed unaffected by the discomfort of the rain or the slides and snakes of the Norton outfit on the slippery surface. world champion sidecar exponent in 1949 and 1950, no roadracing man is more clearly the master of his opponents and more likely, it appeared, to gain the honours (and the hat-trick) this year.' And to confirm this superiority, Berne was followed by wins in the next two rounds, in Belgium and France. With the title assured, the team of Oliver and Dobelli journeyed to Monza for the final Grand Prix of the year.

The Italian GP

An incident occurred at Monza which clearly illustrates the differences in how life and values were in the middle of the 20th century, compared with today.

What happened was this. The Swiss driver Hans Haldemann had become involved in an argument with one of the paddock officials. The result was a

The Gilera Boys

From the start of the World Championship series in 1949 to the end of 1957 when the factory announced its retirement from Grand Prix racing, the Italian Gilera factory made a massive effort on not only two wheels, but sidecars too. It should also be remembered that the company was the only mainstream Italian motorcycle manufacturer to race sidecars during this era and much of this was due in no small part to Giuseppe Gilera's brother Luigi, himself a well-known sidecar competitor (in trials and racing) during the inter-war period.

Gilera had three works riders from 1949 until 1957. The leading one was Ercole Frigerio (born 7 November 1907 in Albiate). Passengered by Ezio Ricotti, Gilera's quest for three-wheel honours was dealt a massive blow when Frigerio was killed during the Swiss Grand Prix at Berne on 18 May 1952. Prior to this, he had recorded three consecutive runner-up positions in the World Championship series in 1949, 1950 and 1951 (all three to Norton-mounted Eric Oliver). Ercole Frigerio won two Grand Prix; the Italian at Monza in September 1949 and the Swiss at Berne in May 1951. The other two Gilera works sidecar men were Ernesto Merlo (born 20 February 1920 in Turin) and Albino Milani (born 11 December 1910 in Garbagnate, the brother of Alfredo Milani).

As far as World Championship positions are concerned, Milani's best results were runner-up in 1952 and fourth in 1951, while Merlo's came in 1952 when he finished the season in fifth place. However, it should be pointed out that Merlo was in the running for the title until the final round in Spain where he was forced to retire, and thus scored no further points.

As far as Grand Prix victories are concerned, Albino Milani (his passengers including Giuseppe Pizzocri and Rossano Milani) was the most successful Gilera sidecar man, with four victories (1951 Italian, Monza; 1952 Swiss, Berne; 1956 Italian, Monza; 1957 Italian, Monza). While Ernesto

The works Gilera of Ercole Frigerio at the Swiss Grand Prix at Berne, 17–18 May 1952.

The 1956 Italian Grand Prix winner, Albino Milani. He won the race at an average speed of 98.13mph from Pip Harris (Norton) and a gaggle of BMWs led by Fritz Hillebrand.

Merlo (passengered by Dino Magri) scored his sole GP win in the Italian round at Monza in 1952.

For 1953 Gilera attempted to sign Englishman Cyril Smith (see Chapter 4), but without success. This, combined with the fact that the Gilera sidecar outfits were little more than their solo 500cc four-cylinder racers with a third wheel added, meant that real success was never achieved. Yes, at Monza they were often victorious, but outside Italy it was an entirely different story. Although power output, at around 70bhp, was at least 10 to 15bhp up on the rival Norton or BMW machinery, the sheer bulk of the machinery and the fact that Gilera did not have any acknowledged international sidecar stars meant their potential was never fully realised. Later, as detailed in Chapter 10, the Swiss Florian Camathias persuaded Gilera supremo Giuseppe Gilera to back a bid for honours in 1964, but this too was not a successful venture. And although Camathias won the opening round in Spain, a combination of mechanical woes and industrial unrest at the Arcore, Milan, factory put a spanner in the works.

fine, which Haldemann refused to pay. This meant that he was not allowed to start. The reason he refused to pay was that payment of the fine would have meant an admission of guilt; and he firmly maintained his innocence. The result was that Eric Oliver paid the fine for him! Haldemann was to finish the race in fourth position. How many world champions today would have responded in a similar fashion?

The race had begun with Gilera's number one, Ercole Frigerio, who had been Oliver's closest rival in the points table, retiring almost immediately the race had begun; however, there was more than one Gilera, and Albino Milani proceeded to engage in what was described by *The Motor Cycle* in its race report as: 'One of the most famous duals Eric Oliver has ever had to contend.'

Their battle was one of the highlights of the meeting. The lead changed hands repeatedly, even several times a lap. The Gilera was quicker, but the Englishman's cornering simply defied description. At the finish there was really nothing in it, but the officials gave it to the Italian by a fraction of a second. Even so, Oliver and Norton were champions for the third year running.

Problems

Then came 1952, and even before the first round of the World Championships got under way, the three-time title holder was in trouble. While competing at the *Circuit de Bordeaux* on Saturday 3 May, Eric Oliver hit some straw bales on the seventh lap of the sidecar event. He and his passenger Lorenzo Dobelli each broke a leg. This incident meant that the pair were non-starters at the first round, the Swiss GP. Even though he had crashed only three weeks before, fellow Englishman Cyril Smith (see Chapter 4) was passed fit by the circuit doctor and surprised everyone by finishing runner-up after a race-long dual with the factory four-cylinder Gileras of race winner Albino Milani and Ercole Frigerio. Sadly, the latter crashed on his last lap and was fatally injured.

Spa Francorchamps

The second round of the 1952 Championship series was the Belgian GP at Spa Francorchamps, in early July. Although not fully recovered, Eric insisted on competing and stunned everybody by winning! Milani was second and Cyril Smith, who had been loaned a spare works Norton engine, third. Rebuilt from the Bordeaux crash, the Watsonian sidecar was now using lighter experimental square tubing, the wheel diameter being reduced from 18 to 16 inches, and the sidecar had been much lightened, including the sidecar wheel spindle support, resulting in the sidecar spindle support fracturing, forcing Eric Oliver's retirement while holding a commanding lead. This effectively eliminated all chances of his retaining the world title.

With Eric out of the running, victory at Solitude went to Smith, who followed this up with a second at Monza and a third in the final round in Barcelona to take the title.

A Change of Passenger

For 1953 Lorenzo Dobelli, twice world champion, was unavailable due to an ongoing leg injury sustained the previous year at Bordeaux, so the three-times champion, now fully recovered, had been joined by Stan Dibben, a member of Norton's testing staff.

The GP calendar for the new season stayed at five events; however, although Spa, Berne and Monza remained, the German and Spanish rounds had been replaced by the French GP (Rouen) and Ulster GP (Dundrod).

But more important on the Oliver/Norton front was an all-new outfit which debuted mid-season. This looked very different from its predecessor. There were now extensive front and rear streamlined fairings, with the front section blending into the sidecar nose cowl. Since this streamlining had been evolved round a kneeling position for the driver, the previously used Featherbed-type frame was unsuitable and thus a new frame had to be constructed. This was on similar lines to the one used on the experimental Norton solo streamlined 'kneeler' built that year and used by works rider Ray Amm a few times.

Eric Oliver and Stan Dibben with the first Streamliner in 1953.

The aluminium fairing completely enclosed the front wheel, forks, steering head and handlebar. When tucked in, the driver was shielded effectively by the streamlining. Experiments also took place with a brake for the third wheel. Even so, Eric Oliver chose to rely on his 'old' featherbed-framed outfit with its conventional solo-type 'sit-up' driving stance for all the World Championship rounds that year.

Four Out Of Five
Although Gilera did not compete that year, following Ercole Frigerio's death the previous season, the German BMW factory entered the fray, with the veteran Wiggerl Kraus and the up-and-coming Willem Noll and Fritz Hillebrand (both destined to become champions). Even so, Eric Oliver was to emerge victorious in four of the five rounds. The one race he did not win (or even finish in) was in Ulster. After a battle royale between Eric and Cyril Smith – and after he had set the fastest lap – the former's engine seized on the descent into Leathestown, leaving Smith an easy winner. Incidentally, the 1953 Ulster GP was the first one staged over the 7.5 mile (12km) Dundrod circuit.

Into 1954
For 1954 Eric Oliver used the streamlined 'kneeler', now considerably modified. Meanwhile, Stan Dibben had joined Cyril Smith (whose daughter he later married). The classic season on three wheels started in the Isle of Man – only the fourth time that a sidecar TT had been run (the previous ones being in 1923, 1924 and 1925). But unlike the earlier races, the 1954 event was held not over the famous Mountain circuit, but over the much shorter 10.79-mile (17.36km) Clypse course. And to Eric went the honour of winning the first modern era TT sidecar race. His time for the 10-lap race was 1 hour 34 minutes 0.2 seconds, an average speed of 68.87mph (110.81km/h). He also set the fastest lap, in 9 minutes 9 seconds, a speed of 70.85mph (113.99km/h). Leading from the start, he was never overtaken. But a warning for the future came in the form of three BMWs, who secured second, third and fourth (Hillebrand, Noll and Schneider). The next two rounds were the Ulster and Belgian GPs, which Eric won.

Fate Takes a Hand
But just a week prior to the German round at Solitude, both Eric and his passenger Les Nutt were injured when their outfit skidded on a wet track at a non-Championship meeting near Frankfurt on 18 July. Eric broke his arm, while Les injured a shoulder. Without the four-times champion, the German

Oliver and passenger inspecting their Norton, at Hockenheim in 1954.
Photo W. Gruber/Archiv

Grand Prix was simply a walkover for the factory BMW team, their twins now featuring Bosch fuel injection.

The Swiss GP took place a month later. Somehow, although far from fit, Eric turned up. But with four works BMWs in the race and his best practice lap some 10 seconds slower than the BMW team leader Noll, the Norton driver looked up against it. And so it proved; at the end of lap one Noll was in the lead, with the world champion down in sixth, obviously not his usual self. In the end Noll won comfortably, with the British machine down in fifth spot.

The End Game

Eric Oliver was a notable absentee from the Italian GP in mid-September. The fractured arm was still proving a problem and was not strong enough to allow him to take part – a bitter blow. In retrospect he had attempted to come back too quickly in Switzerland. Wilhelm Noll took the victory, his third that year. This left both drivers with three wins apiece. But the Championship went to the German because of his superior placings in the other three events.

After a poor start to the 1955 season, Eric Oliver announced his retirement. Then 44 years old, the maestro finally called it a day.

The Mark II Streamliner during the 1954 Ulster Grand Prix at Dundrod.

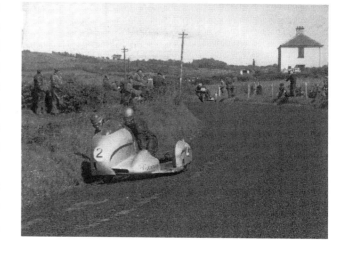

Four-times world champion Eric Oliver took the title in 1949, 1950, 1951 and again in 1953.

Besides his four world titles, he had pioneered several important innovations in three-wheels, including rear springing (1951) and the streamlined 'kneeler' (1953). He then retired to his motorcycle business in Staines, Middlesex, which had opened earlier that year.

A Return To The Isle of Man

The former world champion, then aged 47, made a sensational return to racing, in no lesser an event than the Isle of Man TT, in 1958; however, the machine he chose was a series production twin-carb Dominator 88 Norton with a Watsonian Monaco single-seat sports chair, while his passenger was Mrs Pat Wise of Louth, Lincolnshire. Both the motorcycle and sidecar came from the stock at Eric's own Staines showroom.

Not only did Eric and Pat complete the race, but they finished 10th; an incredible achievement, for both driver and machine. Yes, that performance on 4 June 1958 was one that would stick in the mind of every enthusiast fortunate enough to witness it.

One Last Return

For 1960, the ACU finally switched the Sidecar TT back to the Mountain circuit. To race a sidecar outfit over the Mountain had long been Eric's ambition. And he decided to make one last, final appearance.

This was to see Eric, together with journalist Charlie Rous, travel to the Isle of Man for what the former described as a 'mild lookaround' over the New Year's holiday period, leaving by train complete with a 500 Norton (Manx) outfit on 31 December 1959.

And at dawn on 2 January 1960 Eric, with Charlie in the chair, set off from the Glencrutchery Road. And as Charlie Rous explained years later: 'He proceeded to demonstrate that much of his mastery came from the very pleasure and fun he got from simply riding a motorcycle.'

Charlie went on to say: 'We left the Island quite convinced that the Bee-Emms would be aware of Eric's presence in June – but that battle never arose. While practising for the race, Eric and passenger Stan Dibben crashed at the Verandah when the forks of their newly-built outfit broke loose. Fortunately, neither Stan or Eric received injuries that were life-threatening, but the incident put them out of the race, and what might have

The standard Norton Dominator 88 and Watsonian Monaco, driven to a superb 10th by Eric Oliver, with passenger Mrs Pat Wise, in the 1958 Sidecar TT.

been never happened. Yet I still have the feeling that a different result may well have come up on the scoreboard had Eric Oliver started in that particular TT.'

After Racing

The motorcycle business finally closed in 1968 – on doctor's advice. But before this, during the early-mid 1960s, Eric Oliver went car racing, 'for fun' says his son Roger. Then in the period 1963–66 he raced a Lotus Elan, having his final meeting at Goodwood on 30 April 1966.

Later still, with the advent of vintage racing he went back to his old love: motorcycles. And he subsequently built a replica of his 1950 Championship-winning Norton outfit. His last motorcycle race occurred in 1979.

Eric Oliver died on 1 March 1980 from a heart attack. In the author's mind, Eric was not only the first world champion, but one of the true greats of motorcycle sport; 'maestro' is the word that immediately comes to mind.

Eric's 1960 outfit pictured with left to right: Ben Willits (sidecar constructor for Watsonian), Ron Watson (Watsonian boss) and passenger Stan Dibben. Sadly, Eric's dream of competing over the Isle of Man TT Mountain circuit came to an end with a practice crash.

CHAPTER 4

CYRIL SMITH

C.J.H. (Cyril John Henry) Smith was born in Birmingham on 2 January 1919 and was destined to become World Sidecar Champion in 1952 – the only man besides four-times champion Eric Oliver to win the title on a Norton, or for that matter a British-engined outfit.

Pre-war Days

Growing up in the English Midlands, the young Cyril went through his schooling with ease, leaving Coleshill Grammar School in Warwickshire during 1935 at the age of 16.

As an occupation he chose engineering and in due course served his apprenticeship. During this period he began his interest in motorcycles, which at that time meant using them as his daily transport. And it was via his two-wheel transport that the young Cyril travelled to Yardley to visit his future wife Irene Evens, niece of the famous Worcester football player Frank Evens, a well-known star of the mid-1930s. Cyril and Irene were married in 1938.

Grass Track

During the late 1930s Cyril Smith competed in several grass-track events as a member of the King's Norton Motor Club with an ancient twin-port Ariel outfit originally belonging to Arthur Goddard. He competed, with Wilf Wellstead, at meetings including Lilleshall, Monkmore (Shrewsbury) and latterly at Rushmere on 3 September 1939 – the fateful day that Great Britain and France declared war on Germany, after the latter had invaded Poland a couple of days earlier.

Only three days earlier Cyril had become the father of a daughter, Kathleen. And before the baby was no more than a few months old, the

Cyril Smith (centre with cigarette) at Castle Bromwich grass-track races, 1947. The machine is an Ariel outfit.

grass-track outfit had been put into storage and Cyril had joined the Royal Tank Regiment, where he was to remain throughout the conflict and beyond. Much of it was spent in the Middle East in campaigns from Alamein to Tunis, and later through Sicily and Italy to Germany. His army career was not without incident, either, including a fractured skull when he stepped on a mine.

Demob

Finally demobbed from 26 Group in 1946 at the age of 26, Master Sergeant Smith, his Eighth Army service over and two mentions in despatches to his credit, made a return to the world of grass-track racing at an event at Crown Meadow, Evesham, one Sunday in 1946.

And it was on that day that Cyril Smith re-engaged his association with the sidecar world. A competitor that day was Tommy Dedman, whose passenger had failed to make an appearance. Could Cyril help? The answer was a very positive 'yes'. And so began a partnership which was to last until 1948. And it only ended when Cyril, who was later to admit that: 'I was never passenger material' decided to build his own outfit. This turned out to be single-port Ariel Red Hunter which he raced from 1947 to 1948. He also teamed up again with his pre-war passenger, Wilf Wellstead.

In 1949 Cyril had got the 1934 ex-Gordon Johnson/Howard Hill Norton outfit and concentrated on road racing; Robert Clements taking over in the chair in 1950 until he had to return home from the continent, being replaced by Les Nutt.

A Road Racing Debut

Cyril made his road racing debut at Ansty, near Coventry, in 1949, but it was to be Cadwell Park in the Lincolnshire Wolds that was the scene of his earliest triumphs on the tarmac, winning the Sidecar Cup in that first year, and again in 1951 and 1952.

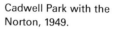
Cadwell Park with the Norton, 1949.

'In some all-too-brief spare time' as *Motor Cycling* were later to report, Cyril built a grass-track outfit for his younger brother Dennis to race; however, impatient of the slow progress made by Dennis, who said it was not fast enough, Cyril took over

the machine for the 1951 National Grass-track Championship event at the then new Kirkby Mallory circuit and romped home the winner!

The Mallory outing was almost the last on grass for Cyril, as he now turned his attention towards achieving success on the road. And there is no doubt that he had chosen wisely in deserting grass for tarmac, as from 1949 the name C.J.H. Smith began to appear at ever more regular intervals in the results. By now Cyril had teamed up with Robert Clements. As *Motor Cycling* commented in their 30 October 1952 issue: 'An ideal passenger Robert. He can't drive an outfit and doesn't want to. Which means he does what the driver wants him to. Which they don't all do.'

Norton

Every year from 1949 until his retirement from racing, Cyril produced a new or radically altered road-race outfit. For example, his 1949 road racer (a grass track machine with road tyres) had a more specialised platform for 1950 with a nose fairing. For 1951 it had a proper Mark 1 Watsonian racing chair.

Cyril used the 1934 Norton with various engine sizes from 1949–51 inclusive. Because the World Championship went to 500cc (from 600cc) Cyril (along with Pip Harris) got a *new* double knocker 500 Manx engine to fit into the 1934 Norton with 'adjustments ' to the top tube. Pip recently said that: 'Norton normally would only supply full solo race bikes, but they were concerned about them defecting to another manufacturer.' Even the Norton records disguise the truth that both Pip and Cyril got only engines – Cyril's diary recording his engine number as 35895, Pip Harris stressing that: 'The long stroke 500s were good engines.'

Brough, East Yorkshire, 1950. Overhead camshaft Norton with girder forks and Watsonian sidecar.

Throughout the 1950 season Cyril used a 1934 overhead-cam Norton single, with Watsonian sidecar. This engine, at various times, was raced as 490, 528 or 596cc, but invariably on petrol. Probably the highlight of 1950 was winning the massive Mellano Trophy at Bemsee's big end of season meeting, the Hutchinson 100 at Silverstone. This was the first time that trophy had ever gone to a sidecar competitor, although Eric Oliver followed Cyril's example the following year.

A Continental Trip

It was in the summer of 1951 that Cyril Smith made his continental racing debut, in no lesser an event than the Belgian Grand Prix over the super-fast Spa Francorchamps circuit in the eastern area of the country known as the Ardennes, only a few miles from the German border. And what an excellent race it was for Cyril (this time passengered by Bob Onslow) with fourth position, behind Eric Oliver (Norton) the winner, runner-up Ercole Frigerio (Gilera 4) and third place man Pip Harris (Norton).

The rest of the 1951 racing season was spent at home, sharing the spoils of victory on the British short circuits with men such as Bill Boddice, Pip Harris and Jackie Beeton. The 1934 Norton frame had been given one of the new for 1951 double knocker engines.

Going For Broke

As far as work was concerned, Cyril had become chief tester at the Norton works in Bracebridge Street, Birmingham. But in planning for the 1952 racing season he decided to 'go for broke' and take in a full Grand Prix season.

During that winter Cyril, together with his regular passenger Robert Clements, 'practically disappeared from the Birmingham social round'

Cyril Smith's 1952 outfit fitted with Norton chassis, prior to the final round of the Sidecar World Championship, the Spanish Grand Prix. He was crowned champion that year.

(*Motor Cycling*). Instead, the pair could be found in Cyril's home burning the midnight oil. One of their jobs was carving up a second-hand Featherbed frame and making the rear end rigid; while the crankcase of the old engine was being modified to accommodate the new frame. In addition, some sponsorship had been acquired from Charles Headland, proprietor of the Birmingham-based Saltley Motors.

By New Year's Day 1952, the outfit was ready for action, while an ex-city of Birmingham ambulance (a 14hp Commer) was being fitted out as a mobile workshop and living quarters for Cyril and Robert. But probably most important of all the pair had been given permission from their respective wives to be away from home racing, for weeks on end.

Mettet

In those days the international racing season got off to a start in Belgium, at Mettet. And 1952 was no different. During practice Cyril and Robert looked impressive. However, one of the slower local competitors veered across the track, just as the Smith Norton was about to pass them going much quicker. The result was disaster. And although Robert Clements was able to walk away from the subsequent crash unscathed apart from bad bruising, the same could not be said for Cyril Smith. Instead he was rushed to Namures hospital in an ambulance with a fractured skull, broken collarbone and dislocated shoulder. The Belgian race authorities were, obviously, very concerned at what had happened: it later transpired that the slower competitor lived locally and had decided to take a short cut home rather than finish the lap – and was so shocked and remorseful at the resulting crash that he never raced again!

No Money, What Next?

Even though Robert had escaped uninjured he was a worried man. Unable to speak a word of French, without money (the pair had sunk their last pence on the channel crossing and journey to Mettet) and unable to drive the van, he was extremely depressed. However, Robert had reckoned without the motorcycle crowd in Belgium, who soon rallied round. These included Englishman Martin Whitney from the Vanderschrick team, the Masuy family and Jules Tachery, the latter the organiser of the Mettet event.

An Amazing Recovery

But what of Cyril Smith himself? Well, he was a tough individual, and amazingly within a week he was back in Birmingham, persuading his wife and his doctor that he had suffered nothing more than a few scratches! And three weeks later Cyril and Robert were racing in the Swiss Grand Prix at Berne, the first round of the World Championships.

Not only did they appear on the start-line in Berne, but he came home in second place behind the factory four-cylinder Gilera outfit of Albino Milani. Even more surprisingly, the Smith entry even led the race for a few laps. And one has to remember that Cyril's shoulder was giving him considerable pain throughout the race. One positive outcome of the Swiss GP was that Cyril had to: 'Grossly over-rev to slip stream the Gilera 4s, teaching him to over-gear' (Pip Harris).

Following this, Cyril received works engines for use in the rounds in Belgium, Italy and Spain – Pip Harris remembering bashing the frame with a hammer to accommodate the large bell mouth!

Next came the Belgian Grand Prix. Here Cyril led the race but was forced off the track when he was lapping a tail-ender at the treacherous Blanchimont corner, putting his shoulder out in the process. Following this incident, he completed the remainder of the race virtually single-handed, yet still finished third, behind the winner Eric Oliver (works Norton) and Milani's four-cylinder factory Gilera. But perhaps the most surprising aspect of the race in Belgium was that even with his problems Cyril Smith still managed to beat the second Gilera four outfit of Ernesto Merlo!

Victory In Germany

The third round of the 1952 Championship took place over the tree-lined Solitude circuit just outside Stuttgart. This race saw Eric Oliver forced out with a broken sidecar wheel bush. Then both Cyril and the Gilera of Merlo ended up in the straw bales early on. However, unnerved Cyril pressed on and in the process beat the early leader Albino Milani (Gilera) to take a famous victory.

Next on the Championship trail came the Italian Grand Prix at Monza in early September. Here, the Gileras had virtually every advantage – home track knowledge (Cyril never having raced there before) and of course a significant speed advantage. Even so, the British pair and their single-cylinder Norton outfit managed to split the two Gileras, with Merlo taking the win and Milani third behind Cyril and new passenger Les Nutt. This change in the chair occurring after Cyril, on hearing that Robert Clement's wife was unhappy actively encouraged Robert to go home, even though he had no replacement lined up; Cyril was a 'thoroughly decent bloke' (Pip Harris).

Then, finally, came the Spanish Grand Prix at Montjuich Park, Barcelona, in October. With a Norton Championship in sight, the Watsonian chair was replaced with a special sidecar, made with the hope of claiming a Norton/Norton victory. Eric Oliver (remaining loyal to Watsonians) won, with Jacques Drion second and Cyril third. Designed by Collier, and tested the new sidecar at the early September Castle Combe meeting by Pip Harris, the chair was fitted with castors if it tipped up – the verdict being that the castors were laughable and generally very poor.

But, of course, it was not quite as clear cut as it might have seemed. Because the frame broke on the first lap at Barcelona! Actually, the front downtubes had both broken. In fact, Les Nutt had to keep hooking his arms through the frame to keep the crankcase off the tarmac when the outfit was braking for the many sharp corners at Montjuich.

Asked why he did not retire when his nearest challenger for the Championship, Merlo, went out of the race on the 20th lap, Cyril replied: 'What? Retire with only another four laps to go. Not likely! We'd have finished if we'd had to carry it over the line.'

The Champion

And so Cyril Smith became 1952 world champion.

Asked if he subscribed to the view that the passenger contributed little more than his weight to the proceedings, Cyril replied as follows: 'Good gracious, no. In sidecar racing it's a three-way split – the machine, the driver and the passenger. Each contributes a full share to any success that comes. I couldn't have got where I have without Wilf Wellstead, Robert Clements or Les Nutt.'

Sport Rather Than Money

Besides his views on passengers, Cyril Smith also said the following immediately after winning the title in Spain, in reply to how much money he had netted through racing that year: 'As a matter of fact, by the time I've squared up with Charles Headland and paid for this and that I'll just about break even. In a week or so I'll be back at work getting the pennies together for next year.'

And the interviewer also asked: 'You think you'll be in the money next year?' to which Cyril replied: 'No, I don't. I think there's quite a lot of nonsense talked about the money attaching to a Championship. But so long as I get a good season's racing and don't finish out of pocket, I'll be happy.'

Other Continental Events

Besides his Grand Prix activities in 1952, Cyril had journeyed around Europe at lesser, but still international, events where he was often up near the front, if not winning. And he did score some significant successes, including coming home first at venues as diverse as Avus (Berlin), Sombreffe Monschon and Luxembourg.

In retrospect, as this was in reality Cyril's first real season of continental racing, the experience gained with the non-Grand Prix event was to prove valuable as the season wore on. As *The Motor Cycle* commented later that year: 'He was gaining experience fast, and the period proved of immense value. Run out of road in a Continental race and, instead of mixing with a straw bale, as you would on an airfield, you were in a voluble Frenchman's front parlour, or a German biergarten!'

The Championship-winning Machine

So what of Cyril Smith's Championship-winning machine? As one commentator of the period described the outfit: 'He embarked on the project with a shallow purse and with a sidecar which had already served two racing seasons. The machine was a Norton, but an unusual hybrid version since it was largely built from second-hand bits and pieces – some of them very second-hand!'

The engine Cyril used in 1952 was essentially a production 499cc Manx double overhead assembly, prepared to the highest standard which the Smith camp could achieve. And, certainly, it was Eric Oliver who was the official Norton works entry, having already won the three previous Championship titles.

And as we know, thanks to the Spanish GP when the frame broke on the first lap, it was the chassis rather than the engine which posed the biggest problem. We also know that frame had been a second-hand assembly which had been modified from swinging-arm rear suspension. But why did Cyril take what on paper was clearly a retrograde step? Well, as he was to later comment, he had no previous experience of rear-springing on sidecar outfits, and therefore considered it would be foolhardy that such experience should be gained in the fierce arena of international racing on European circuits. There was also the matter of his sidecar chassis being of the type designed for fitting to a solid (rigid) frame. And to purchase the correct 'chair' would have entailed an unwanted visit to his bank manager; however, Pip Harris recently reminisced that he himself never paid for anything from Watsonians, and it would seem unlikely that Cyril had to either.

A Problem Solved

So, to achieve what he required and in line with his hesitant nature to embrace rear springing at this time – plus the financial implications as explained above – Cyril, assisted by Robert Clements, converted their swinging-arm Featherbed frame to an unsprung one. This was achieved by locking up the rear pivot, and bracing the fork ends to the top-rear curve of the main frame. This rigid sub-frame was encased with aluminium sheet and topped with a long, one-piece racing seat. The Manx telescopic fork legs (of the latest centre-axle type) were shortened so that the overall height of the machine was reduced by some 2 inches (50mm) to lessen wind resistance. All this work being carried out in a small back bedroom in Cyril's Birmingham home. And as *The Motor Cycle's* George Wilson was to later tell his readers: 'Everyone who has seen the bedroom, the French windows leading from it, and the narrowness of the passage from the French windows to the road, considers that getting the completed outfit out of the house was as brilliant an achievement as winning the world title.'

The Gilera Offer

So, what of Cyril Smith's plans to defend his title during the 1953 season? The month following the Spanish GP, Cyril was to be found on the Norton Stand at the London Earls Court Show. But when asked what his plans were he was non-committal. But behind the scenes he was someone who had won a world title, which even he would have admitted only weeks before he had never thought of winning. This had, of course, been achieved against genuine factory entries.

Also, sadly, while Gilera and BMW were planning works teams, British manufacturers (including Norton) were reigning in. But Cyril refused the overture to join them, including later one from Geoff Duke, after the former Norton works riders and multi world champion had joined Gilera in spring 1953. There is no doubt that Cyril was patriotic, also unlike Duke he had spent the war fighting the Germans and Italians, notably in the North Africa campaign. He also, wrongly, believed that he could still equal and even surpass them on his own Norton.

Cyril Smith/Stan Dibben, Brands Hatch, 16 April 1954. Note early attempts to provide some form of streamlining.

Ever Downwards

With the benefit of hindsight, Cyril Smith should without doubt have followed Geoff Duke's lead and gone foreign. And the fact is that from 1953 onwards Cyril's racing career took an ever downwards spiral. Not only this, but the decision to remain with Norton came at a considerable cost, both in terms of track results and financial implications.

As a privateer, Cyril had to pay his own way. And once the BMWs in particular began to dominate international racing from 1954 onwards the Norton was at a distinct disadvantage. Not only was it down on power, but

Cyril with wife Irene and daughter Kathleen in 1954.

A 1957 shot of the Cyril Smith équipe. Lovely period photograph of an era long gone – not a motorhome in sight!

also, in the case of the BMW with its flat cylinder configuration, much too high. Of course this meant that the BMW with its lower engine height could cheat the wind far better. Also from the end of 1954 Norton retired from actively entering official works machinery anyway.

Expensive Blow-ups
And so until he finally accepted the inevitable during 1959, Cyril was being faced with ever-increasing cost to maintain his engine. This was because the only way he could attempt to be competitive was use all 100 per cent of the

The 1958 TT. As in other years this ended in retirement. The Isle of Man played a major role in breaking Cyril's finances after suffering expensive blow-ups.

Norton's available power. The results are clear for everyone to see – second in the World Championship (to Eric Oliver) in 1953, third in 1954 (with Stan Dibbon as passenger), fifth in 1955, way back in 1956, sixth in 1957 and fifth in 1958.

A special mention must, however, be made of the 1957 Italian GP at Monza, where Cyril (with Eric Bliss as passenger) finished runner-up to the Gilera of Albino Milani, and in the process beat all the BMWs!

The Isle of Man TT had seen the Sidecar event added from 1954 – but in all six TTs up to 1959, Cyril's Norton retired every year.

To help the cause, Irene, his wife, continued to work full-time and, to further supplement the finances, even sang two nights a week with a band!

The End

The end of Cyril Smith's racing career came halfway through the 1959 season – and after yet another disastrous Isle of Man TT. Quite simply a succession of expensive engine blow-ups had forced this decision upon him.

After his retirement he joined the northern dealers Cowies, of Stockton-on-Tees. While his only daughter, Kathleen, married Stan Dibben, one-time passenger to both Cyril and Eric Oliver.

The racing world was shocked by the news that Cyril had been found dead in an hotel in Keswick, Cumberland on Saturday morning, 24 November 1962, aged 43. At that time he was service manager at Cowies and lived in Redcar.

As *Motor Cycling* reported in its 5 December 1962 issue: 'A streamlined racing outfit modelled in flowers' was among the many tributes at Cyril's funeral in Redcar on Thursday 29 November. Not only did almost the entire staff of Cowies attend, but also many racing personalities, including: Bill Boddice, Fred Hanks, Chris Vincent, Robert Clements and Eric Bliss. There were also many representatives from the likes of Norton, Watsonian Sidecars, Dunlop and Perry Chains.

CHAPTER 5
WILHELM NOLL

Wilhelm Noll has the distinction of not only being the first in a long line of BMW sidecar world champions, but also the man who brought to an end British supremacy in the class.

Born in Kirchhain, Germany, on 15 March 1926, Wilhelm Noll had the appearance of a college professor rather than a motorcycle racer and record breaker. The protégé of Ludwig (Wiggerl) Kraus, the 'old man' of BMW's racing squad, Wilhelm was also a close friend of the Munich factory's press officer, Carl Hoepner.

The First Grand Prix
Throughout his career as one of BMW's sidecar aces, Wilhelm Noll had one passenger, Fritz Cron (born 31 March 1925). The two had been close friends since boyhood, both growing up in Kirchhain. And the German pair's first Grand Prix came on home ground at Solitude in July 1952. Here, with the new normally-aspirated 492cc BMW double overhead camshaft flat twin engine in its first year as a replacement for the now banned supercharged unit, Noll and Cron finished sixth, behind the winner Cyril Smith (Norton) and the runner-up Gilera's Ernesto Merlo. Then came a trio of Nortons. At this stage it was not evident just how successful Noll and, of course, BMW, would be in future seasons. Noll and Cron finished the season 11th in the World Championship table.

The 1953 Season
Like 1952, in 1953 there were five rounds counting towards World Championship points. However, the German and Spanish rounds had been axed in favour of Ulster (Dundrod) and France (Rouen), the three other venues being Berne (Swiss GP), Spa Francorchamps (Belgian GP) and Monza (Italian GP).

Future world champions Wilhelm Noll (right with glasses) and passenger Fritz Cron. Photo W. Gruber/Archiv

Wiggerl Kraus

Ludwig (Wiggerl) Kraus was born on 12 March 1907 and was destined to become a vital figure in BMW's motorcycle racing activities during the 1930s and then in the immediate post-World War Two era of the late 1940s and early 1950s. Like many of his generation, Wiggerl Kraus was multi-talented in motor sport and rode BMW machines in both solo and sidecar events. Also he competed on both supercharged and normally-aspirated engined-machines, as his career spanned the era of German supercharged racing motorcycles.

Kraus was also a valuable test rider for the BMW Munich works. And much of the success garnered by stars such as Georg Meier and Jock West was down to the track testing already carried out by Wiggerl Kraus, often behind closed doors. In fact, he had been involved with BMW since 1921, when he joined the company as an engineering apprentice at the age of 14.

Then in 1933 Wiggerl began his BMW racing career as a passenger to Hans Mauermayer. But even then it was not simply racing, but also other motorcycle sporting disciplines – including hill-climbing, sand-racing and even participating in long-distance trials, including the ISDT (International Six Days Trial). In fact, he was a member of the German team for the ISDT in 1935, 1936, 1937 and 1938 – with a 600 BMW outfit (passenger Müller).

From 1938 Wiggerl Kraus was to become an official member of the BMW works team. And in 1939 he won the 500cc German Championship title – his only major solo road-racing success. Then came the war, and it was not until 1948 that Kraus returned to racing on a private BMW. From 1950, as the 'Grand Old Man of Racing' he made a return to the full BMW works team, mainly with sidecars, with his co-driver Bernhard Huser.

By now well into his 40s, Wiggerl Kraus and his younger passenger won the German national 1200cc Sidecar Championship. Then, in 1951, the pair won the West and East German sidecar titles. But perhaps their most

impressive showing was when they emerged victorious in a battle with the reigning World Sidecar Champion Eric Oliver (Norton) at the non-Championship international meeting at Hockenheim that same year.

After winning the German Championship title yet again in 1953, Kraus, now 47 years of age, decided to at last hang up his leathers and let younger men such as Wilhelm Noll take up the BMW mantle; however, this was far from the end of the old man's motorcycling career. Instead, he now

Wiggerl Kraus was a BMW works star both before and immediately after World War Two.

concentrated upon long-distance trials, notably the International Six Days. In 1955, riding a 600 BMW at Gottwalov, Czechoslovakia, he won a silver medal; this was followed in 1956 when he went one better, gaining a 'Gold' when the ISDT was run at Garmisch-Partenkirchen, Bavaria. He then took his leave from motorcycle sport at the age of 49.

Although no longer taking part in competitive events, Wiggerl remained very much involved with the sport he loved and was head of the racing services and jury member of the ERG (the German equivalent of the British Auto Cycle Union) until 1973. He was also competitions manager for the Metzeler tyre company, and he remained in this post until his last event at Erzebirge in 1972.

After his retirement from both sport and business, Wiggerl Kraus continued to maintain his links with former competitors and officials alike, in particular his passenger from the 1950s, Bernhard Huser.

Wiggerl Kraus died on 3 November 1987 at his Bavarian home, aged 80.

The first round was in Belgium, where the Norton men Eric Oliver and Cyril Smith took first and second places respectively. Wiggerl Kraus was third – the first podium position for BMW in World Championship sidecar racing. Marcel Masuy of Belgium and Hans Handemann of Switzerland, both with Nortons, were fourth and fifth. While in sixth position Wilhelm Noll and Fritz Cron brought their BMW home successfully.

Third in Switzerland

The German pair's only other top-six placing that year came in Switzerland, where they came a brilliant third behind the Norton duo of Eric Oliver (first) and Cyril Smith (second). At this stage there is no doubt that Norton rather than BMW ruled the roost in the sidecar racing stakes. And to be fair, the BMWs had not seemed a really serious challenger, but all this would change the following year. Even so, Noll and Cron finished sixth in the 1953 world rankings.

Oliver v Noll

The 1954 season was very much a case of Britain versus Germany, Oliver verses Noll. In the first three of the six round series the Englishman held sway, but in the second three Noll took charge. However, the German had fortune on his side as Oliver crashed at a non-Championship meeting breaking an arm, which effectively put him out for the remainder of the year. With three victories each, the Championship title was decided by the fact that Noll and Cron had also scored points in their three other races, whereas Oliver (passengered by Les Nutt) had not, due to the accident already mentioned.

Showing Their Hand

Right from the very first round, the Isle of Man TT, the BMW team of Fritz Hillebrand, Walter Schneider and Wilhelm Noll had taken three of the first four places – with Oliver taking the victory; the final result being Oliver, Hillebrand, Noll and Schneider. Then in the second round, the Ulster GP at Dundrod, Oliver had won, with fellow Norton man Cyril Smith runner-up. The BMW trio were next, with Noll third, Hillebrand fourth and Schneider fifth.

Getting Closer

At the third round in Belgium, Noll moved ahead of Smith to take second behind the winner, Oliver. Hillebrand was fourth, Schneider fifth. There was no doubt now that the BMWs were rapidly closing the gap on the Norton. And not only this but, as the results proved, the German machinery was proving ultra-reliable.

Victory on Home Ground

And so to the German Grand Prix at Solitude. Over this difficult course, Noll and passenger Cron finally got the victory that everyone could by now see coming, winning at an average speed of 76.3mph (122.8km/h) from teammate Schneider. Nortons brought up the next four places, headed by Smith.

Another Victory

The next round, the fifth in the series, was run over the Bremgarten circuit in Berne, the home of the Swiss Grand Prix. Here Noll and Cron won again, with Smith passengered by Stan Dibben runners-up. Third and fourth places were secured for BMW by Willi Faust (passenger Karl Remmert) and Walter Schneider (passenger Hans Strauss).

Wilhelm Noll and Fritz Cron during the 1954 Isle of Man TT when they came third – their debut in this most demanding of road races.

Three Wins In a Row

With another victory, this time at the final round, the Italian Grand Prix at Monza, Wilhelm Noll and Fritz Cron were crowned 1954 Sidecar World Champions and became the team that put an end to the reign of British supremacy. At Monza their BMW was fully streamlined, in stark contrast to the naked machine they had begun with at the beginning of the 1954 GP season.

Breaking 18 World Records

On 30 October 1954, only a few weeks after winning the world title for BMW, Noll and BMW staff including the likes of the former works rider and

When sportsmanship really existed, Wilhelm Noll (with laurel wreath, extreme right) and next to him the four times former champion Eric Oliver.
Photo W. Gruber/Archiv

By the end of the 1954 season Noll and Cron had not only won the World Championship, but also laid the foundation for an unparalleled series of success for BMW, which was to be achieved over the next two decades in sidecar racing.

TT winner Georg Meier travelled to Montlhéry in France to make a successful bid for a number of world speed records.

Driving a streamlined sidecar combination (actually little more than an empty outrigger wheel) powered by a specially prepared works GP racing engine, Wilhelm Noll succeeded in taking the world's Category B records in 500cc, 750cc and 1000cc categories.

First the newly crowned world champion gained the 10-mile distance record at an average speed of 114.93mph (184.93km/h) and the 50-kilometre record at 112.63mph (181.22km/h); then the 10-kilometre record at 132.17mph (212.66km/h), the 100-kilometre at 113.06mph (181.91km/h) and the 100-mile at 105.95mph (170.47km/h). Finally, Noll gained the one-hour record, also in all three capacity classes, with a speed of 106.39mph (171.18km/h).

The 1955 Season

Noll and Cron did not feature in the first two rounds of the 1955 Championship (which was staged once more over six rounds: Spain, Isle of Man, Germany, Belgium, Holland and Italy).

Faust/Remmert won the first race, at Montjuich Park, Barcelona, while Schneider/Strauss took victory in round two, the Isle of Man TT. So it was going to be difficult for Noll and Cron to retain the title.

And when Faust and Remmert won round three over the famous Nürburgring in Germany it looked all over, even though the victors were

The works BMW outfit
which Wilhelm Noll
debuted at Monza on 12
September 1954.

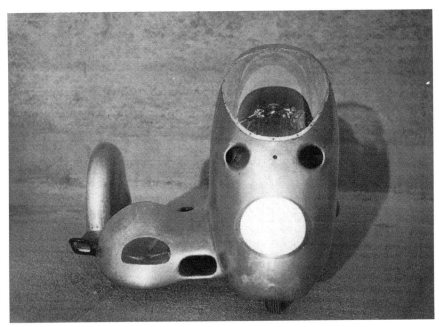

The works BMW outfit which Wilhelm Noll debuted at Monza on 12 September 1954.

closely followed by Noll and Cron, with Schneider and Strauss making it a BMW 1–2–3. By now BMW was the dominant marque, the Norton challenge having faded after round one, when Smith had been second and Oliver third.

A Win in Belgium

And BMW showed that they certainly had the speed over the super-fast Spa Francorchamps course in Belgium, the scene of round four. Here Noll and Cron scored their first win of the year, with Faust/Remmert runners-up and Schneider/Strauss third. The Belgian pair of Deronne/Leys was fourth.

When Faust and Remmert won at the next round at Assen in Holland the Championship was theirs. But Noll and Cron were second.

Victory at Monza

With victory at Monza, Noll and Cron finished the 1955 season as runners-up in the title chart. And with Schneider and Strauss third, BMW made it a 1–2–3 for the first time.

More Record Breaking

A year after his Montlhéry record-breaking adventures of 1954, Wilhelm Noll was back in action in this area, but this time at home in Germany, on an autobahn near Munich. Using one of the latest fuel-injected engines fitted into a machine equipped with an all-enclosing aluminium streamlined shell, complete with aircraft-style canopy and a rear stabilizing fin. These new records included the flying-kilometre, 174mph (280km/h); flying-mile, 174mph (280km/h); 5-kilometre, 168.5mph (271.12km/h); 5-mile, 165.5mph (266.29km/h); standing-start kilometre, 86.5mph (139.18km/h); and standing-start mile, 103mph (165.73km/h).

By capturing the world's flying kilometre sidecar record, BMW and Wilhelm Noll had also become the world's

Wilhelm Noll seen here with BMW's press officer Carl Hoepner after setting a new world record for the German company on 4 October 1955.

fastest on three wheels; the previous best being by the New Zealander Bob Burns (998cc Vincent) at 162mph (261km/h). The new speed of 174mph (280km/h) was subsequently confirmed by the FIM, and therefore Noll and BMW were able to officially claim the 'world's fastest' tag.

This was to prove the swansong of BMW factory record-breaking – for two reasons. The first was financial: in the period 1956–60 BMW and the rest of the German motorcycle industry went through a period of severe recession. The second was that on the one hand the prestige of gaining records was falling, while the costs were rising! So from then on BMW left it to privateers to carry the flag in this area.

The 1956 Racing Season

And so Wilhelm Noll ventured into what was to prove not only his second Championship-winning season, but his final one as a sidecar racer. As in 1954, Noll and his passenger Fritz Cron won three of the six rounds; these were in Belgium (round three), Germany (round four) and Ulster (round five). In addition the pair came home as runners-up (in round two, the Dutch TT) to the winners Fritz Hillebrand and Manfred Grünewald. After winning their second world title they retired from road racing.

During 1957 Wilhelm Noll tried his hand at car racing, but without success.

CHAPTER 6

WILLI FAUST

Willi Faust, who was born on 10 January 1924 in the German town of Fulda, won a single World Championship title, in 1955, together with a trio of Grand Prix events that same year. But during his successful year, none other than four-times champion Eric Oliver was quoted as saying that the German was the best there was at that time. This remark came after Faust and his passenger Karl Remmert had beaten both Oliver and fellow Norton world champion Cyril Smith at Barcelona in the opening round of the 1954 series, the Spanish Grand Prix.

One has to remember that of all the Grand Prix racing circuits, the Montjuich Park, Barcelona, course was the one with the tightest bends and placed everything on riding skill. Yes, the Isle of Man TT course and the Nürburgring were much longer, but they placed much more emphasis on speed, whereas the Spanish course was slow by comparison, due to its undulating nature and tortuous hairpins.

Trained as a mechanic, Willi Faust began his competitive motorcycle career on a solo 250cc split-single German Triumph (TWN) aged 27, in 1951. In his first five races he scored five victories. And that same year he competed on a 500cc BMW flat-twin, in both solo and sidecar classes. He then teamed up with passenger Karl Remmert in 1952, and the pair were to stay together for the rest of their respective racing careers, which was to from then on be exclusively on three wheels.

Willi Faust during one of his earlier sidecar outings – still BMW mounted.

No Points in the Isle Of Man

After setting the fastest lap Faust and Remmert, the BMW pair, were to retire in the Isle of Man TT, after they collided late on in the race; however, they made amends in the next race, the German Grand Prix at the magnificent 14.165-mile (22.791km) Nürburgring, for the first time since 1931.

And right from the start it looked like a BMW benefit, as neither Eric Oliver or Cyril Smith started. From the start the Australian Bob Mitchell (Norton) led briefly, before the BMWs went past, headed by Faust and Remmert. Soon they pulled out a significant lead over their BMW teammates Noll/Cron and Schneider/Strauss. And that was how it finished, Faust and Remmert winning with an average speed of 72.53mph (122.52km/h). They also set the fastest lap at 73.15mph (117.69km/h).

Controversy in Belgium

At the next round, at Spa Francorchamps, Belgium, there was considerable controversy, when just as Noll and Faust were preparing to do battle over the eighth and final lap, an official wrongly displayed the flag and the race was stopped – a lap early! At first the FIM took the approach that as the race had not run the required 100km (62.1 miles), that it would not count towards the Championship title. But thankfully, the officials saw reason, and this decision was later overturned. Also it is worth mentioning that before he had been forced to retire with a broken fuel pump Cyril Smith (Norton) might well have emerged victorious; his only consolation was that he set the fastest lap at 98.43mph (158.37km/h).

Victory At Assen

Willi Faust and Karl Remmert scored their third and final Grand Prix in the Dutch TT at Assen. There was an excellent entry. But it was not to be Norton's day as both Oliver and Smith retired, both with broken valves. Probably caused in over-revving their engines in a vain attempt to keep the BMWs in their sight.

Wilhelm Noll had led Willi Faust, but on the final lap, Faust assumed the lead at de Strubben and in an attempt to re-pass, Noll made an error and went off the track. This left Faust a comfortable winner, but Noll managed to recover and still finished second, albeit some 15 seconds adrift.

A Retirement in Italy

Both Eric Oliver and Cyril Smith were non-starters at the final round of the 1955 series at Monza, in Italy. However, in their place

Faust and Karl Remmert leading the field at the Nürburgring in 1955 on the streamlined works-supported BMW. Photo W. Gruber/Archiv

Willi Faust (centre) and passenger Karl Remmert after winning the German Grand Prix at the Nürburgring in 1955.

A postcard celebrating the 1955 sidecar world champions, Willi Faust and Karl Remmert.

was the four-cylinder Gilera of Albini Milani. Milani was the last to get away, but after five laps had passed the entire field, including the works BMWs of Noll, Schneider and Willi Faust. Milani quickly opened up a massive lead over his German opponents, only to suffer a rear-wheel puncture, three laps to the finish. Willi Faust then retired, leaving Noll to take the victory from Schneider and Jacques Drion (Norton). Into fourth spot came the colourful Florian Camathias to secure his first-ever World Championship points.

An October 1955 Castrol advert showing the oil company's world champions that year on two, three and four wheels.

Champions

But even before Italy, Willi Faust and Karl Remmert had secured the Championship title. So even with his Monza victory Noll could only amass a total of 28, compared to Faust/Remmert's 30.

But their glory was to be short lived, as not long after the Championship season had come to a close, while carrying out official BMW testing at the Hockenheim circuit on 18 April 1956, the champions, piloting a completely new BMW outfit, crashed at a high-speed corner. In the accident Karl Remmert lost his life, while Willi Faust suffered severe injuries (brain contusion and two broken legs). After months in hospital, including six weeks in a coma, Willi Faust made a recovery. And he subsequently opened a petrol station in his home town of Fulda. He also retained his interest in motorcycle racing, but only as a spectator.

He died on 27 November 1992, following a long battle with cancer.

CHAPTER 7

FRITZ HILLEBRAND

Next in the line of 1950s BMW sidecar world champions came the former Luftwaffe pilot, Fritz Hillebrand, and his passenger Manfred Grünewald. The pair totally dominated the 1957 title series, with victories in the first three rounds, and so, with five rounds that year, could not be caught. However, after establishing the unassailable lead, and coming home third in Belgium, the pairing suffered an horrendous crash while competing in a non-Championship international meeting in Bilbao, Spain, in August that year. In the accident Hillebrand suffered fatal injuries; Grünewald sustained head and chest wounds from which he was to recover but decided not to race again. Fritz Hillebrand was buried in his home town of Amberg, Bavaria, the funeral being attended by many well-known racers, both sidecar and solo and by representation from the BMW factory.

Early Days

Friedrich (Fritz) Hillebrand was born in Erlangen, Munich, on 22 November 1917, Fritz was always mechanically minded. And on leaving school at 16 years of age he joined a local motorcycle dealer as an apprentice mechanic and attended night school to further his engineering experience.

Strangely, his first motorcycles were British rather than German, the first a late 1920s three-fifty Bradshaw, followed by a much-loved Velocette GTP 250cc two-stroke.

First Sidecar Action

In 1935, at 17, Fritz had his first taste of sidecar racing, as a passenger to Hans Strohmeier, the latter campaigning an NSU with a Walter Moore-designed overhead camshaft single-cylinder engine. But then, in 1936, the young Fritz decided to set out to be a civil airline pilot.

By then, however, the Nazis were firmly in control of Germany, and aviation supremo Hermann Goring decreed that all potential civil airline pilots would have to serve a four-year spell in the Luftwaffe. And so Fritz became a member of the fledgling German Air Force and, luckily, was posted quite near to his Bavarian home.

A Switch to Speedway

Joining the Luftwaffe meant that Fritz was no longer able to keep up his passenger duties for Strohmeier, and so his competitive instincts were instead channelled into speedway-type events which were then flourishing in southern Germany, Czechoslovakia and Yugoslavia at this time. For this new sport Fritz raced a 350cc JAP and a 250cc supercharged split-single Puch two-stroke, with considerable success.

War Clouds

But war clouds were gathering, and in September 1939 the dirt bikes were put away, never to be raced by Fritz again.

During the war, Fritz Hillebrand flew an assortment of aircraft, ranging from heavy transports to lightweight fighters. But without doubt it was the unspectacular but highly dangerous job of flying the tri-motor Junkers Ju52s fully laden with petrol from Sicily to North Africa to keep Rommel's tanks running, which was the most stressful. He did this for two years (1941–43). And Fritz later recalled that the most dangerous aspect was the return trip – one incendiary bullet in the highly explosive mixture that lingered in the empty cans and...no more Junkers or Fritz!

Next he flew twin-engined Junkers 88 and 188s on Atlantic patrols in the support of the U-boats, the idea being to bring down Allied aircraft who were searching for German submariners.

Shot Down

Two days after the D-Day invasion of Europe in June 1944, Fritz was shot down when strafing the landing beaches by a Spitfire. But he managed to crash land and was taken prisoner; he escaped during a German artillery barrage and managed to reach German lines.

After his escape, Fritz was sent to northern Germany to help try and stem the daylight bombing raids by the Americans which were paralysing the Ruhr and Hamburg areas. Fuel was so short by now that Fritz flew very few missions in the new Focke Wulf 190D fighter, and then when the Allies finally reached the Rhine he was shot down by flak when attacking a bridge and taken prisoner.

It was in this last crash that Fritz was to injure his left ankle – the very joint which is all important when it comes to speedway.

Working For The Americans

After two years working for the Americans as a supervisor in charge of German mechanics who serviced American vehicles, Fritz moved with the

Americans to Amberg, near Munich, and when his compulsory service ended, made this Bavarian town his home.

With dirt-track racing now out of the question, Fritz turned to road racing. As he had not raced for eight years (it was now 1947), Fritz decided sidecar racing was the way to go. And so for the next three years he campaigned an NSU very similar to the one used by Strohmeier in pre-war days. But even though it gave him three years of reliable service the pre-war bike was simply not competitive enough.

The First BMW

So, in 1950, Fritz constructed a totally home-brewed sidecar racing machine from surplus war material BMW components. The frame was essentially an R51 with 16-inch wheels from an ex Afrika Corps R75. The 745cc ohv transverse twin also came from the R75 and, suitably modified, gave a maximum speed of some 105mph (169km/h) at 7,000rpm – with no streamlining. On this machine Fritz went from success to success, culminating in being crowned 1952 German Champion.

At the end of 1952 the 750cc class was abandoned in favour of the 500cc engine size. So, retaining the same frame, Fritz modified his 750 engine and, with hotter cams and new carburation, created a faster higher-revving power unit than the old 750 – even from the 500s very first outing.

Other competitors and officials thought he was still using a 750 – and soon an official engine measuring took place...however, it was found to be within the 500cc limit!

The First Rennsport

At the end of 1953 Fritz put in an order for one of the first pukka racing Rennsport dohc engines from the BMW works. And with this he made his first journey to the Isle of Man in 1954 and immediately proved his and the machines worth by taking runner-up spot behind Eric Oliver, the four-times world champion.

Following the TT, Hillebrand went on to score points in Ulster, Belgium and Italy, finally finishing the season fifth in the points standing – and at his first-ever attempt at this level.

Fritz Hillebrand and passenger Prätorias, Schotten, 1950. The photograph shows the totally home-built outfit which Fritz had constructed earlier that year, using surplus BMW components including those from an ex-Africa Corps R75.

Fritz Hillebrand and Manfred Grünewald, the pair went on to become world champions in 1957.
Photo W. Gruber/Archiv

An Untimely Crash

But if 1954 had ended well for the Hillebrand team (he only ever had one passenger, Manfred Grünewald), 1955 began in disaster, when they crashed in the opening round in Spain. Fritz had broken a thigh bone in the pile-up; normally such an injury can take a full six months to mend, but an operation by one of Germany's leading surgeons out Fritz back in action in half this time.

In his very first comeback race the pair beat Julianne Deronne (BMW) at Gedinne in Belgium; however, the accident had destroyed all hopes of a World Championship placing and so Hillebrand and Grünewald had to wait until the following year to make a return to the world stage.

A Good Start

The 1956 Championship season got under way in the Isle of Man. Fritz won the TT on his privately entered and run BMW Rennsport outfit, after Noll piloting the works model retired when leading. Fritz followed this up by winning the next round, the Dutch TT at Assen (beating Noll in the process!). Then, the following week in Belgium, all hopes of victory evaporated when his spark plugs played up, dropping him to fourth.

The next round was on home ground at Solitude, and the factory had finally given Fritz a fuel injection motor, but Noll came out on top with Hillebrand second.

It now all rested on the Ulster GP in August. But when well in the lead at Dundrod, Fritz had the misfortune to retire, leaving Noll to win both the race and the Championship.

1957

In 1957 Fritz made no mistake, and by winning the first three rounds of the five-round series (at Hockenheim, the Isle of Man and at Assen) he was declared the first world champion of 1957. In Belgium he cruised round to finish a steady third to cement his position.

Hillebrand and passenger
Manfred Grünewald
finishing a fine second to
four-times world
champion Eric Oliver
during the 1954 Isle of
Man TT.

These successes had been achieved on the previous year's works BMW – Fritz having purchased it from the factory following Noll's retirement. He had modified this over the winter, fitting his own flywheels and replacing the fuel injectors with conventional carburettors.

The Fatal Crash

On 24 August 1957 a shocked nation heard the tragic news that their newly crowned world champion had lost his life during practice for an

Winner of the Ray B.
Westover Trophy and the
Overseas Newcomer
Trophy, 1954 TT, Fritz
Hillebrand and Manfred
Grünewald (front left),
plus Cron, Straus, Noll
and Schneider. Photo W.
Gruber/Archiv

Hillebrand and Grünewald
with their streamlined
BMW outfit at Monza.
Photo W. Gruber/Archiv

Ex-Luftwaffe pilot Fritz Hillebrand (then 40 years old) partnered by Manfred Grünewald in the course of winning the 1957 Sidecar TT. Their average speed of 71.89mph was a new record.

international meeting at Bilbao in Spain. Fritz was killed instantly when his machine struck a kilometre stone on a fast section of the course, throwing him into a lamp-post. His passenger Manfred Grünewald received injuries to the head and chest but was to make a good recovery, although his racing career was at an end.

The motorcycle racing scene had lost one of its brightest stars.

Fritz Hillebrand Strasse – a recent photograph showing the respect shown by his home town of Amberg, Bavaria.

CHAPTER 8
WALTER SCHNEIDER

Walter Schneider was the last of the four German BMW world champions of the 1950s, following Wilhelm Noll, Willi Faust and Fritz Hillebrand.

Born in Weidenau on 15 January 1927, Walter Schneider, together with his passenger Hans Strauss, took the final two Championships of the 1950s, in 1958 and 1959. They won a total of seven Grand Prix races, beginning in June 1955 with the Isle of Man TT and ending with the Belgian Grand Prix in July 1959. In fact, six of the seven races were at these two venues (Isle of Man TT 1955, 1958 and 1959, Belgium GP 1957, 1958 and 1959). Their only other victory in the Championship series came at the German Grand Prix (Nürburgring) in 1958.

How It All Began
Walter Schneider began his racing career in 1949 as passenger for the Berlin driver Kurt Bäch. From 1950, the trained motor mechanic was competing as the driver of his own BMW R66. And was to soon score victories in Dieburg, Lorsch and Recklinghausen. In 1951 Walter won again at Dieburg, and later that year at Lizenzfahrer. Two years later he raced a Norton and with this outfit became one of the top German privateers.

Then came 1954 and BMW introduced its 500cc RS54 Rennsport racing machine. And with this Walter Schneider and Hans Strauss joined forces.

An Immediate Impact
Together with the BMW, the pair made an immediate impact on the World Championship racing scene. The first race was at round one of the 1954 series, the Isle of Man TT (the first held there since the mid-1920s). Here they came home an impressive fourth; one place behind Wilhelm Noll and Fritz Cron (destined to become world champions that year). Then, at round two in Ulster, Schneider and Strauss finished fifth, behind the BMWs of

Walter Schneider (BMW) with passenger Hans Strauss during the 1955 Isle of Man TT, which they won, with Englishmen Bill Boddice (Norton) runner-up and Pip Harris (Matchless) third.

Noll/Cron (third) and Hillebrand/Grünewald (fourth) and the 1–2 Nortons of the winner Eric Oliver and runner-up Cyril Smith.

This result was repeated at the next round in Belgium a week later.

The Highlight

But the highlight to the Schneider/Strauss season was without a shadow of a doubt at round four – the German Grand Prix at Solitude. Here, Noll and Cron scored the first ever BMW World Championship race victory, with Schneider and Strauss finishing second behind them – impressive to say the least in what after all was their debut season at this level.

After Solitude the final two rounds were something of an anti-climax, with the best result being a fourth in the Swiss Grand Prix at Berne. And so Walter and Hans ended the year fourth in the Championship behind Noll/Cron, the winners; Oliver/Nutt, runners-up; and Smith/Dibben who were third.

The 1955 Season

The pair went one better in 1955, finishing not only third in the Championship, but also scoring their first GP victory, with the win in the Isle of Man. They also finished runners-up (to Noll/Cron) in the final round at Monza, and also scored a brace of third positions, in the German GP at the Nürburgring and in the Belgian GP at Spa Francorchamps.

The 1956 Season

In contrast, the 1956 season was not a successful one, with only two top-six finishes; a fourth at the German Grand Prix (Solitude) and a sixth in the final round in Italy (Monza).

The 1957 Season

It was much better in 1957 – with Schneider and Strauss coming home runners-up in the title hunt, behind the winners Fritz Hillebrand and Manfred Grünewald. Sadly, the newly crowned champions were not to enjoy their success, with Hillebrand suffering a fatal accident shortly after becoming champion (see Chapter 7). At the first two rounds Schneider and Strauss followed Hillebrand and Grünewald home in both Germany (Hockenheim) and the Isle of Man. They did not score in Holland, but at round four in Belgium took a great victory, beating Hillebrand/Grünewald into second position, with Camathias/Galliker third.

Again, no points were gained at the final round in Italy. But these results had been good enough for Walter and Hans to be made BMW's sole official works entry for the 1958 season, following the death of Fritz Hillebrand.

The 1958 TT. This photograph, taken immediately after the race, shows the winners Walter Schneider and Hans Strauss, and to their right, the runners-up Florian Camathias and passenger Hilmar Cecco.

World Champions

For the 1958 season the Championship was reduced from five to only four rounds: the Isle of Man, Belgium, Holland and Germany (the latter run at the Nürburgring).

And with victory in three of these events (Isle of Man, Belgium and Germany), Schneider and Strauss became the new champions with 30 points. But the BMW privateers Camathias/Cecco, with one victory (Dutch TT) and three second places, scored 26 points. And just to show how far these two teams were from the rest of the pack, the third place went to the up-and-coming Helmut Fath with a score of eight points!

Champions For A Second time

Walter Schneider and Hans Strauss became world champions for a second time in 1959. And again this was achieved from the main opposition Camathias/Cecco, who they again beat to the title by four points. Now with five rounds – the French Grand Prix at Clermont-Ferrand being added – Schneider and Strauss won in the Isle of Man and the Belgian Grand Prix. Camathias/Cecco also had two wins (at Hockenheim, Germany, and the Dutch TT at Assen). The other victory went to Scheidegger/Burckhardt at the season opener in France.

A lovely shot of Schneider, Strauss and friend with their streamlined BMW outfit. Photo W. Gruber/Archiv

The 1959 TT which Walter Schneider and Hans Strauss also won.

Schneider and Strauss in Retrospect

When looking at Walter Schneider and Hans Strauss in retrospect, the obvious thing is how they coped so well with the demanding Isle of Man TT course. In the six years they competed, the German BMW stars scored three victories (1955, 1958 and 1959), they were runners-up once (1957), fourth once (1954 – their debut year) and suffered one retirement (1956). The Isle of Man demands a combination of great skill and bullet-proof machine preparation; in the author's opinion, Schneider and Strauss had both.

After winning their second world crown, Walter Schneider and Hans Strauss retired from the sport. Walter tried motor racing in 1960, but without success. It should also be recorded that later he was to become a leading dealer for VW (Volkswagen), which might seem strange when one considers his close ties with BMW. However, the reader has to remember that during 1959 (the year of Schneider's last Championship) the entire BMW group was on the verge of financial collapse and was only saved at the eleventh hour by the intervention of the Quant family (major shareholders) and the company's bankers; otherwise BMW would have either gone out of business or faced takeover. This may seem far fetched half a century later but is absolutely true. And also the BMW car presence was a fraction of what it is today, whereas Volkswagen was, even in 1960, a major automobile name.

Schneider and Strauss leading the 1959 Belgian GP at Spa, the last round of that year's Championship, which they won. And so after securing their second world title the pair quit three wheels. Schneider subsequently tried car racing, without success.

CHAPTER 9

PIP HARRIS

PV (Peter Valentine – but more commonly simply known as 'Pip') was born in the Staffordshire village of Wombourne on 6 August 1927. Actually, Pip's arrival was to bring to an end his father Henry's (known as 'Curly') own motorcycle racing career. Curly had enlisted with the Shropshire Yeomanry during World War One and was to soon become a dispatch rider. On leaving military service after the end of the conflict he quickly gained a position with the AJS factory then based in Wolverhampton, in the West Midlands.

Curly's Racing Career
During the 1920s Curly was to become a talented racer (on solo machines) and competed in 12 Isle of Man TTs (one Lightweight, six Juniors and five Seniors), between 1921 and 1927. Besides riding for AJS, he also rode New Imperials in 1924 and thereafter campaigned HRDs in 1925 and 1926. Finally, in 1927, he competed in the Senior on a Triumph.

His best TT was the 1923 Junior, when he was to narrowly miss victory, beaten by none other than the legendary Stanley Woods (Cotton). Curly, however, had been leading the event by some eight minutes, and would have won easily if he had not stopped to repair a broken rear stand clip.

Curly Harris kept in touch with Howard Davis after the latter quit AJS to form his own company HRD (Howard Ronald Davies). Curly, having done quite well financially from his racing activities (including being paid the then vast amount of £400 by the Hutchinson tyre company), invested some of this money in the fledgling HRD concern. As journalist Roy Poynting pointed out in a recent *Classic Racer* article: 'That at least guaranteed him HRD works machinery for a couple of years.' But sadly, he was to lose his investment when HRD went bankrupt a few years later.

Pip Arrives
As previously mentioned, Pip Harris's arrival into the world in August 1927 saw his father decide that the time had come to end the racing activities and instead settle down as a family man. Not only this, but he opened a garage in Wombourne – much later Pip himself would take over the business when his father retired.

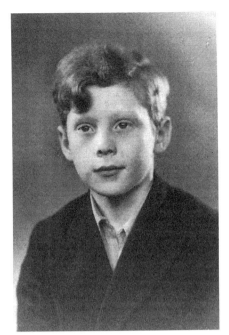

A young Pip as a
schoolboy.

In those far off days garages did not specialise as they do now. Instead, they catered for all varieties of wheeled transport. And so, the young Pip's first interest in this direction was to be in the humble pedal cycle and, together with his brother John and sister Margaret, the trio built a replica Rushmere circuit at the bottom of the family's garden, where they used to compete against each other and their friends. At the tender age of 7, Pip was put on his older brother's motorcycle and told to steer, which he promptly did – straight into the wall of the house! Luckily no real damage was done to him or the wall. After that rocky start, his natural competitive instinct and sheer determination took over, despite being born with a weakened right leg.

The Family

Both his brother and sister loved motorcycles. John was to have a reasonably successful grass-track racing career. And although Margaret never raced herself, she would travel the length and breadth of the country on various motorcycles, with her dog sat on the petrol tank.

Pip never liked school, having attended the local primary, St Benedict Biscop in Wombourne. He then went on to one of the first modern comprehensive schools in Kingswinford, where apart from woodwork and metalwork he failed to shine in any subject and promptly left at the earliest legal age, at that time 14.

A Powered Two-wheeler

In 1945, at the age of 18, Pip graduated from pedal power to horsepower, and his first motorcycle. This was an ancient Sunbeam, which had been manufactured in 1929. And when the local milkman updated his Harley-Davidson outfit, Pip purchased the redundant sidecar, fitting it to the Sunbeam, commenting recently: 'That was just so that I could keep the Sunbeam going in a straight line and it had the benefit that I could get six of my friends in the tradesman's box-body.'

But the old Sunbeam was to be the only street-legal motorcycle which Pip was destined to own, and it was obvious early on that he had inherited the need to go racing from his father. And his older brother John was already racing a Velocette. John soon commandeered the Sunbeam outfit – with the express purpose of transporting the Velocette to meetings. And so Pip was introduced to the 'addictive atmosphere of speed, smoke and paddock camaraderie' (Roy Poynting).

Sidecar Rather Than Solo

It was to be his older brother's influence which was to spark Pip's sidecar racing career, as John had told his father: 'I reckon that if Pip goes racing a solo, he's likely to fall off and do more damage to his dickey leg, so perhaps he ought to have a go with a sidecar outfit.'

'Fair enough,' said Curly Harris. 'You find something suitable and I will buy it for him.'

As Pip was to explain later: 'Dad was a bit taken aback when the very next day John announced that he'd found a suitable outfit at Smokey Dawson's emporium in Dudley, but he kept his word and bought it for me.'

It should be explained to readers that Smokey Dawson was a pre-World War Two grass track ace, who after the war became equally well-known as the manufacturer of DMW motorcycles. The machine in question turned out to be a Grindlay Peerless, though it was far from standard, having, for example, a Rudge cylinder barrel and many other non-standard components.

Racing on Grass

Pip made his debut with the Grindlay Peerless on grass; but in truth it was far from competitive. But at least he was able to show that it was worth his father providing the finance to find a more competitive piece of machinery. In fact, this turned out to be none other than a pukka Manx Norton outfit. Pip explains: 'It was on sale in Jack Surtees's south London dealership.' He continued: 'Dad drove down there and paid £110 for it, and I remember seeing young John Surtees, who was still a schoolboy, hanging around looking sorry to see it go. We didn't even have a trailer at the time, so we bolted the Norton's forks to the rear bumper, put some ballast in the chair and simply towed it home.'

Brough Airfield races 1949. Pip Harris Norton (66) leads another competitor on one of the Bracebridge Street, Birmingham, machines.

A Shrewd Buy

The camshaft Norton soon turned out to prove a shrewd buy. In fact, first time out on it – at a Redditch grass track meeting – Pip surprised everyone by gaining not only a debut victory, but a comfortable one too.

However, as they say 'pride can come before a fall', and that's exactly what happened to young Pip, as his second race saw him crash and end up in hospital with a cracked shoulder blade.

Taking to the Tarmac

But, of course, Pip's Manx Norton was really built for the road, not grass, and confident in being able to show his abilities on the tarmac he made the switch. When interviewed recently, Pip says he thinks that he: 'Probably had just one race at Cadwell Park', before setting off to race in the 1950 Belgian Grand Prix.

And his confidence was not to prove misplaced as the raw novice from rural Staffordshire came home in the top 10 finishers at Spa Francorchamps – the fastest circuit in the GP calendar!

Domestic Rather Than foreign

As Pip recalled himself: 'I quite liked the near continental GPs.' Continuing: 'And I did both the Belgian and Dutch rounds fairly regularly, but I didn't venture much farther afield, apart from going to Monza for the Italian a couple of times.'

Why? Well, in Pip's own words: 'It was too expensive without works sponsorship.'

In fact, these continental events were essentially family holidays, Pip continuing: 'John and I went with our parents in their car and we took the outfit on a trailer.'

As Pip's daughter, Caroline, told the author: 'Motorcycle racing was a family affair, his mother, father, sister and later wife and children plus numerous friends would follow Pip all over the country when he raced.' Caroline went on to say: 'Over time it became obvious that the "family" was getting bigger and bigger, and he joined the sidecar racing world family, which Pip remembers as being both supportive and fun with friendly rivalry.' A vivid example came later at the 1960 Isle of Man TT when the big-end went on his BMW-engined outfit. As soon as Helmut Fath realised the situation, he told Pip he would rebuild his engine for him if he could get the parts required. Jock West then worked for the British BMW importers and said simply: 'Leave it to me.' And Jock was as good as his word, as within 48 hours the parts were flown over from Germany and Helmut began rebuilding the engine…no money ever changed hands.

The British Scene

So Pip concentrated on the home circuits. In those early days his biggest rivals were Eric Oliver, Cyril Smith and Jackie Beeton. All four, including Pip, were using Nortons. As we know from other chapters in this book, Eric, Cyril and Jackie were all top-class competitors – with two of the three gaining World Championship titles to prove it.

Both Eric Oliver and Cyril Smith had close associations with the Norton works and its racing team manager Joe Craig, whereas both Pip and Jackie were on their own – privateers.

The Vincent

Pip's single knocker 600 in 1950 was going well. Norton offered to fit a double knocker head to it, which proved slower until a factory fitter quickly sorted the problem.

In 1951, with the World Championship sidecar down to 500cc, both Pip and Cyril Smith got new 500cc double-knocker engines to fit in their old Nortons with some modifications to the frames. The new engine proved both fast and reliable.

In fact, it can now be revealed that Norton, in the shape of Joe Craig, were unhelpful to say the least. Not only did they sell Pip a second-hand double-overhead cam Manx engine (to replace Pip's existing single knocker assembly) at full price, but then in 1952 when Pip attempted to purchase a brand new Featherbed Manx Craig claimed that none were available, certainly not before the TT.

So having already sold his old Norton – in the expectation of taking delivery of a new Manx – Pip journeyed to Stevenage, where he had learnt that the legendary record-breaking 'Gunga Din' was gathering dust at the Vincent works. And Pip was given the green light by the management to borrow the beast, providing he agreed to place an order for a new Black Lightning, a production bike that had been developed from Gunga Din, and took it up to Watsonians in Birmingham to have a chair fitted.

While at the Watsonians factory, Eric Oliver was there and told Pip that he was 'wasting my time' with the Vincent. However, the Vincent had its first outing the following Saturday at Silverstone, where Pip not only set a new lap record some eight seconds faster than the old one, but won the handicap race. This was despite having to start after Oliver and Cyril Smith. As Pip was to recall later: 'I flew past them on the straight and had an easy win.' Continuing: 'to be fair, Oliver was the first to congratulate me, even though he did emphasise the difference in engine sizes [998cc to 499cc].'

Pip with passenger Henry
Mykos (Featherbed
Norton), Brands Hatch,
April 1953.

Another outing for the Gunga Din outfit was at the Boreham track, near
Chelmsford in Essex. Here Pip set a new sidecar record – and for a short
period faster than the solos too! Then Gunga Din went back to Vincent
when the production Black Lightning was ready. But Pip only raced this
once – at the Welsh Eppynt road circuit – before selling it to fund the
purchase of the new Manx which was finally offered in mid-1952.

As Pip recalled: 'I should probably have stuck with the Vincent as it was
the fastest thing I ever raced.' But the Stevenage factory didn't seem
particularly interested. And neither were Norton as: 'They charged me the
full market price of more than £400 for the Manx.'

Besides the circuits already mentioned, the name P.V. Harris was to be seen
in the entry lists of programmes from Castle Combe, Ibsley, Thruxton,
Snetterton, Gamston, Brands Hatch and many others during the early 1950s.

Pip also had a succession of passengers during this period, including Charlie
Billingham (up to the end of the 1952 season), Henry Mykos (1953), Graham
Holden (1954), before, finally, teaming up with Ray Campbell, the latter
destined to stay with Pip for many, many years from the 1955 season onwards.

The Isle of Man TT

In June 1954 the Isle of Man TT included a Sidecar race for the first time
since 1925 (see Chapter 1). And from then until 1961 Pip Harris was to
compete annually in the event (there were also further appearances in 1963
and 1965). During that first year, on the Norton, he retired. However, Pip
was back the following year to finish third on a Matchless G45-engined

outfit. But back on a Norton for the 1956 TT he was runner-up behind the German world champion, Fritz Hillebrand (BMW). The next two years (1957 and 1958) he also had the Norton, but retired on both occasions. Things did not improve in 1959 when, now BMW mounted, he posted another retirement. Then came another runner-up spot in 1960, this time behind Helmut Fath (BMW), while in 1961 Pip was third, this time to Max Deubel (winner) and Fritz Scheidegger – needless to say, all were on BMWs. His final two TTs in 1963 and 1965 saw the big 'R' posted on the giant scoreboard opposite the pits on both occasions.

Third in the Championship

In 1956 Pip had finished third in the World Championship series – the last time a Norton was to appear in the top three as the BMW twins took over and began their domination of the sport. His only Grand Prix victory came at the Dutch TT in 1960. He later recalled: 'We led the Dutch TT on a Norton three times. We had half a mile to go the first time and the con-rod broke, we had two laps to go the next year and the frame broke and I can't remember what happened the next time, but mechanical failure put us out.'

The Matchless G45

As we know, in 1955 Pip had a spell with the Matchless G45, but he was soon back on Nortons. Oddly, his Matchless period came via the trade rather than the company itself. At the annual Bemsee (BRMC) dinner, the Mobil representative had asked Pip if he would like a works G45. Perhaps naturally,

Pip Harris and Ray Campbell 499cc Norton (132) lead Walter Schneider, BMW (137); Ernie Walker, Norton; Willi Faust, BMW; Scarborough International Gold Cup meeting, 16–17 September 1955.

Belgian Grand Prix 1956. Pip Harris is number 22 with his streamlined Norton outfit. Numbers 2, 10 and 12 are all members of the factory BMW team.

he jumped at the chance, only to discover that, while the engine was free, he had to pay for the transmission! Although on paper more powerful than the Norton – and that he finished third in the TT on it – Pip was never entirely happy with the way the Matchless engine delivered its power.

A Works Norton Engine At Last

After finishing runner-up in the 1956 TT, Pip had asked Norton's managing director Gilbert Smith (Joe Craig having retired at the end of

The 1957 Isle of Man TT. Staged over the 10-mile Clypse circuit, Pip Harris was runner-up to that year's world champion, Fritz Hillebrand (BMW).

1955) for a short-stroke engine. Initially, Smith said 'No'; however, after a certain dealer intervened an engine was provided. But this 'works' motor proved a major disappointment, being both slower and less reliable than Pip's own engine!

Following this, Pip was offered an MV motorcycle to race as an outfit at about the same time as Surtees and Hartle being MV Agusta works riders – this not coming to fruition as, to quote Pip: 'I took too long to make a decision.'

Switching to BMW

If truth be told, in sidecar racing at least, the Norton single had by then had its day. As a solo, the frame's superb handling could still make up the power deficiency, but with a third wheel added this was lost. Added to this was that the tall engine did not lend itself to lower and more streamlined outfits. And this was just where the flat twin BMW scored so heavily.

And so came the 'big move' as Pip was later to describe his switch to BMW. Initially, Pip went 50/50 with fellow sidecar star Jackie Beeton (see Chapter 2) on a second-hand Rennsport. The machine (in solo guise) was purchased from the Australian racer Jack Forrest in 1958. At first, after fitting a Watsonian sidecar Pip was 'disappointed', but after realising that he had to concentrate on the German engine things were to rapidly improve.

The BMW came with four and five-speed gearboxes, and after experimenting with the sidecar chassis he soon found that the BMW was very much a love affair, commenting: 'You went from the Norton which vibrated and leaked oil, to something that didn't vibrate or leak. Effortless to ride, really.'

Before racing the BMW power unit Pip took it over to the BMW works in Munich, saying: 'They did everything while I was there and were incredibly efficient. They were also extremely expensive, charging an astronomical £1500 in a bill that even included the petrol they'd used to wash the parts.' Although Pip and Jackie Beeton shared the bill, they later realised that sharing an outfit was not such a good idea, so Pip purchased Jackie's share and became the sole owner. Jackie then purchased his own BMW.

A Grand Prix Victory

In 1960, Pip became the first British sidecar driver to win the Dutch TT, achieving this against all the top Continental Europeans, several of whom had more powerful works engines. The result was as follows:

1st   Pip Harris passengered by Ray Campbell

2nd   Helmut Fath

3rd   Fritz Scheidegger

4th   Edgar Strub

5th   Bill Boddice

6th   Max Deubel

All except Boddice (Norton) were using BMW engines.

With a runner-up berth at the Isle of Man TT (behind Helmut Fath) that season was to see Pip and Ray Campbell finish the season third in the Championship table – behind Fath and Scheidegger, a magnificent result.

Pip and Helmut Fath after the former had finished runner-up to the latter in the 1960 TT. Helmut had earlier helped Pip rebuild his BMW engine.

The Boddice Family

W.G. (William George – or more commonly simply Bill) Boddice was born in Smethwick, Birmingham, on 11 May 1913.

The first motorcycle the young Bill ever rode, at least legally, was a Rex Acme TT Replica model with a 350cc Blackburne engine and outside flywheel. Then in 1932 or 1933 (Bill could never remember) he and a fellow group of motorcyclists attended a race meeting at Donington Park. And he was the proud owner of a 1929 TT Replica New Hudson (which had replaced the Rex Acme), as Bill was to recall in 1958: 'I thought – if I could afford it – I would try my hand.'

Very early in his racing life (at this time exclusively on solo machines) Bill realised that it was: 'Almost essential to have some form of race transport.' His first was a Morris Cowley car, bought for £7 10s – the first of a long line of Boddice transporters. And after some 25,000 miles (40,225km) he sold it on for the same figure. After racing the New Hudson until the outbreak of war in September 1939, and early in the conflict, the machine was sold – Bill realising that it would be a long time before he would be able to use it again.

And it was not until 1945, with the war over, that thoughts of competitive motorcycling returned. By now his mount was a five-hundred Ariel Red Hunter. And as he could not reach the floor the idea occurred to Bill of solving this by fitting a sidecar. At this time the local Kings Norton club had plans for a grass-track meeting near Hollywood,

Bill Boddice was a major British sidecar star of the late 1950s and early 1960s, being particularly successful at the Brands Hatch circuit.

and this included a three-wheeler class. So he purchased a 'very second-hand' Norton sidecar chassis. And so Bill Boddice became a sidecar man. His first passenger was Bob Oldridge.

By 1948 things were beginning to settle down. And Bill had added a solo Ariel 500 in road-race trim and running on 'dope'. This latter machine was used mainly at Cadwell Park, while the Ariel outfit was going very well on the grass. In fact, Bill, Cyril Smith (Ariel) and Pip Harris (Norton) were all leading figures in British sidecar grass-track events.

By the beginning of 1949 (the first year of the World Championships) road racing in Britain was beginning to take hold. And it was also the year that Bill made the switch from Ariel to Norton.

As the 1950s began, Bill was still taking in both grass and road-racing. But during early 1952 he suffered a serious eye injury which nearly finished his hopes of ever racing again; this was caused when he was drilling a hole in an engine plate and the drill snapped, a fragment flying into his eye. Later that year Bill had his first taste of Continental European racing, or for that matter a race counting towards World Championship points (the Belgian Grand Prix). However, after only two laps his race was over due to a clanking big-end.

For the Belgian GP and several British short-circuit events Bill had been using a 500cc engine built out of a combination of pre-war bottom-end components and a modern double-knocker top-end. But for grass-track events a 596cc 'dope' engined machine was used.

In 1954 the Isle of Man sidecar TT was revived, but on the shorter Clypse circuit. But a new twin-leading shoe front brake proved too effective at Creg-ny-Baa, resulting in tipping Bill and his passenger on their ears, although they still finished sixth. And 1954 proved a very successful year, with 13 wins, 14 seconds, sundry thirds and fourths, and the Watsonian and Minnie Grenfield trophies. Sharing the name plate of the latter with Geoff Duke: 'Made me very proud' said Bill later.

Then in 1955, Bill Boddice suddenly went on a winning streak, with victories at Brough, Brands Hatch, Crystal Palace, Silverstone and several other British short circuits. He also finished runner-up in the TT behind Walter Schneider (BMW). Part of this success was due to a new short-stroke Norton outfit and streamlining. Very soon Boddice and Brands Hatch were being talked of in the same way as Derek Minter in the solo class – 'King of Brands'. In fact, it was Bill who was to suggest Derek's name to top tuner, the legendary Steve Lancefield.

Into 1956 and Bill came home third in the TT, behind Fritz Hillebrand (BMW) and Pip Harris (Norton), the latter he had beaten the previous year. But after lying fourth in the 1957 TT, Boddice crashed with only a few miles to go. Then Bill did not take part in the TT again until 1961 (after the Clypse circuit had given way to the Mountain course), considering the Clypse: 'Not to my liking'. Although Bill and new passenger Bill Canning finished fifth in the 1958 Dutch TT and the same position at the Belgian GP a year later, it was really on British short circuits that they shone. But once again, in 1960, they were fifth in Holland.

As already mentioned, Bill became top man at Brands Hatch, a position which lasted until the early 1960s, when men like Chris Vincent began to take over. Another feature of the Boddice camp in those days

Mick Boddice took over the family's sidecar exploits from father Bill. Mick is seen here with his 654cc BSA A65 outfit at Mallory Park during the late 1960s.

was the family's massive converted bus, which was used as transporter and living quarters. Also, Bill was to become a leading ACU official. Together with wife Iris the couple had two children Julie (who later married future 125cc World Champion Dave Simmonds) and Mick who was to become a sidecar star in his own right and multi-TT winner (born in Birmingham on 22 November 1947).

In fact, right from the very start Mick (and Julie) were very much a part of the Boddice racing scene. A vivid example of this came in June 1959, when at the Dutch TT Derek Minter bent a valve on his Manx Norton engine. Father Bill was 'too busy' to carry out the repair himself, so Mick, then 11 years old, set to and stripped the Norton cylinder head and fitted the new valve!

As for Mick's own racing career (all on three-wheels), his first competitive outing came at Brands Hatch on Good Friday 1965, driving 'Dad's Manx Norton'. This was followed later that year with a first national victory, at Snetterton.

His first Isle of Man TT came in 1966, when his twin cylinder BSA outfit was a non-finisher. This was when the under-floor fuel tank was punctured by a stray bolt, forcing his retirement. Twelve months later he finished eighth, gaining the first of more than 40 replicas! His first TT win came in 1983, and he continued to notch up victories up to and including 1993. At that time, Mick shared the record of nine wins in the Sidecar TT, with Germany's Siegfried Schauzu and fellow countryman Dave Saville. In 1966 father Bill and son Mick emulated the feat achieved two years earlier when they raced against each other in the Sidecar TT.

Besides his TT successes Mick also won the prestigious Grovewood Award in 1967, as well as three British Championship titles; the Open Class in 1987 and the F2 in 1992 and 1993. Mick was the first Sidecar driver to lap the Thruxton and Castle Combe circuits at over 100mph (161km/h). During his racing career Mick competed on Norton, Triumph, Kawasaki, König, Yamaha and Honda machinery.

In 1994 he formed the Mick Boddice Track Training (TT) Racing School, which has been at the Darley Moor circuit ever since. And he has been an official at the Isle of Man TT since he quit racing. The race school had had the satisfaction of seeing several of its pupils go on to make the big time, including Bradley Smith, Carl Crutchlow, the Lowes twins and the Bridewell brothers.

As for father Bill, he passed away in May 1985, aged 72.

Ultra-reliable

The Rennsport engine which Pip raced was a long-stroke production assembly with bore and stroke dimensions of 66 x 72mm. But the works engine used 70 x 64mm dimensions. As for power output, the production Rennsport put out a claimed 45bhp at 8,000rpm; the works engine 58bhp at 9,000rpm with carburettors or 61bhp at 9,000rpm with fuel injection. These are BMW factory figures for the 1956 season. Later works motors probably exceeded these figures, certainly in the later years.

But, says Pip, although: 'I lost touch with the factory when my initial contact, Müller, had a heart attack and retired, it didn't really matter because the long-stroke engine was incredibly reliable.'

The British Short Circuit Scene

Even though Pip did enjoy success at World Championship level, it was on the British short circuits that he really made his mark. In addition, it was with the BMW power unit that he made the transition from sitter to kneeler position, commenting: 'Once I was used to it I appreciated the advantage. So much better. You didn't have to hang on – you were sitting in it and not on it.'

Pip Harris (BMW, 3) leads Colin Seeley (Matchless, 14), Bill Boddice (Norton), plus another competitor at Cascades, Oulton Park British Championship meeting, 1963.

The Big Crash

His one big crash in a career which spanned 28 years from 1945 until he finally hung up his leathers for the last time in 1972 came at Snetterton in September 1963. In retrospect, Pip admitted that he: 'Tried too hard that day.' Getting a poor start against the six-fifty BSA of Chris Vincent he upended the BMW outfit at Riches and still remembers: 'Flying through the air expecting the worst', only to have a surprisingly soft landing. This, as he subsequently discovered, was because he had landed on top of Ray Campbell. Even so Pip broke a vertebrae; this keeping him out of racing for the entire 1964 season. It also left him with restricted movement in his left arm caused by a trapped nerve.

Pip Harris leads Florian Camathias a lap before the Swiss star's fatal crash, Brands Hatch, 11 October 1965.

The Short-stroke

Pip won the British Championship title on more than one occasion. But, eventually the long-stroke BMW became increasingly uncompetitive, particularly up against machinery such as Chris Vincent's 654cc BSA and Owen Greenwood's controversial Mini. So, in 1969, he purchased a short-stroke works BMW that had previously been campaigned by the German Georg Auerbacher; however, in practice this did not improve results because of yet faster machinery from the opposition, notably the four-cylinder URS. However Pip described the short-stroke in the following manner: 'That was a revelation, so fast and smooth.'

The Cadwell Crash

At Cadwell Park in 1971 Pip had what he described as 'a bit of a crash' and in this his long-time passenger Ray Campbell broke one wrist and sprained the other. Perhaps understandably, Ray decided there and then to quit. And although Pip subsequently had some 'enjoyable' races with new passenger John Thornton, he decided himself to retire after an Oulton Park meeting in 1972.

Other Interests

Pip had two other interests. One was gliding, which he had taken up when he had been forced to miss 1964 due to the accident the previous year already described left him 'bored'. He managed to glide solo on his 21st flight over the Long Mynd in Shropshire, no mean feat.

He also loved yachting and would often sail his brother John's yacht. So after he retired from racing Pip built a ketch rig ocean-going 35ft yacht which he moored in Salcombe.

Pip was married twice. Firstly to Ann, with whom he had three daughters, Caroline (1958), Jane (1962) and Jennifer (1965). He married his second wife (also Ann) in 1970 and had two children, Ruth (1974) and then at last a son, Peter (1976); the latter working with horses since leaving school in 1994 and competing at many show-jumping events across Britain, including county shows and The Horse of the Year Show of which Pip says: 'I take pleasure in going to watch'.

It is also worth mentioning that all his children (and grandchildren) share his competitiveness and have gone on to represent their country and various counties in a variety of sports including tennis, netball, rugby, soccer, badminton, swimming, gymnastics and show jumping.

Asked in 2010 to sum up his racing career, Pip replied: 'I enjoyed every single minute of it!'

CHAPTER 10
FLORIAN CAMATHIAS

If Stirling Moss (cars) and Bob McIntyre (solo motorcycles) are great competitors who never won a world title in their sport, then Florian Camathias was sidecars' 'Mr Hard Luck'. Born on 23 March 1924 in Saint-Gall near Lake Constance in the north-east of Switzerland, the young Florian spent several boyhood years mountain climbing, before being bitten by the motorcycle bug; he was destined to become one of the sport's all-time greats.

A self-employed motor mechanic (by then based in Montreux, and known to his many friends simply as 'Flo'), he tried no fewer than nine times to win the World Sidecar Championship title. He was runner-up no fewer than four times, even though he was forced to wear spectacles for short-sightedness.

Early Days

From his earliest years Florian grew up with motorcycles as his father was a keen competitor in the road races and hill-climbs of the local area, riding Harley-Davidsons and NSUs, scoring many successes and holding several hill-climb records.

Unfortunately, when Florian was only a few years old his father was killed while testing an engine fitted with aluminium pistons (at this time many engines used cast-iron pistons rather than aluminium as is the case now); however, this incident did not deter the Camathias family from inheriting the motorcycling bug, and as soon as they were able his three brothers and two sisters all purchased their own machines.

The First Motorcycle

Florian's first motorcycle was a Swiss-made Zender two-stroke with a 200cc single-cylinder engine. His initial efforts at riding on the street were frowned on by the local police due to the fact that he was only 12 years old at the time!

They came round to the Camathias's home and removed the drive chain from the Zender – so that young Florian would not be able to ride it. As one journalist later commented: 'This may explain his [Florian's] love of shaft-driven BMWs!'

After leaving school Florian was apprenticed as a motor and motorcycle mechanic, and when he became eligible for a licence – in 1942 – he purchased a five-hundred BMW of 1937 vintage.

During the following three years, with war raging all around neutral Switzerland, Florian together with his brothers transversed virtually the entire road network of their homeland on their BMWs, logging over 30,000 miles (48,270km) a year and competing in unofficial hill-climbs that rival motorcycle clubs had organised.

A Racing Debut

Florian's racing debut came at Lausanne during 1947 when he rode a tuned standard road-going five-hundred BMW solo. From then on he competed regularly with a pre-war sports BMW modified and as he described later 'souped up.'

During May 1949 came a crash which all but ended his fledgling career, and one from which he was to suffer the after effects for many years. This came about when, leading a race at Basel, he hit a patch of oil left by another competitor's machine, after the oil tank had fractured. Florian, together with several other riders, crashed.

Paralysed

With his skull fractured in three places, Florian was on the critical list in hospital for several days. Then, when he finally regained consciousness, it was discovered that he was almost completely paralysed down the left side of his body.

The very first thing Florian did was to give away the remains of his once prized motorcycle, but then, as he gradually recovered the urge to compete came back and a year after the crash he bought a 1939 racing BMW with rear springing, and began where he had left off, although he said at the time: 'I am now very much steadier.'

The ISDT

In 1951, 1952 and 1953 Florian rode the BMW solo, and during 1953 he also competed in the ISDT (International Six Days Trial) for the first and only time. Amazingly, he had never seen the ISDT before and had only a vague idea of what to expect. It was a rude awakening…even so, he struggled through five days and then retired with a minor mechanical problem on the sixth and day's speed tests. The machine he rode in the event was a 600cc BMW.

A Sidecar Debut

Then in 1954 came his very first outing with a sidecar. This was at Bourg en Bresse in France, and his ancient 1939 BMW provided the motive power. In truth the addition of a third wheel gave Florian a whole new outlook on racing. One which was soon to see the name Florian Camathias known to all followers of motorcycle sport as one of the outstanding sidecar personalities of all time. He was to build himself a reputation of going out to win every race he was to compete in, and his never-say-die spirit would endear him to enthusiasts wherever he competed.

The Rennsport

Making the decision that he liked racing chairs, Florian purchased one of the 20 or so pukka racing models which BMW manufactured during the closed season of 1954–55. Of course, the machine in question was the legendary RS54 Rennsport. The 492cc (66 x 72mm) air-cooled, dohc, horizontally opposed twin featuring bevel/shaft driven camshafts and two-valves-per-cylinder.

The purchase of the Rennsport was to be a wise decision, because this engine was to dominate sidecar racing for the next two decades at the very highest level.

Solo and Sidecar

But to begin with, and until the end of the 1950s, Florian Camathias was to race both solos and sidecars. In fact, it would be true to say that although ultimately it was sidecars which made his name; 'Flo' was also a more-than-capable solo rider. He once won three out of five classes in France, racing MV Agusta (125) and NSU Sportmax (250) machinery, a brace of Manx Nortons (350 and 500), plus his BMW sidecar outfit – at the time this was an almost unheard of event. In fact speed was a preoccupation which was to see Florian travel the length and breadth of Europe, often overnight, to race or make record attempts.

Return to Bourg en Bresse

With his new BMW Rennsport outfit he returned to Bourg en Bresse at the beginning of the 1955 season – and as related competed in all four solo classes plus the sidecar race.

At the end of that year Florian set up a number of both solo and sidecar records with the NSU at Montlhéry near Paris; however, the real turning point had come at the Italian GP at Monza in September 1955, when he brought his BMW outfit home fourth behind Noll, Schneider and Drion.

Against Streamlining

It should be mentioned here that Florian Camathias had been strongly against the use of streamlining. In fact, he delayed his use of it as long as possible, and it was not until the end of 1956 that he adopted a fairing at all. That same year Florian had finished fifth in the Sidecar World

Championship, with a fifth in Holland, a fourth in Italy and a third in Ulster. His passenger that year being the fellow Swiss Maurice Büla (later to become a photographer and author).

At the final big European event of the year, at Zaragoza, Spain, Florian showed his sporting nature when he lent his only engine to the 1955 world champion Willi Faust after the latter had blown his own in practice. As it happened, this was to be the German's last-ever race as he crashed during the following winter while testing a new machine and eventually decided to retire.

1957

1957 saw Florian finish third in the Championship, this time with Jules Galliker as his passenger. At the first round of the Championship, at Hockenheim, Camathias and Galliker were fourth, behind Hillebrand, Schneider and Knebel. Next came the Isle of Man TT, where the pair came home an excellent third behind Hillebrand (destined to become world champion that year) and future double champion (1958 and 1959) Schneider.

A lovely portrait photograph of Florian Camathias by Grand Prix photographer Wolfgang Gruber. Photo W. Gruber/Archiv

After a retirement in the Dutch TT, the team finished runners-up (to Schneider) in the Belgian GP, before, finally, at the fifth and final round in Italy took another third.

The Machinery

1957 had also seen Florian gain a measure of works support and use works long-stroke engines in his own machine – and ex-works sidecar special sold to him early in 1956.

Into 1958, with works support from BMW being restricted to Walter Schneider only, Florian used his own long-stroke BMW units into which he incorporated one or two special features he had gathered through racing BMWs over the previous 10 years.

A Brilliant Year

The 1958 Championship was run over four rounds: the Isle of Man TT, Belgian GP, Dutch TT and the German GP at the Nürburgring. And even though Walter Schneider, passengered by

Although he was destined never to win the World Championship, the Swiss star Florian Camathias was still destined to become a true sidecar racing legend. He is shown here competing in the British Championship meeting at Thruxton in August 1958.

Hans Strauss, eventually won, it was a close affair, as the works BMW outfit met with relentless opposition from Florian and his passenger Hilmar Cecco.

Yes, Schneider did win three of the four races, but not only did the Camathias team win the other (in Holland), but came home close behind Schneider and Strauss in the other three, to finish runners-up in the title race. Florian also had the satisfaction of winning the British Sidecar Championship race at Thruxton on August Bank Holiday Monday that year.

More Grand Prix Victories

As in 1958, 1959 saw a tremendous battle between Schneider and Strauss, and Florian and his passenger Hilmar Chico. This time there were five rounds and in the event Schneider won two, and Florian won two, with Fritz Scheidegger victorious in the opening round at Clermont-Ferrand in France. At the end of the season a mere four points separated the two teams, with Scheidegger third in the series. Schneider then announced his retirement – probably fearing that if he continued Camathias would emerge the victor.

A Poor Year

But in reality Schneider need not have worried as 1960 was to prove a poor year for Florian. For a start his passenger Hilmar Cecco defected to rival Edgar Strub, so Florian seemed to have a different passenger in every race. These included Englishman John Chisnell, Roland Föll and 'Fiston'

This 1960 photograph shows left to right: Fritz Scheidegger, Horst Burkhadt (passenger), Alfred Wohlgemuth (passenger), Roland Foll (passenger and solo rider), Helmut Fath, Florian Camathias and John Chisnall (passenger).

(meaning youngster), whose real name was Gottfried Rufenacht who resided in Geneva. Florian's best result (passengered by Rufenacht) came at the final round, in Italy, in which the pair finished runners-up to that year's champions Helmut Fath and Alfred Wohlgemuth, who had succeeded Schneider and Strauss as BMW's official entry.

Tragedy

The 1961 Grand Prix season kicked off with the Spanish round at Montjuich Park, Barcelona. Everyone expected a straight fight for the Championship that year between Helmut Fath, the existing champion, and his number-one challenger Florian Camathias.

But although Fath won in Spain, with Florian being forced to retire with a broken drive shaft, the remainder of the GP season did not pan out as the pundits expected.

First, at the Nürburgring, Helmut Fath crashed in very wet conditions and his passenger was killed, while Helmut was left very badly injured. Then only 11 days later while competing at a special attraction at a national meeting at the Moderna circuit in Italy on Thursday 11 May, Florian Camathias and his passenger Hilmar Cecco crashed on the last lap while leading from Max Deubel/Emil Hörner.

They were negotiating a high-speed left-hand bend and observers reported that their BMW outfit spun off the circuit into a wall. Both received extremely serious injuries, which in the case of Hilmar Cecco were to prove fatal as he died the following day. As for Camathias himself, he survived but suffered injuries including a fractured skull, broken arm and ribs, plus back injuries. These keeping him out of racing for the remainder of that year.

The BMWs of Florian Camathias (4) and Pip Harris (2) battle it out at Mallory Park Race of the Year meeting in 1961.

Back In The Grove

If 1961 was an awful year for Florian, the following one, 1962, was to be just the reverse. Straight from round one of the title chase, again in Spain at Montjuich Park, Barcelona, Florian was back in the groove, finishing runner-up to the 1961 champion, Max Deubel. Passengered during the early part of the season by Horst Burckardt, for the second half of the season by Englishman Harry Winter swapped places with Burckardt in the chair.

In a six-round series Florian finished runner-up in the points table, with a trio of second places – Clermont-Ferrand and Solitude plus Barcelona – victory at Spa Francorchamps and finally two retirements (Isle of Man and Assen).

Cadwell Park International Road Races, 16 September 1962, Florian Camathias and passenger Harry Winter.

Harry Scholes

Harold (but known as Harry in the racing world) Scholes was born in Rochdale on 1 December 1935. After his father died in 1948, his mother ran a fruit and vegetable shop. Harry was one of four children, the others being two brothers, James and Jack, and a sister, Jean.

From five to 10 years of age Harry spent five years in a children's hospital with a chest condition. And, after the then compulsory national service, he took up scrambling and also began work at Alan Taylor Motorcycles in Oldham. Then, after attending auctions to buy ex-WD (war department) army machines, he invested the profits gained into buying his shop during the late 1950s, at Halifax Road, Rochdale.

It was through his dealership that he was to meet his wife, Sandra McDonaugh; the latter having to visit Harry's business several times after her NSU scooter kept breaking down.

Harry began racing in 1959 with a G45-powered Matchless outfit, but as his motorcycle emporium in Rochdale prospered so he improved his machinery, first with an ex-Bill Beevers BMW Rennsport and finally early in 1962 he purchased the immaculate BMW-Watsonian that Pip Harris had raced in 1961.

And equipped with this ultra-fast machine Harry Scholes put in some impressive performances, including Oulton Park 23 April 1962, third; Charterhall 29 April, first; Spanish Grand Prix 6 May, fifth; Snetterton 29 July, fifth and Oulton Park (British Championship) 6 August, fourth.

In the 1962 Isle of Man TT he was forced to retire with an electrical fault and the year before, in the 1961 TT on his previous BMW (ex Bill Beevers), Harry had come home 10th. His other TT outing had been 1959 with the Matchless when he had been forced to retire on the second lap – with the G45 Matchless (the last year the shorter Clypse circuit had been used).

Then came that fateful day at Brands Hatch where at a national meeting over the full 2.65-mile (4.26km) Grand Prix circuit at the Kentish track,

Harry Scholes and Ray Lindsay on their BMW at Mallory Park, 1961.
(© Courtesy of R. Nixon)

Harry's 492cc ex-Pip Harris outfit (with Keith Scott in the chair) was shunted from the race at Clearways while all the competitors were bunched up by a safety vehicle due to a previous accident which was being attended to.

The subsequent crash saw Harry taken to hospital, from what was believed at the time to be concussion; however, the head injuries were in fact much more severe, and the following day it was reported that Harry Scholes was 'seriously ill'. He was to succumb to these injuries at the Brook Hospital in Greenwich, South East London, on 28 August 1962. And he was later buried in Rochdale Cemetery.

And so came to an early end a career which had begun to blossom.

Another New Passenger

For 1963 Florian had yet another new passenger, Alfred Herzig. And yet again the Swiss star was to finish runner-up in the Championship – to Max Deubel. This came following victories at Hockenheim and in the Isle of Man TT. 'Flo' was later to recall that his TT win was: 'Probably the highlight of my career.'

Arriving in Liverpool

But before his TT victory came an amazing incident which vividly displays the unique nature of Florian. The following is a descriptive account from the book *From Rocker to Racer* (Breedon Books, 2009), which I helped my friend Reg Everett compile:

'Suddenly the air was filled with a deep throated, echoing, roaring sound. We all listened for some while. It turned out to be the noise of a twin-

Isle of Man TT, 1963. Winner Florian Camathias with passenger Alfred Herzig, here leading Bill Boddice (Norton, 4). Photo W. Gruber/Archiv

cylinder open megga BMW racing sidecar outfit coming through the Mersey tunnel and skidding to a halt on the dockside. It was none other than the Swiss Florian Camathias at the controls with his passenger, toolbox and various other bits in the chair! The police pulled up shortly thereafter. Apparently his Citroën Safari Estate had broken down on the M1 between London and Birmingham and, not wanting to miss the boat, he decided he would ride his machine to Liverpool instead – and probably broke every traffic law in existence on the way. There was much cheering, arm waving and shouting, but eventually he was loaded on the boat to another great cheer and we got underway.'

The Race Itself

A record entry of 45 outfits lined up for the start of the 1963 Sidecar TT, over three laps of the 37.73-mile (60.70km) Mountain course. Max Deubel had been fastest in practice, but surprisingly never appeared on the leaderboard during the race. Instead it was a fight between Florian and Fritz Scheidegger. The latter led by some eight seconds at the end of lap one; however, Camathias reversed the positions on lap two and led the race from Scheidegger by 22 seconds. And this was the way it stayed to the end, with a new race record average speed of 88.38mph (142.20km/h). And set the fastest lap at 89.42mph (143.87km/h).

Besides the other win, at Hockenheim, Camathias and Herzig had two third places: in Spain and Holland, while they retired in the Belgian GP. Finally, the intended sixth round in the series at Clermont-Ferrand was

Silverstone 1963, Florian hugs a tight line round Stowe Corner at the Silverstone circuit.

Florian Camathias in his workshop; a Wolfgang Gruber photograph.

Photo W. Gruber/Archiv

cancelled because of fog at the end of the morning, as was the 250cc race, the 50 and 125cc races having been run before the fog descended.

Gilera

When Max Deubel became world champion for the third successive time at the end of the 1963 season, Florian realised that a good part of this success was due in no small measure to Deubel's exclusive use of a works BMW short-stroke engine, rather than the long-stroke Rennsport production engine available to others, including Florian himself. And so it was that Camathias decided to approach certain Italian companies – Bianchi, MV Agusta and Gilera. And it was at the latter that he received a warm welcome. *Commendore* Giuseppe Gilera, the factory boss, and his brother Luigi had been keen sidecar racers themselves before the war and had subsequently supported men such as Ercole Frigero, Ernesto Merlo and Albino Milani in the World Sidecar Championships during the early-mid 1950s.

When Geoff Duke's private Gilera venture ended in late 1963, Florian saw his chance and arranged a meeting with Giuseppe Gilera, resulting in a promise to loan an engine for the 1964 season.

The Debut

The Camathias Gilera made its debut on 4 April 1964, at the international Hutchinson 100 meeting at Silverstone. But: 'In typical fashion Florian indulged in one of his habitual frantic dashes' (Raymond Ainscoe, *Classic Bike*, Autumn 1983). And he thus arrived at Silverstone too late for official practice; however, race officials allowed the Gilera out onto the grid for the

Florian Camathias campaigned this four-cylinder Gilera-engined outfit during 1964, but a series of problems put a spanner in the works.

eight-lap non-Championship event, but Florian had to start from the back. He proceeded to storm through the field and had moved up to fourth place on the third lap. But heavy rain was making things difficult, and when the Gilera outfit spun at Chapel Curve, passenger Alfred Herzig was flung from the chair, sustaining leg injuries. So for the main 12-lap race Florian recruited fellow countryman and solo rider Roland Föll. Although suffering a poor start, the pair blasted their way through to finish runner-up behind the BMW of Chris Vincent. They also had the satisfaction of sharing the fastest lap with Vincent.

Truly Beautiful

As Raymond Ainscoe described back in 1983: 'The [Gilera] outfit was surely one of the most beautiful ever to race; a sleek fairing in traditional Gilera red and white exuded elegance, and a light-alloy dark red panelling shrouded the rear of the machine lent an air of purpose.'

At its heart the Camathias Gilera featured the world-famous 493cc (52 x 58mm) four-cylinder across-the-frame dohc engine with integral five-speed gearbox. Power output was 70bhp at 10,500rpm – at least 10 per cent more than the best BMW.

And to get the weight as low as possible, Florian had designed the outfit with a full kneeler driving layout.

A Gilera Victory

When Florian took the Gilera outfit to victory in the first round of the 1964 World Championship series at Montjuich Park, Barcelona, in early May

The Dutch TT 1964, Camathias (Gilera) leads Deubel (BMW), Vincent (BMW) and Scheidegger (BMW). Photo W. Gruber/Archiv

everyone's expectations were high. This came after other outings in the non-Championship Austrian and Saar GPs. In Spain both his main rivals struck problems, Deubel oiling a plug at the start and Scheidegger spinning out early in the race. So with Roland Föll still as passenger, Florian won much as he pleased. But this promising start was to prove the last Grand Prix victory for a Gilera-engined machine for many, many years. In fact, the Camathias Gilera was not to finish in the top six at any subsequent GP that year.

Typical was the French GP at Clermont-Ferrand (the second in the series), where after building up a vast lead of nearly half a minute, and in sight of victory, Florian over-revved his engine so it was only able to limp home seventh, out of the points. Then, while leading the Isle of Man TT, fuel starvation began to afflict the Gilera (a common problem) and after a series of problems, including stopping and restarting and pushing in with a dead engine, Camathias and his regular passenger Herzig came home in 15th place, to receive a huge applause from the crowd and the final bronze replica – small reward for all the effort.

A Fire

Next in Holland the pair suffered a fire after petrol sprayed on the engine during the race (after taking pole position in practice). In Belgium his luck was no better, with fuel starvation rearing its head again, even though he set the fastest lap of the race.

For the final GP of the season, Florian was back on his own FCS (BMW-powered Florian Camathias Special). This was, quite simply, because there

Camathias in front of his
BMW dealership in
Montreux, Switzerland,
circa early 1960s.
Photo W. Gruber/Archiv

were no more serviceable Gilera engines, and in fact he never raced the Gilera again – although he did use the chassis in 1965 for his own BMW power unit.

The 1964 season ended prematurely and tragically, with a crash at the end of August, while competing in an international meeting at the Avus circuit in West Berlin. In this incident, Florian was knocked unconscious but, far worse, Alfred Herzig lost a leg. And as Roland Föll had already suffered a fatal crash while practicing for the Dutch TT on his 125cc Honda solo in June; 1964 was not a happy year for the Camathias camp.

A Final GP Victory

For the 1965 season Florian Camathias reverted to BMW power, and it was with this that he was to score his final Grand Prix victory, at Rouen, the scene of that year's French round, beating Scheidegger (second) and Deubel (third). But, again there were more retirements; in fact, the only other top-six GP finish in 1965 was a fifth in Belgium.

The Brands Hatch Crash

And so to Brands Hatch and that fateful day on 10 October 1965, when he crashed his BMW at Clearways while attempting to overtake on the outside, sustaining fatal injuries. As with Bob McIntyre's death some 11 years earlier, the outpouring of emotion and grief from friends, fans and the press was exceptional.

The following are just two examples of press reports of the day:

Motor Cycle News

He died competing in the sport to which he dedicated 19 of his 41 years. His loss robs racing of a fanatical supporter, but his enthusiasm will live forever in the memories of those privileged to know him.

Motor Cycling

Florian Camathias, who died on Sunday at Brands Hatch, was not only a wonderful sidecar racer, preparer of BMW engines, but was above all things a great character.

Ever cheerful, ever-optimistic he was, despite his lack of inches a giant among men when it came to perseverance, guts and daring.

Not Just a Sidecar Racer

But Florian Camathias was not just a sidecar racer. He was a man of many parts. Solo racer, record breaker – having established world records on BMW, NSU and Honda-powered sidecars. Animal lover, for example, he thought nothing of deliberately crashing a car to avoid a cat or dog, saying: 'I wouldn't hurt a fly.' Of his wife Margarite, he once commented: 'She is more than just my wife – she is my mechanic and my diplomat.'

CHAPTER 11

CHRIS VINCENT

C.J. (Christopher John – Chris) Vincent was born at Small Heath, Birmingham, on 20 January 1935.

Finding His Way

His first motorcycle, purchased in 1950, was a pre-war Matchless two-fifty single. That same year, at 15 years of age, Chris left school to work at the nearby BSA company.

At that time he had three main interests – guns, boxing and motorcycles – but the first two of these soon faded. His initial job at BSA was on gearbox assembly, but Chris soon became involved in virtually every aspect of motorcycle production (except engine assembly); even including road testing new Bantam models. A total of 90 new Bantams were tested each day by Chris and another tester – 45 machines each!

After leaving BSA, between the ages of 17 and 18, he had over a dozen different jobs including spells on the Velocette company's LE production line and with Percival Brothers and Webb, the latter well known for its frame and girder fork repairs (the latter a specialist job which they undertook). He also put in some time with motorcycle dealers Grey and Kings in Birmingham; even in coal mining.

Next, in 1954, Chris was employed by the long-established Sun firm (who at that time built Villiers-powered lightweights) in Aston Brook Street, Birmingham. But when someone upset him at work, Chris simply walked out and down the street to take a job at the nearby Norton factory's experimental department. His job at Norton was as a works development tester, doing up to 400 miles (645km) a day on prototypes, among these being a 250cc high-cam overhead-valve single mounted in a Featherbed-style frame and equipped with a self-serve clutch. However, in practice that clutch, intended as an improvement, turned out to be just the reverse. Chris commenting: 'When the twistgrip was snapped open the drive couldn't handle the sudden power, and the bike took off in lurches.' The 250 Norton was later to find a home at Beaulieu Motor Museum, where Chris was reunited with the machine some 50 years later.

Besides the prototype testing, Chris also spent time with Nortons at MIRA testing Dominator twins for the annual Daytona Beach races in Florida.

A Competition Debut

Chris Vincent's competitive debut came during 1954, and was on a solo – a JAP-engined grass-track machine at Rushmere, between Telford and Shrewsbury in Shropshire. But following this and a few more relatively unsuccessful rides, veteran sidecar racer Fred Hanks persuaded Chris that he should be on three wheels, not two.

And so to the next stage in the story, by switching from solo to sidecar grass-track racing.

The Iron B33

Chris began his sidecar career with an iron B33 five hundred single, running on alcohol. Built at the BSA works, the engine had been intended for Midlands grass-track ace Dick Tolly. Chris discovered the engine in the Small Heath experimental shop, under a bench; and promptly bought it from BSA.

Testing his early outfits often got Chris into trouble. In 1956 and 1957 he would be found at the old Castle Bromwich airfield (during World War Two the Spitfire test delivery centre). As Chris was later to relate: 'The police would arrive and say "come on, you know you can't do this." He would reply "just a few more laps", asking them very politely if they wouldn't mind placing their cars across the entrance to the airfield to stop anyone getting in the way.'

Birmingham-based Bill Boddice also let Chris loose on his Manx-Norton road racing outfit at Oulton Park in late 1957; Chris's first test of a sidecar racing machine on the tarmac. He was third in the British Championship in 1956 and second in 1957 with the 500 single, then, the following year, Chris won the 1958 grass-track title using a six-fifty A10-powered machine running on petrol. And in so doing he also created a piece of history by being the first to use a British vertical twin-cylinder engine. A high point was beating Bill Evans, who at that time was sponsored by Bill Boddice.

Having proved his point, he immediately retired from grass-track in early October 1958 and the following weekend made his road racing debut at Cadwell Park with his own A10-engined machine.

A bearded Chris Vincent pictured in 1960.

Chris and passenger Eric Bliss (650cc BSA) rounding Gerard's Bend, Mallory Park, at the Race of the Year in 1961.

The Big Breakthrough

The big break in Chris Vincent's fortunes on the road came at Brands Hatch on Boxing Day, 26 December 1960. The meeting was held in brilliant sunshine over the short version of the Kent circuit.

The following report from *The Motor Cycle* dated 5 January 1961 paints the picture: 'One of the most exciting sidecar races to be seen at Brands Hatch for many a day was given immediate impetus when Bill Boddice (Norton) made a flying getaway, only to find Chris Vincent (BSA) on his tail on the first run-in to Druid's Hill. Behind them, the Triumphs of Owen Greenwood and Fred Hanks were harried by Les Wells' Norton, and these three engaged in a separate, thrilling race of their own. The pushrod Golden Flash outfit took, and held, the lead despite determined efforts by Boddice to get through, and amid terrific excitement it crossed the line to win by some five yards.'

At the time Bill Boddice was 'King of the Sidecars' at Brands Hatch – a master of the legendary Kentish track. For Chris Vincent the 27 December 1960 was truly the day when his road racing career switched into top gear.

Almost overnight Chris became a star name. For example, Geoff Murdock (a former solo racer himself back in the late 1940s and early 1950s) approached the Birmingham-based BSA competitor with offers of support from none other than the Mobil oil company.

Already Chris was backed by Dunlop via Dickie Davies, whom Chris described to the author as: 'The best bloke you could ever have as a trade baron.' In fact, ever since he had beaten Bill Evans on the grass, Dunlop (themselves based in Birmingham, at Fort Dunlop) had supported Chris.

The Hanks Family

Fred (born 4 October 1920) and Maisie Hanks had six children: Norman (24 November 1944), Peter (11 October 1946), Roy (30 April 1948) followed by Beryl, Jill and Carol. At various times Fred and sons Peter, Roy and Norman competed, sometimes all at the same meeting. And in 1964 Fred and son Norman made history when they rode against each other in the Sidecar TT.

Typical of the Hanks family was Roy. He started racing in AMCA (Amateur Motor Cycle Association) events at the age of 12, driving an ES2 five-hundred Norton outfit. On this machine Roy took part in both scramble (moto-cross) and grass-track events. Then, in his final year with the AMCA, at the age of 15, he raced an outfit he had constructed himself comprising a damaged Manx Norton frame and a BSA six-fifty A10 engine, and with this won the AMCA Grasstrack Championship title.

Then as he reached his 16th birthday Roy joined the ACU in 1964 as a passenger to his middle brother Peter. But as Roy himself describes: 'Out of five races we had four incidents – crashes – so I then decided to have a go at driving myself!'

His first passenger was life-long friend Fred Holden, who had been with him in the AMCA, and later went on to passenger for many of the great names in sidecar racing. Memories from Roy's early days as a driver include crashing into his brother Peter on the final lap at Mallory Park's infamous Hairpin – and subsequently, as Roy explained to the author: 'Being dressed down in front of everyone by my father Fred.'

Roy's first Isle of Man TT came on 1966 (the year of the Seaman Strike so the races were run in late August rather than the traditional early June dates). And he finished 18th on a BSA twin. Father Fred had made his TT debut back in 1955, finishing seventh on a Matchless – and followed this

The Hanks brothers (BSA outfits 7 and 8) lead Mick Boddice (6) and Brian Rust (15) at Mallory Park's infamous Devil's Elbow, c.1967.

up with a repeat performance in 1956 on the same outfit. Brother Norman made his TT debut in 1964 (on a Triumph), but it was a retirement.

The following year, 1967, a certain Mrs Rose Arnold passengered for Norman. And as Roy says: 'this was a passenger made in heaven, looked good in black leather, cooked great sausage sandwiches, a welder by trade and good looking; this was the girl for me.'

Rose was the first-ever female passenger to stand on the TT podium – in 1968 finishing second as passenger to Norman. Then in 1969 Rose rode in the TT with Roy, finishing seventh.

Roy's first major race victory came at the Hutchinson 100 international at Brands Hatch over the full GP circuit, but that year run in the reverse direction (1966). This came after what had appeared to be a dead heat, awarded to Roy over none other than his brother Norman! Then, as Roy explained recently: 'I had to wait until 1997 to win my first TT, some 30 years afterwards.'

Roy also pays tribute to his 'many good passengers.' These have included Rose (whom he married), Gerald Daniel (brother-in-law), Tom Hanks (nephew, Norman's son), Julie (Roy and Rose daughter), along with Donny Williams, Jim Mann, Vince Biggs and his nephews Phil and Robert Biggs, along with his current passenger Dave Wells. It would be true to say that a special relationship has sprung up over the years between the Hanks and Biggs families.

And so to the year 2010, when Roy Hanks was in his 46th year of road racing and his 44th year of Isle of Man TT. The last word has to come from Roy himself: 'I can't wait to stop enjoying it.'

The family business Fred Hanks Motorcycles began trading at 247 Flade Road, Erdington, Birmingham on Saturday 6 December 1958. And it was still trading at the same address as *Sidecar Champions* was being compiled in the spring of 2010, over half a century later.

Fred Hanks passed away on 3 August 2009, aged 87. He had retired from racing upon reaching 55 years of age, in 1975.

The 1981 Isle of Man TT, Roy Hanks and passenger Vince Biggs (750cc Yamaha) at Ginger Hall.

The Murdoch/Mobil offer had come via journalist Mick Wollett (himself formerly a racing sidecar passenger for Edgar Strub). And it is worth mentioning that part of the Christmas Brands meeting was televised.

Typical of Chris Vincent's new found fame was the fact that he was now being approached to do club talks; not just in the Birmingham area, but, for example, in March 1961 to members of the Falcon Club at the Star Hotel, London Road, Broad Green, West Croydon, in the South London area.

The Kneeler

By 1961 Chris was ready to challenge the very best, certainly on British short circuits. That he was able to achieve this was down to three things – his own riding ability, his preparation, and his new, super-low kneeler outfit design.

As proof of just how successful he was in 1962 is to record the Easter programme. At Brands Hatch on Good Friday he won the sidecar event from Owen Greenwood (649cc Triumph) and Fred Hanks (499cc Norton), with *The Motor Cycle* commenting: 'With a delightful drive Chris Vincent came out on top.' Then, two days later at Snetterton on Easter Sunday the combination of Chris and his passenger Terry Harrison won both sidecar races and made fastest lap in each. Finally, at Oulton Park on Easter Monday the main sidecar race was won by the 1960 world champion Helmut Fath (BMW) and Chris runner-up, in front of a star-studded field – many of them BMW-mounted. Mr Vincent, however, did have the satisfaction of setting the fastest lap. The Oulton Park event was for 500cc machines so this meant that Chris with his A7 Shooting Star and single carburettor were up against the much quicker German BMWs. And it is worth recording exactly what *The Motor Cycle* race report had to say in its 6 April 1961 issue:

'Early leader in the 500cc Sidecar race was Bill Boddice, using his second-string Norton to head Helmut Fath round the opening lap. Boxed in at the start, Chris Vincent closed steadily on the two leaders and, with six laps gone, the three were tightly bunched. Fath went past Boddice then, a lap later, Vincent repeated the dose. Excitement mounted as Chris made a last lap effort, drew level with Fath, dropped back, then tried again – without success – as they dashed for the flag.'

Actually, Bill Boddice was so shocked by Chris Vincent's performance in this race that he put in a protest that Chris had used an oversize BSA engine; however, on being stripped by ACU officials it was found to be just under 500cc! Then Boddice was asked to strip his engine to be measured, but he refused and left the circuit. The result of this was that Bill was banned for a number of meetings…

Scintillating Form

At the international Hutchinson 100 meeting at Silverstone in early April, Chris showed 'scintillating form' (*The Motor Cycle*) and on this undoubted speed track came home fourth in the sidecar event – behind the BMWs of Florian Camathias, Pip Harris and Helmut Fath. But he did win the Sidecar Handicap race – from the BMWs of Jackie Beeton and Camathias – and set a new Silverstone sidecar lap record of 90.01mph (145km/h) in the process. Also, this was the first over 90mph sidecar around Silverstone.

In fact, Chris told the author: 'Silverstone was very special because I knew every bit of it – having just done the 1000 Kilometre Production Machine race there (on a BSA C15 solo).' And: 'The lap record was good against the foreign competition.'

Then, a month later Chris was victorious in both sidecar events and again set a new course lap record – of 80.16mph (129km/h). By now the pairing of Chris and his BSA were being referred to as 'all conquering'. In fact *The Motor Cycle* described him as: 'The most startling sidecar discovery since the great Eric Oliver', and: 'Chock-full of killer instinct.'

A Disappointing TT

But after being seen as having 'a golden opportunity' to have a good TT, Chris was to retire on the first lap with a burst rear tyre. The previous year had also seen an early retirement, when his engine died as he reached Quarter Bridge for the second time; however, as will be recorded later, he was to more than make up for these two glitches in 1962.

Chris Vincent and Eric Bliss during their victorious outing in the 1962 Isle of Man Sidecar TT.

Photo W. Gruber/Archiv

Winning the ACU Star

As proof of just how successful Chris Vincent was on the British short-circuit scene in 1962 is that not only did he win the ACU Sidecar Star, but he did this with a total of 84 points, with Pip Harris the next man with just 54 points! This was to be the first of many British titles to come Chris's way over the next few years.

The Currie Interview

The Motor Cycle dated 15 February 1962 carried a three-page feature by journalist Bob Currie, entitled: 'A Throttle To Steer Her By...', with the sub-heading: 'High Priest of the Travelling Prayer-Mat, Chris Vincent Gives the Low-down on Kneeler Technique.'

Bob Currie began by saying: 'By all the signs and portents, this coming road-racing season will see a big upsurge in popularity of the ground-hugging sidecar outfit. The travelling prayer-mat, Bill Boddice calls it. He, as you now know, has one under construction – and so have many others, Pip Harris included. And you don't need me to tell you that the man responsible for forcing his rivals on to their knees is Chris Vincent, whose exploits with a BSA-powered bombshell electrified many a meeting in the last year or two.'

Yet it was not Chris who had begun this kneeler concept, but Eric Oliver (see Chapter 3), who pioneered so many features of modern sidecar racing – rear springing and full streamlining among them; however, it should be noted that the BSA or even more so a BMW was far more suitable to power a kneeler than Oliver's very tall Norton engine.

But Chris Vincent, then only 19, used to frequent Cyril Smith's workshop, when both Cyril and Eric were in their heyday, in 1954; and it was a close-up of Oliver's kneeler which persuaded Chris that this was the direction in which sidecar racing would eventually evolve.

As we know, Chris began his racing career on the grass and in solo mode, before quickly switching to three wheels. Then, at the end of 1958 he transferred to the tarmac.

For 1958 he had a new outfit on the stocks. Low build, he reasoned, was not the complete answer; the centre of gravity must also be brought as low as possible. And so the assembly (which was, in fact, the one he campaigned up to the end of 1961) featured a home-spun frame which incorporated a rubber-in-tension rear-suspension system mounted below the level of the wheel spindle. Nor was that all, because originally the machine was even lower than it was at the time of the Currie feature – but things did not work out precisely as he had envisaged.

Hub-centre Steering

This was because Chris was enthusiastic about the use of hub-centre steering – both as a means of reducing overall height and ensuring a non-varying wheelbase. As Bob Currie explained: 'So he reckoned on mounting a king-pin within the front hub, carrying the wheel on pivoted arms arranged in parallelogram fashion, and steering by linkage from the handlebar. Unknown to him, Jack Difazio was working along broadly similar lines. But whereas Jack's creation made an appearance in public, Chris, albeit reluctantly, had to abandon the project.'

As Bob Currie was to admit, perhaps: 'Abandon is the wrong word; say shelve.'

Chris had many discussions with his old friend from Norton testing days, Bob Collier. Bob was a great special builder in his own right, particularly frames and suspension. There is no doubt that both Bob and Chris bounced ideas off each other.

And so to the 'sleek projectile' (*The Motor Cycle*) which fellow racers and the public alike came to know so well. There is absolutely no doubt that this had a tremendous advantage over a conventional sit-up outfit in that the front area was so much less and therefore less drag. But as Chris was to admit, he also owed much to the entirely new technique he had developed. This featured more than a hint of speedway practice – readers should remember that by then he had built up quite a reputation as a speedway sidecar star. His sidecar wheel was canted inward at the top and that feature, which he had employed ever since he began road-racing, was a direct legacy of speedway days.

How to Drive a Kneeler

In 1962, to drive a kneeler successfully, Chris said: 'You steer more by throttle than by the handlebar, keeping the steam turned on and sliding the bends in a series of controlled drifts. Sheer momentum and the power at the rear wheel carries the outfit through.'

Bob Currie went on to say: 'It is in cornering, in fact, that he gains those valuable yards on his rivals, but Chris believes that he can develop the technique still further. At present, on his own admission learning just how far he can go with it.'

In the author's opinion, by the beginning of 1962 Chris had perfected the technique of employing delicate throttle control to balance on the razor edge that separated drive from drift.

The 1962 Season Begins

As *The Motor Cycle* dated 5 April 1962 said: 'It would seem that Chris Vincent is set for another bumper season in the sidecar class. Neither in his heat nor in the final was his 497cc BSA twin kneeler headed.' These results came at the very first British national meeting at Mallory Park, Leicestershire, the previous Sunday. Chris also set the fastest lap.

Silverstone

Next, six days later in fact, came the international Hutchinson 100 at Silverstone. Every big-name sidecar racer from all over Europe was there. But it was the veteran Jackie Beeton (BMW) who came out on top to score a famous victory (see Chapter 2). Behind came the Swiss star Florian Camathias, with Chris third, the 1961 world champion Max Deubel fourth, Charlie Freeman fifth, and Claude Lambert sixth.

As the race had an engine capacity limit of 500cc, Chris was using his 497cc BSA engine. At this point it is important to point out that he only had one chassis, this now sporting a single massive front down-tube – so when 500cc and 1200cc classes took place on the same day an engine swap had to take place.

Unlike the later unit BSA engines (A50/A65), pre-unit A7 and A10 only ever used a single carburettor. In the Vincent sidecar racing, the five-hundred employed an Amal TT, while the A10 sometimes was fitted with an RN instrument.

Additionally, a four-speed gearbox was used until the 1962 Dutch, when a six-speed Austrian-made Schaftleitner assembly replaced the four-speed unit. The A7/A10 always used a siamesed exhaust system. An engine change could be achieved in only 45 minutes.

Chris and four times world champion Eric Oliver talking together at Silverstone during the early 1960s. Eric considered Chris could become champion too.

Chris Vincent, Eric Bliss and Colin Washbourne (BSA mechanic) after Chris and Eric had scored their famous 1962 TT win on a 500cc A7 BSA pushrod twin.

TT News

During mid-May 1962 it was confirmed that Chris Vincent was among the additional entries for the Isle of Man TT the following month. He was entered on his BSA Shooting Star-engined outfit, thus scotching rumours that he would drive Jackie Beeton's BMW instead.

There were a total of 35 entries for the Sidecar TT, with Chris and his passenger Eric Bliss at number three. Eleven BMWs were included: Scheidegger, Deubel, Camathias, Kölle, Pickup, Scholes, Lüthringhauser, Salter, Jackson, Lambert and Auerbacher. Plus Seeley (Matchless), Freeman (Norton) and Greenwood (Triumph).

The race itself was scheduled to start at 11am on Monday 4 June and be over three laps (113.2m – 182.1km).

A Historic Victory

Practising had been dominated by Florian Camathias, the flamboyant BMW driver from Switzerland, and by world champion Max Deubel – the previous year's winner – on another of the German twins. In fact, the pundits said it would be the customary BMW benefit. And yes, four of the first six home were BMWs. Yet it was Chris Vincent who climbed the rostrum at the end of the race to receive the winner laurels. It was the first British Sidecar TT victory since Eric Oliver had triumphed back in 1954.

Troubled by mechanical gremlins since the season began, Fritz Scheidegger was a non-arrival. And with the last-minute withdrawal of

Charlie Freeman – on doctor's advice after a practice crash – it meant that the first men away would be Chris and Max Deubel. And it was the latter who led down Bray Hill at the start.

At the end of the first lap Deubel led from Camathias, with Chris third. On lap two Chris moved up to second spot from Deubel after Camathias had retired after hitting a bank on the twisting, leafy section through Kerroomooar.

Unknown to spectators, Chris had a problem, caused at the 33rd milestone the first time around, the BSA having brushed the bank, in the process bending his gearchange lever. This was making swapping cogs difficult.

On the final circuit, and there was a major surprise when race leader Deubel's BMW engine seized at Ballig Bridge, thus leaving Chris and his passenger Eric Bliss heading the field.

The crowds around the last few miles 'gaped in astonishment' (*The Motor Cycle*), but they were soon recovered enough to wave and cheer the BSA. It was incredible, but it was happening. A British driver on a British machine was leading the Sidecar TT, for the first time, on the Mountain course, since 1925; Eric Oliver's victory having been achieved on the short Clypse course.

A celebration by BSA after the 1962 TT victory. Left to right: Colin Washbourne, Brian Martin (BSA competition manager), Chris Vincent, Eric Bliss (almost hidden by Chris), Bert Perigo, Bob Fearon (director and general manager), A.H. Jones (works director) and Bill Rawson.

The final finishing positions for the 1962 Sidecar TT were:

1st   C. Vincent (BSA)
2nd   O. Kölle (BMW)
3rd   C. Seeley (Matchless)
4th   C. Lambert (BMW)
5th   H. Lüthringshauser (BMW)
6th   G. Auerbacher (BMW)

The following is how Chris viewed his 1962 TT success when interviewed by Val Ward in the August/September 1980 issue of *Classic Bike*:

'That TT race was like a fairytale. Eric [Bliss] really knew his way round the Island and gave me a lot of help. We knew that Max Deubel and Florian Camathias on the BMWs had retired. We were lying third. All we had to do was keep going. The only thing that went wrong was when we ran off the course early in the race and I had some trouble changing gear.'

Technical Details

So what went into the TT-winning BSA shooting Star engine? In reality it was pretty standard, just put together correctly. As Chris says: 'the compression ratio was nothing fancy, it had a 358 camshaft – available to anybody – and there was only one carburettor; this being an Amal 1 5/32 in (29mm) type ie GP, TT or Monobloc.' The engine was not highly tuned, but as mentioned above 'put together very carefully.'

1962 Dutch TT

The 1962 Dutch TT was not Chris Vincent's first Continental European venture; actually this had taken place exactly one year earlier, in 1961, at the same Assen venue, in the north of the country.

The 1962 Dutch TT also marked the race debut for the newly-acquired six-speed Austrian-made Schafleitner gearbox. Chris told the author that it 'was worth 10bhp'. Also that during the 1962 season he had 'no less than five A7 Shooting Star engines.' Quite simply if one went wrong another one would be substituted. Chris remarking that 'there was not enough time between meetings to strip and rebuild.'

Getting Married

The remainder of the 1962 racing season did not bring as much joy as the first half. This was typified by what happened at the Race of the Year, at the end of September, Charlie Rous writing in *Motor Cycle News* Paddock

Gossip column that Chris: 'did not have much to celebrate at Mallory Park. The new BSA outfit played up and, when Vincent went out on his Aermacchi for the 250 race, the ignition coil dropped off on the first lap.'

It was also at Mallory Park that news leaked out that a couple of weeks earlier (15 September to be precise) he had married Kay. Charlie Rous remarked about his Mallory Park problems that Chris 'can't be lucky at everything.'

The World Championship Series

As we know, Chris Vincent had won the Isle of Man TT, then a round of the World Championship series, and retired in the Dutch TT with a blown engine. However, earlier that year the BSA star had finished sixth in the Spanish Grand Prix at Montjuich Park, Barcelona, and at the next round, the French Grand Prix at Clermont-Ferrand, finished third – behind the winner Max Deubel and second man Florian Camathias. These results meant that even though he had only finished in three of the six rounds, Chris had finished fifth in the points table; an excellent result for what, after all, was a series production roadster engine, rather than a pukka racing one.

A Winning Farewell to the 1962 Season

The Brands Hatch meeting in mid-October saw the 1962 British road race season come to its finale. *Motor Cycle News* dated 17 October takes up the story: 'The sidecar races saw Chris Vincent right back at the top of his form. He lead from start to finish and set a new race record of 79.68mph [128.20km/h] and equalled his own lap record of 81.26mph [130.74km/h].' The *MCN* report continued: 'Starting from scratch, Vincent was in just as tigerish mood in the four-lap handicap event, but try as he might the deficit was too great over the distance and he did well to finish third.' However, it is also worth noting that this time the Aermacchi kept going and he finished a very respectable third, behind the winner Fred Hardy (REG) and Norman Surtees on another Aermacchi.

This was to mark Chris Vincent's successful foray into the lightweight road-racing classes, and in subsequent years he was to prove almost as successful on two wheels as he did on three.

Testing the BSA Kneeler

Journalist David Dixon tested the Vincent BSA Kneeler at Brands Hatch in November 1962, and the actual date of this appearing in print was the 6 December issue of *The Motor Cycle*. Actually, the Dixon test session was with two outfits, not one.

The smaller-engined machine David Dixon described thus: 'To slide an outfit on a dry road takes power, and plenty of it. Well, that five-hundred BSA twin is a real goer with an extremely useful spread of power between 4,000 and 7,500rpm. From 4,000rpm the revs build up fast – and then some – without hesitation; at all times the unit was vibration free – one of the smoothest twins I've encountered. The exhaust pipes are siamesed, lead into a single, shallow megaphone, and the sharp note from that exhaust is enough to stir the blood of your granddad!'

Dixon followed these comments with ones regarding what he described as a new design, in the following manner: 'Why should Chris want to replace this fabulous outfit with a completely new design? Old faithful, first used in 1959, may have been successful, but it was felt that there was room for improvement. And, of course, the opposition is razor sharp these days. When I tried it, the new outfit had a 646cc engine, a factor which underlined the difference between the old and new.' He continued: 'First the steering. The front fork is different, its movement controlled by rubber bands and a single telescopic hydraulic unit mounted behind the wheel. The steering characteristics were also entirely different, and the steering was incredibly light. The merest suggestion of pressure on either bar produced an almost violent change of direction! So much so that our first passage through the sharp right-hander at Druid's and the left-hander into Bottom Straight was a series of wobbles, with the outfit snaking all over the road.'

But as David Dixon went on to explain: 'Far from being worried by this, Eric Bliss was chuckling heartily; he *knew* the steering set-up and what to expect.'

The test session also showed that: 'The beefier power of the big unit was apparent straight away, especially in the lower and intermediate rpm range. Carburation was clean as a new driving licence right through the range – not surprising, from a single carburettor – and there were oodles of useable power on tap between 3,000 and 6,500rpm. Incidentally, the unit would rev to 7,000, the five-hundred to 8,000rpm.'

Of course, both engines were interchangeable in the frames, and Chris confirmed that he would use a six-speed Schafleitner gearbox for the five-hundred engine.

Another point of interest was the redesigned sidecar. The old outfit carried its fuel in the sidecar wheel mudguard; and electric pump lifting petrol from there to the carburettor.

Unit Engine
1962 had seen the launch by the BSA factory of its new unit construction twin: the 499cc A50 and 654cc A65.

Chris voiced the opinion to the author that the new unit engines had a more robust bottom end. The unit engines had a shorter stroke. This had seen a widening up of the cylinder bores and an increase in crank journal size. This, together with lighter flywheels, meant the new engines revved higher. But a disadvantage of the smaller engine was that the six-speed 'box could not be used.

In fact, the smaller BSA unit was soon to be ditched in favour of BMW power; however, the six-fifty BSA went on to win countless races while under Chris Vincent's control.

Obviously many of BSA's resources were at his disposal, including a dynomomer – as long as it was not required for company use at the time. Also Chris would often work on in the experimental shop late into the night. Then it was out on the Small Heath test track – without a passenger – his van's headlights illuminating the scene.

Unlike many former employees, Chris has only happy memories of the Small Heath factory. In a May 1995 interview by Peter Glover, he emphasised that: 'Everyone seemed to want to help.' And without much formal education, Chris explained that was why he learned things so much more quickly.

Chris worked under Len Crisp, foreman of the experimental department. He also came into contact with the other motorcycle competitors within the BSA organisation, including motocross men such as Jeff Smith and, after the Ariel factory moved to Small Heath in 1962, trials star Sammy Miller.

An example of the help which Len Crisp provided is that he loaned Chris a three-fifty B40 unit single to ride around the TT course during his first visit to the Island in 1960.

During the 1960s at BSA Chris often covered 50,000 miles (80,450km) every year testing everything from a Dandy scooterette to factory racers which would be taking part in the annual American Daytona 200.

Dunlop Tyre Tester

Another string to Chris Vincent's bow was the role of tyre tester. This was carried out at venues such as Mallory Park and the industry's test track at MIRA, just off the A5 near Nuneaton. This worked very well, as not only was he testing tyres for Dunlop with his outfit, but at the same time he was also trying out results of his own experiment; an ideal combination.

At MIRA, Chris says that he would cover up to 20 laps – 60 miles (96.5km) – often in sub-zero temperatures. In these conditions he would block up the air intake on his BSA fairing.

An amusing aside to association with Dunlop and Dickie Davies was that upon hearing that Chris was about to be married, Dickie asked him what he was going to do for a bed. When Chris explained that he did not have one, Dickie said he would solve this, and the next thing a new Dunlopilo mattress arrived!

The 1963 Season

Winning the British Championship (ACU Star) for the second time in 1963 showed that his BSAs, the larger one in particular, were competitive on the short circuits. However, the same could not be said of the smaller engine, which simply was not quick enough to successfully challenge the might of the BMWs on the long GP courses. In fact his only top six placing in a 1963 Grand Prix came at Assen, the scene of the Dutch round. But in the Isle of Man TT he had retired in both Sidecar and Lightweight (250cc) events; the latter on Bob Geeson's REG twin.

Into 1964

1964 was a busy year for Chris. First he finally accepted that he needed a BMW to compete in GPs and purchased one from the Swiss star, Fritz Scheidegger.

The year was also notable because it saw him set something of a record by riding in three solo classes of the TT, as well as in the sidecar race! In fact, as one commentator remarked: 'He put 48 hours into a 24 hour day.'

The 1964 TT entries comprised: Ultra Lightweight (Honda), Lightweight and Junior (both Aermacchi, provided by importer Syd Lawton), and Sidecar (BMW).

With film star good looks, Chris Vincent was utilised by BSA in a publicity role at the 1963 London Earls Court Show with Caron Gardner, one of the blonde pilots from the James Bond film *Goldfinger*.

But he only gleaned a single finish – 12th on the Honda CR93. The machine was actually owned by Liverpool dealer Bill Hannah and Chris had made a victorious debut on the machine at the British season opener at Mallory Park on 22 March. The rider who finished second in this race was none other than Bill Ivy on another CR93, and that is proof of Chris Vincent's ability as a solo rider.

Another notable date was 19 April 1964, when at Brands Hatch he won the 125cc event on the Hannah Honda and also the 1200cc Sidecar with his BSA A65-engined outfit.

Runner-up at Assen

1965 was to see Chris finish runner-up in the Dutch round of the World Championship series in Holland, behind Fritz Scheidegger. He also came home in fifth position in the Isle of Man, behind Deubel, Scheidegger, Auerbacher and Lüthringhauser. But once again, as the previous years, he won the British title with BSA power.

Talking of the Dutch TT, this was always staged on the Saturday. And as proof of the hectic lifestyle, the Brands Hatch 500-mile race was the following day, and to make sure the big names at the Dutch reached the Kent circuit in time, the Brands promoters chartered a special plane. As Chris remarked recently: 'The passenger list was a Who's Who of motorcycling. I flew over with Derek Minter, John Cooper, Dave Croxford, Tommy Robb, Phil Read, Mike Hailwood and other

Chris Vincent (654cc BSA, 38) leads Colin Seeley (650cc Dunstall Norton, 6) and Owen Greenwood (Mini, 48) at Mallory Park, c.1965.

competitors. If anything had happened to that plane, international racing would have come to a full stop.'

The 1965 season was also when Chris Vincent won the 50cc British title (on a Suzuki single) and the Sidecar British Championship (BSA). No other rider has ever achieved this feat.

The Greenwood Mini

In 1966 the home Championship title went to Owen Greenwood and his controversial Mini-based three-wheeler. This inspired Chris to respond by creating a revolutionary three-wheeler. This had two wheels at the front and a five-hundred BMW engine and six-speed Hewland gearbox, but work on this exciting machine came to an abrupt halt when the sport's rulers banned it.

Then he reverted to his orthodox BMW, but with only moderate success. Even so, he had got to know, and become good friends with, Fritz Scheidegger. Fritz gave Chris the run of his workshop facilities when he was abroad in return for a similar arrangement when they were racing in Britain. In 1980 Chris controversially told journalist Val Ward: 'There was an agreement between us about who would win what, but nobody else knew about it at the time.' However, in truth this story was not quite what it seemed – with Fritz asking Chris to go steady once so that the world champion would not be shown up at Cadwell!

Owen Greenwood

No one in sidecar racing (or probably motorcycle sport in general) caused more controversy than Owen Greenwood, when the Leicester man wheeled out his 1071cc Mini-powered Special at the beginning of the 1965 season. The so-called experts said the machine would never work and that Owen was wasting his time. Yes, three-wheelers had been tried before, but had failed to equal the overall performance of conventional outfits.

However, Owen, passenger Terry Fairbrother and mechanic Roger Compton proved the pundits wrong. For in 1965 they won the Brands Hatch Shield for the best performance in their class at the Kent circuit, set a new lap record at Cadwell Park and beat Chris Vincent to win the big Gold Cup meeting at Mallory Park.

Owen's competitive motorcycling career began when he rode in a wartime scramble near Derby when he was 17. That was in 1941. He had never seen a scramble – in fact he thought he was going to compete in a trial! However, when he arrived on his 500cc Norton the others were rushing around on scramblers with great knobbly tyres. Still, he had a go, and that was how it all began. Later, he did a lot of grass-tracking and some speedway. In 1951 he started road racing on a BSA Gold Star in solo events; later still, he took up sidecar racing.

Owen Greenwood raced every year in the Isle of Man from 1951 to 1964 inclusive. First in the Manx Grand Prix (1951–56) all of which was on solo machines (BSA, AJS and Norton), followed by the TT. In that first year (1957) he rode an AJS 7R in the Junior (50th) and with a Norton outfit (13th) in the Sidecar race. From then on he competed every year in the Sidecar class with Triumph-engined outfits, except 1963 when he used the

Leicester-based Owen Greenwood (649cc Triumph), Mallory Park, 19 June 1960.

horizontally-mounted Matchless G50 single 'chair'. His only other solo TT appearance, again on an AJS, came in 1961, when he finished home 32nd. As for his best TT sidecar race, this was in 1959 when he finished sixth.

He had met his wife, Kathleen, in the Isle of Man when riding there in the TT. The couple had a son John, born in 1959, and during the 1960s they lived in Thurmaston, near Leicester, where he ran his own business. Owen admitted that he was very much 'the amateur at heart', racing for the fun and satisfaction it gave him.

Prior to the Mini, Owen had raced a Norton, but mainly Triumph-engined outfits, plus an interesting Matchless G50-engined device with the cylinder lying horizontal. These machines were in addition to his solo efforts.

So what gave him the idea of building the Mini Special? When interviewed by Mick Woollett in October 1965, his answer was: 'I first thought of building a three-wheeler long before I started sidecar racing in 1955.' He continued: 'sidecars didn't seem good engineering to me and I imagined a 500cc Cooper-Norton racing car with a single wheel at the back.'

Then, of course, Birmingham engineer Ernie Earles and the Italian Gilera factory both tried something along the same lines. But both these projects were failures and, Owen said, put him off. Then in 1962 Greenwood, Fairbrother and Compton reconsidered the idea of a three-wheeler, but powered by a 649cc Triumph Bonneville engine.

Their first plan was to revert to Owen's original idea – two wheels at the front with one drive wheel at the rear. But a friend of theirs who worked at BRM on chassis design said that this layout simply would not work sufficiently well for the outfit to be competitive on all types of circuits. This engineer explained that, in his considered opinion, their three-wheeler must have front-wheel drive. And that was not feasible using a Triumph engine. And so the idea came about to use the Austin Mini car engine.

Although he successfully raced conventional sidecar outfits, Owen Greenwood will forever be associated with his controversial Mini, seen here at Mallory Park during 1966.

Contrary to rumours at the time, no help or support was given, or sought, from the Mini's manufacturer, BMC (British Motor Corporation). It took three months, once the concept was mapped out in the trio's minds, to actually construct the machine. As Owen later recalled: 'We worked every evening from seven o'clock till around two in the morning. Then Roger [Compton] had to ride 17 miles to his home in Hinckley. I felt sorry for him.'

The total cost was some £450 and they purchased a 1071cc Cooper S engine with gearbox for £170. Owen saying: 'It was a second-hand unit and we were lucky, for BMC had just started to make the 1275cc engines, which made the 1071cc units obsolete for some types of racing.'

The engine and transmission were built into their own tubular chassis and erred on the safe side by making it strong – and heavy. Later, a five-speed close-ratio Colotti gearbox was added for an additional £100 – plus a limited-slip differential which set the team back an additional £50.

So where did the Mini Special gain over conventional sidecars, and where did it lose? As Owen himself explained back in 1965: 'We gain on acceleration and on most corners, particularly on left-handers.' This was because the passenger could get his weight well over on the lefthanders, but on the right-handers: 'He could only crouch behind me.' In addition, time was lost changing gear, Owen saying: 'You just cannot get a car-type change anything like so fast as a positive-stop motorcycle gearbox'. But, fortunately, he did not have to change gear nearly so much with the Mini, because the engine had a wider spread of power than a conventional motorcycle engine.

Also, interestingly, the Greenwood Mini lost a little on maximum speed. Owen telling Mick Woollett: 'At Silverstone, Florian Camathias on his 500cc BMW could pull away on the straights.'

Who did Owen Greenwood consider the best sidecar racer of his generation? His immediate answer was: 'There's no doubt about it – Chris Vincent. He's in a class of his own.'

A particularly controversial aspect of the Greenwood Mini was the use of two close-set wheels at the rear – actually making it a four-wheeler!

When the Mini was eventually banned during 1966, Owen Greenwood decided to hang up his leathers. But this was not before he had carved a name in motorcycle sport – largely through the controversial Mini Special – which in many ways was more car than motorcycle!

The Innovator

Throughout Chris Vincent's racing carer he was very much an innovator, always trying to push the envelope of development further. In this he can be compared to Freddie Dixon, Eric Oliver and Rolf Biland; all four men intent on developing sidecar racing to a higher level on the technical front. In Chris's case, even the legendary BMW Rennsport engine did not escape his attention, as he converted one of the German units to dry-sump lubrication, even though eventually insoluble problems with scavening drove him to convert it back to wet-sump and cost him the principle advantage of the dry-sump layout, that of a lower centre of gravity.

Eventually for World Championship 500cc races Chris Vincent had to switch from BSA to BMW. He is seen on one of the latter machines at the Dutch TT in June 1965.

The Solo Career

Mention has already been made of Chris Vincent's solo racing career. But in the author's mind he could have been even more successful in this field, had he not been the sidecar ace he was.

What may not be widely appreciated today is that he was a works rider for both Suzuki and Kawasaki. For example, at the 1966 Japanese Grand Prix at Fisco he and fellow Englishman Dave Simmonds (together with Ernst Degner and Naomi Tanaguchi) rode factory Kawasakis in the 125cc event.

Testing a Team Lotus racing car in March 1966. Chris's long-time business manager, Peter Chapman, is next to him. Also in the picture is solo star, John Cooper.

The Kawasaki ride was also to directly lead to Chris's business manager Peter Chapman becoming the British importer of the Japanese company's racing motorcycles (the 250 and 350cc AIR twin-cylinder models), Chapman having accompanied Chris to the Grand Prix. It is also worth noting that Chris rode an ex-works Hugh Anderson single-cylinder Suzuki in the 50cc event at the same circuit the following year.

Before leaving the solos, Chris also rode Suzuki machinery in the 500-miler at Brands Hatch and the first-ever Isle of Man Production TT in 1967. Although he usually rode a two-fifty T20 Super Six for Suzuki GB, Chris competed in at least one 500-miler on the five-hundred T500 twin. In both cases Chris was a class winner.

The 1969 Season

As Chris Vincent was to remark to the author: '1969 – phew, what a season!' There were a host of victories, including Oulton Park, Snetterton, Mallory Park, Brands Hatch, Cadwell Park, Castle Combe, Crystal Palace, Thruxton and Lydden Hill. And, yet again, the British Sidecar Championship title.

The Münch URS

Eventually, Chris decided to concentrate solely on three wheels, and his big break came during the winter of 1971. The German Horst Owesle (see Chapter 16) had just won the Sidecar World Championship title with a developed version of Helmut Fath's four-cylinder URS, but after winning the title decided to retire, together with his passenger Englishman Peter Rutherford. And so, Chris Vincent's name was put forward as the team's

The four-cylinder URS Münch outfit with which Chris contested the 1972 World Championship series.

replacement for the outgoing Owesle. So, at last mounted on truly competitive machinery, Chris Vincent – and his many fans – looked forward to 1972 as the year he would challenge the world.

When the URS-Münch engine and gearbox assembly arrived from Germany, Chris and his team set about designing and creating an outfit, a task they completed in just six weeks. The new chassis was of entirely British origin. However, it was not to be the dream season that everyone connected with the Vincent camp had hoped for. The first three rounds of the World Championship took place in Germany (Nürburgring), France (Clermont-Ferrand) and Austria (Salzburgring). But trouble with ignition and cycle parts led to retirement in all three. Things were no better at the fourth round, the Isle of Man TT.

Success at Last

Then, at the fifth round, the Dutch TT at Assen, Chris and his passenger, Peter Cassey, finally managed to complete the race – with a magnificent second to the rapid BMW of Klaus Enders passengered by Ralf Englehardt. And the pairing of Vincent and Cassey had beaten Siegfried Schauzu, already winner of the German GP and the Isle of Man TT that year. During this race, Chris set a new sidecar lap record by over four seconds – incredible. Then came a whole string of finishes in Belgium, Czechoslovakia and Finland.

The first race after Assen came at Spa Francorchamps in the heart of the heavily wooded Ardennes, in eastern Belgium, a few miles from the German border. Here, Chris and Peter Cassey came home fourth, behind Enders, Lüthringhauser and Schauzu. Things improved in the Czech GP at Brno, with another second behind Enders, with Schauzu back in fourth.

Then at the final round in Finland at Imatra, everything clicked into gear, with an impressive victory, with Enders this time runner-up and Schauzu third. This left Chris and Peter fourth in the overall ranking, finally bettering the 1962 result, when on the BSA Chris had won the TT and claimed fifth in the title rankings.

Besides his Grand Prix success, that year Chris won several big international events on the British short circuit with a 750cc version of the URS Münch, in place of the 500cc unit.

In 1973 Chris had occasional outings on the URS-Münch engined machine, but did not contest the World Championship series. Then, with two-strokes coming on to the scene (first König and then Yamaha) Chris, with a Yamaha 700cc four-cylinder engine, bowed out after emerging victorious from the big international meeting for the fifth year running. Chris Vincent then decided to retire.

Up to that time probably no one else in the world had won more sidecar races, and since he began road racing at the end of 1958 he had won over 200 races and that was not including heats, or grasstrack or speedway events! But even though he had quit racing, Chris retained his interest in motorcycles and in 1976 opened a dealership at Earls Shilton, Leicestershire, becoming a solus Yamaha agent.

By the late 1970s he also had a small number of personal bikes – an RD200 Yamaha (suitably modified to Chris's tastes including Ariel Arrow front forks), a Sunbeam S7 and a Ducati 860 GTS; the latter rebuilt with spares supplied by the author. Chris's two sons, Max and Jason, were both to become successful solo racers in their own right.

The motorcycle business was sold as a going concern in the late 1990s, but today Chris still has the Yamaha RD200 and the URS-Münch racing outfit. And he attends various motorcycle events and shows, such as the TT Riders annual dinner and the Stafford classic show.

CHAPTER 12

MAX DEUBEL

Max Deubel, who was born on 5 February 1935 in Mulhenau, Germany, first came to the public, the media and, most importantly of all at that time, BMW's attention when he finished third at Hockenheim in June 1959, the scene of that year's German Grand Prix.

At that time Walter Schneider (see Chapter 8) was the world champion (a title he won in 1958 and was to retain in 1959).

A TT Debut

The 1960 season saw Max and passenger Horst Holer take in every round of the Championship. That year there were five races: these being held in France (Clermont-Ferrand), the Isle of Man (TT), Holland (Assen), Belgium (Spa Francorchamps) and Germany (Solitude).

Interestingly, Max and Horst made their Isle of Man TT debut that year – the first year since its return in 1954 that it had been run over the full 37.73-mile (60.70km) Mountain circuit, rather than the much shorter Clypse course. Allocated race number 17, Max and Hans were to retire in the race.

The TT had been preceded by the French GP, where the pair had finished fourth, with Helmut Fath, Fritz Scheidegger and Florian Camathias taking the top three positions in that order. Like Max Deubel, the trio all drove BMW outfits, with Fath's the official works entry that year, following the retirement of Walter Schneider.

The third round of the 1960 Championship came at Assen, with the Dutch TT, Deubel and passenger Holer finishing sixth. But eight days later at the Belgian Grand Prix the pair posted another retirement.

The final round was held at the 7.1-mile (11.4km) Solitude circuit, just outside Stuttgart, and it was deemed a real rider's course, particularly the tricky back-leg section. The sidecar race was staged over drenched roads on the Saturday afternoon (the solos raced the following day), and took in nine laps – a total distance of 63.8 miles (102.65km). Won by Fath, from Camathias and Scheidegger, Max Deubel was fourth ahead of Otto Kolle.

Montjuich Park

When the first round of the 1961 World Championships began in Spain, over the tortuous Montjuich Park circuit in Barcelona, no one could have predicted the outcome of the title that season. Once again, Helmut Fath emerged victorious, with Fritz Scheidegger runner-up. As for Florian Camathias, he had been forced to retire with a fractured final-drive shaft.

There was no mention of Max Deubel at all, and he certainly was not listed as a finisher.

All-change

Then fate intervened and before the next round of the Championship there were a couple of incidents which would change the course of history.

First, on 30 April only a few days after the Spanish GP, world champion Helmut Fath and passenger Alfred Wohlgemuth crashed heavily in the annual Eifelrennen at the Nürburgring. As *The Motor Cycle* was to report: 'The Eifel Mountains were in a treacherous mood.' Continuing: 'Mist and rain on the 5.1-mile [8.2km] South circuit made conditions decidedly grim for the international Eifelrennen.' As fully explained in Chapter 14, Helmut Fath suffered several serious injuries, but did, eventually, make a recovery, whereas Alfred Wohlgemuth died in the accident.

The many well-known mourners included Florian Camathias, Fritz Scheidegger and Max Deubel. It was also attended by pre-war solo star and TT winner Georg Meier and, representing BMW, Carl Hoepner (the company's publicity chief).

As if this was not enough, only a couple of weeks later on Thursday 11 May, Florian Camathias and passenger Hilmar Cecco crashed their BMW outfit at Modena in Italy. Cecco sustained fatal injuries, whereas Camathias, although originally feared to have sustained head injuries, had in fact suffered multiple fractures to the lower ribs, but was able to return to his home in Montreux, Switzerland, later in May.

Victory at Hockenheim

With both Fath and Camathias sidelined, it was to be Max Deubel (now passengered by Emil Hörner) who was to emerge as the new challenger for the world title. The first chance came only a few days after the Camathias accident, on Sunday 14 May, when the German Grand Prix was staged over the 4.8-mile (7.7km) Hockenheim loop, and as *The Motor Cycle* reported in its 18 May 1961 issue: 'A circuit detested by all riders proud of their craft, and loved, if at all, only by development engineers anxious to prove the top speed of their machines.'

Deubel and Hörner led the 13-lap 62.4-mile (100.4km) race from start to finish, and also set the fastest lap at 105.88mph (170.36km/h).

Max Deubel
acknowledging the crowd
after emerging victorious
in the 1961 TT. Also in the
picture are his passenger
Emil Hörner and other
competitors including Pip
Harris.

The French Grand Prix at Clermont-Ferrand was staged one week later, but this time it was Fritz Scheidegger who won, with Max Deubel runner-up – a reversal of the positions gained by the two drivers at Hockenheim.

The Isle of Man TT
As the 15 June issue of *The Motor Cycle* began its Sidecar TT race report: 'the only surprising thing about miracles, it is said, is that they sometimes happen.' And continued: 'The miracle of Monday's Sidecar TT was that Max Deubel (BMW) of West Germany beat the favourite for a win, the dashing Swiss, Fritz Scheidegger (BMW).'

Actually, Deubel had led throughout, completing the three-lap 113.2-mile (182.13km) race in 1 hour 17 minutes 29.8 seconds, an average speed of 87.65mph (141.02km/h). Scheidegger's time was 1 hour 18 minutes 2.6 seconds and his speed 87.03mph (140.03km/h). Third was Isle of Man favourite, Pip Harris, also on a BMW in 1 hour 19 minutes 40.4 seconds, a speed of 85.26mph (137.18km/h).

The Dutch TT and Victory Number Three
Round four of the 1961 Championship took place at Assen. But Englishman Pip Harris was unable to repeat his 1960 Dutch TT victory. Having led Max

Deubel and Hörner with the victors' laurel, after winning the 1961 Dutch TT at Assen. Photo W. Gruber/Archiv

Deubel's BMW 'by an eyebrow' (*The Motor Cycle*) for six laps, Pip's BMW seized and Max was able to win as he pleased. Fritz Scheidegger, meanwhile, had his light-alloy sidecar wheel collapse after three laps, while Chris Vincent (BSA) who was second to Max for four laps, had carburation bother and a rear chain off once; he struggled home ninth. Edgar Strub and Jackie Beeton (BMWs) provided a storming finish for second place, Edgar just getting the verdict. The fastest lap, a new record, was set by Deubel at 78.07mph (125.6km/h).

The final round of the 1961 Sidecar Championship season came at the Belgian GP over the ultra-fast 8.76-mile (14.09km) Spa Francorchamps circuit in the Ardennes. And it was long remembered due to its near-tropical heat and the high standard of racing. Quite simply, Max Deubel had to follow Fritz Scheidegger home to secure the title; and that was precisely what he did.

There had been a sidecar race scheduled during the Swedish Grand Prix, but this race was not taken up. So that meant that Max Deubel and Emil Hörner were the new world champions. Taking each driver's best four performances, Max and Emil had three wins and a second (30 points) to Fritz Scheidegger and passenger Horst Burckardt's two wins and two seconds (28 points); Edgar Strub ranked third with 14 points.

Skill This Time Around

As Maurice Bula described in the book *Grand Prix Motorcycle Champions of the World 1949–1975* (Foulis): 'If luck favoured them in 1961, it was skill alone which brought them their second title.' As Max and Emil turned up the pressure on their rivals in the 1962 season.

Florian Camathias made a return to the scene (now with Horst Burckart as passenger). While Fritz Scheidegger had a new passenger too, in the shape of Englishman John Robinson.

Before the GPs began Max Deubel visited Britain and took part in the 30th international Hutchinson 100, staged at Silverstone. But on a clockwise circuit, Deubel's right-handed outfit 'seemed at a slight disadvantage' (*Motor Cycle News*). And this seemed to be borne out in the

Max going around the outside of Bill Boddice (Norton) on the approach to Gerard's Bend during the Race of the Year at Mallory Park in September 1961.

results, with a fourth place in each of his two events at the Northamptonshire venue.

Victory At Oulton Park

Max and Emil scored impressive victories at Oulton Park on Easter Monday 1961, when as *Motor Cycle News* described, they: 'Scorched away to resounding victories in both the sidecar scratch and handicap events'. The German BMW teamsters also set the fastest lap in both races.

And Victory in Spain

At the first round of the 1962 Championship – again in Spain – Max won setting a new race record average speed of 67.2mph (108.11km/h); he also set the fastest lap at 68.58mph (110.21km/h).

At round two at the 'circuit in the mountains' (*Motor Cycle News*), in other words the French GP at Clermont-Ferrand, Max Deubel won again, increasing his lead in the title race.

TT Prospects

Then on the eve of the TT, Britain's former world champion (in the 350 and 500cc classes on Norton and Gilera) Geoff Duke, writing for *Motor Cycle News* in their 30 May 1962 issue, saying: 'Max Deubel my choice.' Going on to explain: 'Although Camathias will no doubt give Deubel more than a run for his money, I don't subscribe to the theory that Mr C's troubles are

Max Deubel during the 1962 Isle of Man TT. Although a clear favourite to win, Max was forced into retirement with engine trouble. However, this setback did not stop him from being crowned world champion for the second time.

always "bad luck". Let's face it, he rides and drives very hard, and in a longish race my money would always favour Max Deubel.'

And what a sensational start to the Isle of Man TT week. Chris Vincent, with Eric Bliss (see Chapter 11) as passenger, won the race on his BSA outfit to give a British machine and crew their first TT success since Eric Oliver and Norton won back in 1954.

So what happened to the BMW brigade? The Max Deubel–Florian Camathias 'no-holds-barred, no-quarter-given' (*Motor Cycle News*) battle ended with Florian retiring unhurt after crashing, although his passenger broke a leg, and Max was forced into retirement with engine trouble.

Scheidegger Returns

Fritz Scheidegger made a return to the GP scene at the Dutch TT, at the end of June, and won the race at Assen. But by coming home second Max retained a comfortable lead in the Championship; Florian Camathias retired with clutch trouble.

However, a week later in Belgium roles were reversed and Camathias won, with Scheidegger second and Deubel third.

Victory in Germany and a Second Championship Title

Victory in the last round of the Championship, the West German Grand Prix at Solitude, by Max and Emil gained them a winning points lead of 34. Next came Camathias (passengered by Bob Winter on this occasion), his second place meant that his points total that year was 26.

Deubel and Hörner working on their factory BMW in a Continental European paddock during the mid-1960s. Photo W. Gruber/Archiv

In the race itself Camathias led for the first four of the nine laps, but then the German pair went ahead and finished comfortable winners. There were 26 starters in the 63.8-mile (102.7km) race, and Max Deubel set the fastest lap at 89.4mph (143.8km/h).

Short Circuit Meetings

From early August 1962, Max and Emil took part in several international meetings both in Continental Europe and Great Britain. In the latter, his first visit came in early August at the ACU British Championships, staged at Oulton Park in Cheshire. There were two sidecar events: one was won by Max, the other by Fritz Scheidegger; in both cases the one who did not win came second – a reversal of positions in fact.

Next at Cadwell Park in early September, after being forced to retire with a blown-up motor in the 12-lap 500cc Sidecar event (after winning his heat), 'Feverish work in Deubel's pits saw him out in the Handicap event with a new engine fitted to his outfit' (*Motor Cycle News*). He went on to win his heat, but in the final the handicap proved too much. Riding brilliantly, he came through the field to finish fifth and set the fastest lap.

To Quit?

But much more significant was the story in the same issue of *MCN* which began: 'World sidecar racing champion Max Deubel, one of the greatest artists of the three-wheeler world, may be in his last season on the international circuits.' Max had told *Motor Cycle News* at Cadwell Park that he had purchased a guest house in Germany which he would be opening soon. Going on to joke that: 'I may be too busy washing up to go racing.' However, Max's decision whether to continue racing was more likely to be influenced by the BMW factory's attitude to road racing the following year.

Scarborough

A week after the Cadwell meeting came the Gold Cup at Oliver's Mount, Scarborough. Max and Florian Camathias both won their respective heats, with the former getting the verdict in the final, with Max runner-up.

Next came the Mallory Park 'Race of the Year' meeting, but although Max won his heat beating Camathias, he was a non-finisher in the final, which was won by the Swiss driver.

The 1963 Championship

The 1963 world Championship series got off to a winning start for the existing champions. The Spanish Grand Prix at Montjuich Park, Barcelona,

After suffering a practice crash, Max was forced to take on a new passenger, Barry Dungworth, for the 1963 TT race. The pair came home, for Max, a lowly eighth.

saw Max and Emil comfortable winners from Otto Kolle who finished runner-up and Florian Camathias.

At round two, the West German GP at Hockenheim, Camathias won with Max second. The next scheduled round was at Clermont-Ferrand in France. Unfortunately the sidecar race (together with the 250cc solos) was cancelled, due to thick fog at the end of the morning.

And so to the Isle of Man TT. A practice crash left the reigning world champions and TT lap record holder in less than perfect condition for the

Oulton Park British Championship meeting August 1963. This photograph clearly shows the colourful emblem which was painted on the front nearside of the world champion's BMW.

Max Deubel leads Fritz
Scheidegger during the
Austrian Grand Prix – note
the cobblestone surface.
Photo W. Gruber/Archiv

race. Not only this, but he was forced to take on a new passenger, Englishman Barry Dungworth, in place of his usual ballast Emil Hörner, who had been slightly injured in the spill. And so Max was to finish, for him, a lowly eighth.

After the Isle of Man came the Dutch TT at Assen. Here Max, with Emil Hörner back in the chair, made no mistake and took the victory from Scheidegger and Camathias. A week later they secured a third successive title with runner-up spot to Fritz Scheidegger in the Belgian Grand Prix.

The 1964 Championship

The 1964 Championship series followed the same pattern as the previous year, except this time the race at Clermont-Ferrand took place, while the German round saw the switch from Hockenheim to Solitude; however, unlike the 1963 result Max Deubel did not win in the season opener in Spain, but finished fourth; Florian Camathias taking the victory with the four-cylinder Gilera he had been loaned for the season by the Italian factory.

In France, at Clermont-Ferrand, the German duo came home second behind Fritz Scheidegger. Next came the Isle of Man. Here Max won his second TT; and he also set the fastest lap at 89.63mph (144.21km/h). In fact, right from the start he was the firm favourite, and he led from start to finish and broke the race record – but not the lap record.

Then came the Dutch TT at Assen, when Colin Seeley became the first Englishman to win a World Championship sidecar race since 1960 (FCS-BMW). And it was no fluke victory because Seeley and his passenger Wally

Rawlings led from start to finish. Second was Chris Vincent (BMW), third Fritz Scheidegger and a distant fourth Max Deubel. Meanwhile, after 4 laps Camathias' Gilera outfit had burst into flames when a petrol union came loose spraying fuel onto the engine!

Then it was on to Spa Francorchamps for the Belgian round, where Max, referred to as 'cool, calm and collected' (*MCN*), won after setting the fastest practice lap, thus putting him in pole position on the grid. And at the start, he flashed ahead – staying there to win easily from Fritz Scheidegger. As for Florian Camathias (Gilera), he held third place until the second lap, when he stopped with fuel-line trouble.

A Fourth World Title

After setting the fastest lap of the race at 88.43mph (142.28km/h) at Solitude during the German GP, the final round of the 1964 Championship, Max Deubel was content to let Fritz Scheidegger take the victory, secure in the knowledge that second position would be sufficient for a fourth world title. This put him on level terms with Eric Oliver.

At Solitude there were no fewer than 200,000 spectators. And the final points tally for the 1964 series was Max Deubel/Emil Hörner 28 points (34 gross) and Fritz Scheidegger 26; Colin Seeley was third on 17.

1964 saw Max Deubel score his fourth and final World Championship crown.

Colin Seeley

C.J. (Colin Jordan) Seeley was born on 2 January 1936 at Crayford, Kent. From his early childhood, motorcycles were very much a way of life in the Seeley household. Colin learned to ride on his father Percy's Vincent Rapide v-twin sidecar outfit at the age of 14 in 1950; he passed his driving test to ride a motorcycle a couple of years later, in 1952. As proof of how keen he was to become part of the motorcycle industry, the young Seeley, at 15 years of age, gave up an engineering career to join Dartford dealers Schwieso Brothers, as a mechanic; Harold and Les Schwieso having been leading grass-track riders at the local Brands Hatch circuit.

In 1954, at 18 years of age, Colin started his first motorcycle business venture, a repair shop in Belvedere, Kent; two years later he opened his first showroom and was appointed main agent for Matchless and AJS. Thus began a long association with the AMC (Associated Motor Cycles) works in Plumstead Road, Woolwich, in south-east London. Other agencies soon followed, including at various times Francis-Barnett, Ariel, Velocette, Greeves and NSU, plus sidecars from Busmar, Canterbury, Watsonian and Wessex.

Colin Seeley's name first began to appear in many sporting programmes during 1957. His first competition motorcycle being a five-hundred Triumph T100C Trophy, with which he took part in scrambles, sprints, hill-climbs and grass-track events. With 'Colin Seeley – The Rider Agent' emblazoned proudly on the sides of his company's pick-up truck, he then turned to a Greeves two-stroke, riding at Canada Heights near Swanley, Kent, at that venue's inaugural meeting.

In 1961 Colin piloted his first Matchless G50-engined machine, this being fitted with a Canterbury racing sidecar, and finished a brilliant sixth in his very first event to the Isle of Man TT, averaging 77.93mph (125.39km/h) for the four-lap, 150.92 mile (242.83km) race. This was a major turning point in his life; as he recalled to the author recently: 'What

Colin Seeley made his sidecar racing name with his Matchless G50-engined outfit; he and passenger Wally Rawlings are seen here at Silverstone, 6 April 1963.

With the FCS (Florian Camathias Special) BMW Dutch TT, Assen, 1964; his only Grand Prix victory.
Photo W. Gruber/Archiv

a proud moment for me, my passenger Wally Rawlings and the AMC factory.' Two more TT silver replicas were to be followed on the Matchless, with third and sixth places in 1962 and 1963 respectively.

Colin's racing career then moved up a gear with the loan in 1964 of a BMW outfit entered as the FCS from the Swiss star, Florian Camathias (who used a Gilera that year) and with it a leap on to the world stage. Seeley and Rawlings finished third overall in the 1964 World Championship series; their best placing being a win in the Dutch TT at Assen, and runner-up in the Isle of Man TT. Another third place in the Championship table came in 1966, with runner-up spot in France, and third places in both Belgium and West Germany. Colin later purchased his own BMW.

Colin Seeley and passenger Wally Rawlings with their immaculate Matchless G50-engined outfit; Race of the Year Mallory Park, September 1963.

Meanwhile, on the commercial front, the first Seeley G50 Matchless and 7R AJS racing solos appeared in 1966; these being ridden by Derek Minter and John Blanchard that season on the British short circuits. And when the AMC works went into liquidation later that same year, all the racing assets of the group (Matchless, AJS and Norton) were purchased by Colin Seeley Racing Developments. The Norton side was later sold off to John Tickle in 1969. Based at Forge Works, Stapley Road, Belvedere CSRD soon built up an enviable reputation among racers not just in Britain, but all around the world, for its high standard of craftsmanship.

In 1967, Colin Seeley also formed a connection with Helmut Fath (see Chapter 14), to build a Seeley-framed URS four-cylinder solo racer; this was ridden by John Blanchard. In 1969 the AJS 7R engine was dropped in favour of the newly released Japanese TR2 for the 350cc class, and so the Yamsel was born.

Then came the 1970s, and the Seeley organisation was forced to change direction and consider alternative power units to the G50 Matchless. These included the Dr Gordon Blair QUB (Queens University Belfast), a 500cc single-cylinder two-stroke (1970), the Suzuki T500 Daytona (1972), and various big twins of 750cc from Norton, Triumph and Westlake. Later still came a succession of Honda-powered bikes, including a 200cc ohc single (for trials) and various across-the-frame, four-cylinder models for fast roadwork, the latter being produced in 750, 900 and 1,000 engine sizes. And, in fact during the late 1970s complete Seeley bikes were almost exclusively powered by Japanese engine. Also during the mid- and late-1970s Colin Seeley was actively involved with the Brabham car concern.

Then came the worst recession in post-war motorcycle industry history, and Colin Seeley bowed out as a manufacturer.

Later still, he was involved with the Duckhams-supported Norton rotary race team, during the mid-1990s. More recently still, Colin has produced a two-volume autobiography, and for this reason only I have given him a box, rather than a chapter on his racing career and business.

Runner-up in 1965 and 1966

During 1965 and 1966 Max and Emil finished runner-up in the World Championship to Fritz Scheidegger and passenger John Robinson on both occasions.

In 1965 Max also scored his third Isle of Man TT victory and in the course of this set new race and lap records at 90.57mph (145.72km/h) and 91.80mph (147.70km/h) respectively.

The second victory in the 1965 series came in the Spanish Grand Prix at Barcelona. But Scheidegger scored four victories (West Germany, Holland, Belgium and Italy).

Incredible But True

Incredible as it may seem, Max and his passenger Emil Hörner rode in two sidecar races on Sunday 7 July 1965 on two circuits 300 miles (483km) apart, in two different countries – and finished second in both events!

Deubel and Hörner after winning the German Grand Prix at Solitude (Camathias is also in the car).

Photo W. Gruber/Archiv

In 1965 Max scored his third Isle of Man TT win and in the process set new race and lap records for the famous 37.73-mile Mountain course.

In the morning, the pair competed in a German national meting at Nürnberg – and were narrowly beaten by Otto Kolle (BMW). Then a friend flew them from Nürnberg to Aachen where a car was standing by to whisk them to Spa Francorchamps for the Belgian Grand Prix.

The whole affair was as carefully worked out as a military exercise. First, Max and Emil practised on the number-one machine at Francorchamps. Then, leaving the machine in the care of the BMW factory mechanic, they left Belgium at 3pm on Saturday and travelled to Aachen where their friend was waiting to fly them to Nürnberg.

Arriving there, they practised on their number-two outfit late on Saturday afternoon. Luckily, the Sidecar race at Nürnberg was at 11am on Sunday. It finished at midday, and soon after 3pm they arrived back at Francorchamps in good time for the sidecar event there which began at 4.45pm.

After Florian Camathias's fatal crash at Brands Hatch on 10 October 1965, Max Deubel came very close to retiring, but he carried on for another season, gaining another second position in the Championship; however, this time without a victory – in the five rounds he gained four second places (Hockenheim, Isle of Man, Assen and Spa) and in the remaining round (Clermont-Ferrand) he was third. Fritz Scheidegger won all five rounds.

Max and passenger Emil Hörner continued to take in the important British short-circuit meetings, however, and it was at one of these at Brands Hatch on Sunday 12 October 1966 that the pair had their very last meeting before retiring from the sport. In fact the 500cc sidecar race at the Kent circuit was named in Max's honour. But sadly failing light caused it to be cut from 10 laps to six. Just for the record, the result was:

Fritz Scheidegger, Colin Seeley, Pip Harris, Tony Wakefield and Max himself, with Mick Boddice sixth on the first non-BMW (a BSA).

And so Max Deubel returned to Germany to run his hotel in Muhlanau, while Emil Hörner returned to his former trade as a car mechanic. Although he had a business to run, Max did not divorce himself from the motorcycle sporting scene, as he became a senior official for his country's version of the British ACU, a position he retains to the present day.

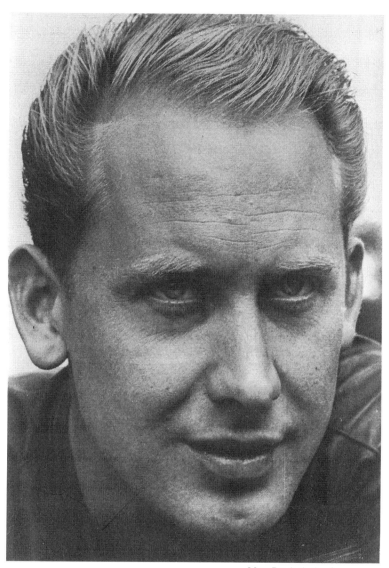

Max Deubel, the four-times world champion (1961 to 1964).
Photo W. Gruber/Archiv

CHAPTER 13

FRITZ SCHEIDEGGER

Born in Langenthal, Switzerland on 30 December 1930, Fritz Scheidegger became interested in motorcycles at a very early age, but he had to wait until he was 18 before he actually owned one. This was because, in Switzerland that was the youngest age at which a licence was granted to motorcyclists.

Apprenticeship

By that time young Fritz had already served three years of an apprenticeship as a motor mechanic with a local dealership and on that memorable day his boss presented Fritz with his first motorcycle, a three-fifty Royal Enfield Bullet. Actually, in reality, Fritz was not really given the machine at all. Instead, he worked many hours' overtime to pay the invoice!

A BSA Gold Star

The following year the Royal Enfield gave way to a 348cc BSA Gold Star in grass track racing guise. And this quickly resulted in Fritz being bitten by the racing bug and he just had to have a go himself.

His very first race was a 350cc class at a grass track event at Belp, not far from Berne, and he was later to recall that he finished third that day in the final. That was June 1950, and later that same year he rode the Gold Star in a road race at Lausanne, but was forced to retire with carburettor problems.

Manx Norton

In 1951 Fritz purchased a five-hundred Manx Norton from fellow Swiss racer Hans Haldemann which he proceeded to race throughout the season in local events, finishing third in the Swiss national Championships.

From then on he gathered yet more experience with this machine and others on both road and grass until 1954, when Fritz thought he would: 'Like to have a go at sidecar racing.'

Switching To Three Wheels

And so he made the switch to three wheels. It took him almost a year to get the hang of it, but when he did the results suddenly began to flow and he became virtually unbeatable in Swiss events. This resulted in him winning the Swiss grass track Championship three years running: 1955, 1956 and

1957. During 1957 he also carried off the 350cc solo title, riding a modified Manx Norton; again on the grass. This form of racing was popular in Switzerland at the time, where the tracks were hard, long and fast.

1957 turned out to be an eventful year, as Fritz also competed in his first-ever sidecar road race. Actually, this came about by chance. Fritz lived only a few kilometres from another Swiss sidecar racer, Edgar Strub. The latter found that he was unable to take part in a meeting at San Sebastian, so he telephoned Fritz to suggest that he take over Edgar's entry.

So with a holiday in Spain in mind Fritz agreed, and with a road-racing chair attached to his grass-track Norton and shod with the appropriate tyres, Fritz set off south to San Sebastian. But it was not to be a fairy-tale debut, in fact just the reverse, as he was forced to retire with engine trouble. But the seed had been sown...

Getting Organised

Immediately, Fritz returned from Spain and set the wheels in motion to find a suitable machine so that he could go sidecar racing himself. And so Fritz contacted that other great Swiss sidecar of the 1950s and 1960s, Florian Camathias. Florian had just such a machine for sale, a BMW Rennsport. And so, only a few days later Fritz was travelling back to Spain to compete with the BMW at Bilbao. He found the BMW to his liking and finished fourth. From there he was soon off to Monza for the Italian Grand Prix – this was only his third sidecar road race and the first time that he was up against world-class opposition.

A Great Result

But with seven years of racing Fritz was certainly not worried and soon showed his potential by finishing a hugely respectable fourth behind Albino Milani (Gilera four), Cyril Smith (Norton) and Florian Camathias (BMW). As Mick Woollett was to remark: 'He had arrived!'

The Garage

His Italian GP success came in September 1957 and the following year, 1958, Fritz started his garage business in his home town of Langenthal. This meant that during that year the garage came first, racing second. However, the racing which he did undertake in 1958 was useful as it provided more experience of international events.

Then, into 1959 and a return to more racing activities, and this was to pay dividends as Fritz, together with his passenger German Horst Burckhardt, finished the year third in the World Championship table.

Fritz Scheidegger made his Isle of Man TT debut in 1959 – the last year before the Clypse circuit was replaced for the sidecars by the much longer Mountain course. Fritz and passenger Horst Burckardt finished third.

A First Grand Prix Victory

The 1959 French Grand Prix at Clermont-Ferrand saw Scheidegger and Burckhardt gain their first Grand Prix victory counting towards the Championship. That year the pair were also victorious in the non-Championship Austrian GP at Salzburg. With a couple of third places in the Isle of Man and Belgium, plus fifth at Hockenheim in the West German round, they had a successful season.

Runner-up Two Years Running

Then, in 1960 and 1961 Fritz and Horst were runners-up in the Championship series two years running.

In 1960 the pair began with runner-up berth at Clermont-Ferrand, behind the eventual champions Helmut Fath and Alfred Wohlgemuth. In the Isle of Man TT, the first held on the Mountain course since 1925, Scheidegger was lying fourth, but was then suffered a retirement. In Holland they came home third, in Belgium second (behind Fath again) and third in the final round at Monza in Italy.

Fritz and Horst during the 1960 TT; they finished 11th.

More Victories

Then came 1961 and two more Grand Prix victories; in France and Belgium. These results, together with a trio of third places (Spain, Hockenheim and the Isle of Man), meant that Scheidegger and Burckhardt were again runners-up, but instead of Fath (sidelined by a serious crash early in the season) the new champions were Max Deubel and passenger Emil Hörner (who were BMW's official entry that year). It is also worth pointing out that the Scheidegger team were lent engines by the BMW works for both the Dutch TT and Belgian GP in 1961 – the only factory support received by Fritz up to that time.

Finishing runner-up (to Max Deubel) in the 1961 Isle of Man TT.

A Major Setback

Then in August 1961 came a major setback for Fritz, when his passenger Horst Burckhardt had to return to his home in Germany to help his father with the family business. As he was to comment at the time: 'This is a big blow as Horst has been with me since the early grass track days in 1956.'

Enter John Robinson

And so came onto the scene Englishman John Robinson as the replacement for the departed Burckhardt. His first encounter with Fritz came in August 1961, at the non-Championship Grand Prix de Vitesse d'Avignon in France.

John had gone to the Avignon event to passenger for John Tickle, whose usual passenger, his wife Cathy, was unable to travel. Previously John had been regular passenger for first Geoff Clark and later Jim Jakes; and had an international licence. And it was at Avignon that Fritz Scheidegger asked John if he would passenger him in 1962.

As John said in an article published in *Motor Cycling* during January 1963: 'How can I possibly explain my reaction to his offer?' And continued: 'In a flash, I had World Championship laurels around my neck and a passport with every European country's stamp on it. Even so, nothing had been decided when we left Avignon on that Sunday evening.'

In the 1963 article John went on to reveal: 'Maybe this kind of offer is the secret dream of every passenger. But let's face it; there was no future in it for me. It meant giving up a secure job, losing a girlfriend and living in Switzerland.'

Then in October 1961 John went to Switzerland as Chris Vincent's passenger for a couple of grass-track meetings. And on both occasions the pair finished second to that man Fritz Scheidegger.

Finally, in January 1962 a telegram arrived from Fritz offering John the 'job' of passenger for the 1962 Grand Prix season. And so as John explained: 'At 9am the following Thursday I hopped off the train in Berne to be met by my present "govnor".'

The Debut Meeting

The debut meeting for the Scheidegger/Robinson partnership came at the international Silverstone Hutchinson 100 in April 1962. Travelling to England with the pair were Rudi Kurth (later a sidecar racer himself) and the former Swiss sidecar star Hans Haldemann. But that British venture, which also took in meetings at Brands Hatch and Oulton Park, was fraught with mechanical problems.

Early Problems

The first half of the 1962 season continued in the same vein as had the English venture – a series of problems, including blown up gearboxes, mechanical gremlins and crashes – even a fire! In fact, after not finishing any of the first three GPs (Spain, France and the Isle of Man), Fritz was seriously considering retirement from the sport.

Then came the Dutch TT as Assen.

The 1961 Dutch TT at Assen; Fritz Scheidegger (12) leading Chris Vincent (6, BSA), Florian Camathias (11), Max Deubel and further back Jackie Beeton (9, BMW).

ASSEN, Dutch T. T.

An amazing photograph showing Fritz grass-tracking with his road-race outfit, Switzerland 1962, with John Robinson in the chair.

A Victory At Last

After all the problems, heartache and expense, Assen at last provided a moment of glory, when Fritz and John soundly beat the Championship pairing of Max Deubel and Emil Hörner on the factory BMW. In fact, in the final three races of the six-round series, besides the Assen victory, they finished runners-up in Belgium (behind Florian Camathias) and third at the

In 1962 Fritz Scheidegger constructed this 500cc engine from a pair of watercooled Adler units. Reliability issues saw him decide to stick with BMW power.

final round in Germany at the Solitude circuit (behind Deubel and Camathias), thus finishing third in the Championship table – even though they did not score any points in half the races.

1963

The following year, 1963, Fritz and John repeated their third place in the Championship. And once again they did not figure in the first three rounds: Barcelona, Hockenheim and Clermont-Ferrand.

Next came the Isle of Man TT, and here the pair finished second to Camathias/Herzig. Another second was gained at the next race, at Assen, behind Deubel/Hörner. Finally, in Belgium, Fritz and John scored another victory, beating the three-time champions Max Deubel and Emil Hörner.

Second in the Championship

In 1964 Fritz and John scored two GP victories, in France (Clermont-Ferrand) and West Germany (Solitude), but they again suffered from mechanical problems. As Maurice Bula commented: 'His revolutionary engineering intrigues more than one enthusiast, but had no future.' In Spain and the Isle of Man the pair did not finish, but in the three remaining rounds it was not only a finish every time, but the Solitude victory, plus a second in Belgium and a third in Holland.

The First Championship Title

It was Fritz Scheidegger who brought to an end the long reign of German Sidecar Champions. The year was 1965. And Fritz and his passenger John

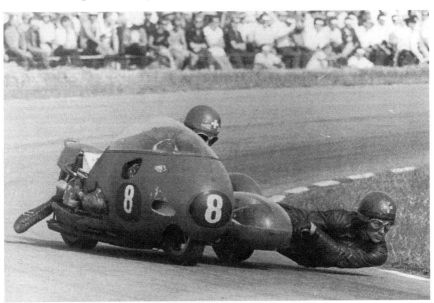

Fritz Scheidegger and John Robinson during the 1964 Dutch TT in which they finished third behind the BMWs of winner Colin Seeley and runner-up Chris Vincent.
Photo W. Gruber/Archiv

Scheidegger leads Deubel during the 1965 Belgian Grand Prix at Spa.
Photo W. Gruber/Archiv

Robinson won four of the seven-round series, in West Germany (Nürburgring), Holland (Assen), Belgium (Spa Francorchamps) and Italy (Monza).

One also has to remember that he not only beat the combination of four-time world champion Max Deubel and Emil Hörner, but also men such as Camathias, Schauzu, Butscher, Auerbacher, Seeley, Vincent, Harris and Luthringshauer. Another notable achievement for Scheidegger was that his BMW finished every Grand Prix; in early years it had been retirements that had cost him so dearly. Besides the four victories, the pair were also runners-up in every race that they did not win.

Actually, as the front page of *Motor Cycling* dated 10 July 1965 revealed: 'The first 1965 world road-racing title is in the bag. Fritz Scheidegger, the Swiss ace who came out of retirement for a last try at the Sidecar Championship this year, achieved his life's ambition when he won the three-wheeler class at Sunday's Belgian Grand Prix at a record 107.23mph [172.53km/h].'

FIM Rule Changes

At the time several observers thought that Fritz and John had become world champions at the previous round, the Dutch TT. But this was not so.

This was because the FIM radically changed the method of deciding ties at the Autumn Congress the previous year. Prior to the Congress, if two riders finished the Championship with the same number of points from the significant number of races then their next best performance was to count.

Scheidegger's BMW Grand Prix outfit in 1965, the first year of his two World Championship titles.

Under this system Scheidegger and Robinson would have been champions after their Dutch victory. For their main rival Max Deubel, if the latter had managed to win in Belgium he would only have tied with Fritz and John on the results from four meetings – and they had a 'spare' second place.

But at Prague the previous October, the FIM decided that, in the event of a tie, the number of first places in the significant number of races would be the deciding factor. So if Deubel had won the Belgian his three wins and one third would have got the verdict over Scheidegger's two wins and two second places.

But, ultimately, all this did not matter anyway, as in the final two rounds – Belgium and Italy – the Swiss star and his English passenger emerged victorious.

1966

1966 was the year that the Isle of Man TT almost never was. A national seaman's strike caused the postponement of the traditional TT dates. But thanks to the co-operation of several organisations, including the FIM, ACU and, most of all, the Isle of Man government, the races were held towards the end of August, rather than the normal June dates. This also meant a hectic month of practising and racing with the TT immediately followed by the Manx Grand Prix (the author taking part in the latter).

An Historic and Controversial Victory

There were 56 starters for the 1966 Sidecar TT, making history as the first-ever TT race to be held on a Sunday. On the first lap Max Deubel led Fritz by 12 seconds, Georg Auerbacher was third, 13 seconds down, followed by Colin Seeley, Klaus Enders and Otto Kolle. At the end of lap two, Deubel had increased his lead to 15 seconds and looked therefore to be the likely race winner, with just one lap to go. However, at the Bungalow it was indicated that Fritz Scheidegger was leading, but only just. Deubel crossed the line and there was 40 seconds to wait (readers should remember that in the Isle of Man, unlike other races, competitors are started individually or in pairs and results are determined on time not finishing order). Fritz arrived almost exactly 40 seconds later, and the official times were awaited eagerly. Scheidegger had beaten Deubel by 0.8 of a second! But there was still drama to come, Fritz being excluded for a fuel technicality. He appealed against this but it was turned down. He appealed again, and it was many months before he was granted first place, together with the prize money he had won – and the vital World Championship points.

Public And Trade Support

Long before the officials finally passed judgement in Scheidegger's favour, the general public and members of the trade had come down firmly in Fritz and John's favour. Typical were Castrol, with whom the pair were under contract. The company deciding only a couple of weeks after the TT that they would pay the £150 bonus money they would have paid had he been *officially* declared the winner of the Sidecar TT.

Commenting on their decision, Castrol's motorcycle competition manager Malcolm Edgar said: 'We feel Fritz and his passenger John Robinson are, in the eyes of the public, the winners of the race and that they should be rewarded.' A typical press comment of the time simply said: 'As every racing enthusiast knows, Scheidegger was excluded for a minor infringement of the loosely-worded regulations.'

Continental GP Success

Besides the Isle of Man, there were four other rounds counting towards the 1966 world title, in West Germany (Hockenheim), France (Clermont-Ferrand), Holland (Assen) and Belgium (Spa Francorchamps). And Fritz and John won them all. So with the Isle of Man TT (when confirmed) the pair had won every round; a feat unmatched by any other competitor in the series that year. Maurice Bula commenting: 'A unique achievement, this brilliant partnership won every race of the Championship. Their superiority was such that no opponent could offer any challenge.' And it was also a fact that, at the end of that year, the four-time former champions Max Deubel and Emil Hörner announced their retirement.

Fritz Scheidegger and
John Robinson, the 1965
and 1966 world
champions. Photo W.
Gruber/Archiv

End-Of-Season British Victories

With the end of the GP season, Fritz and John took in a number of
international British short-circuit events. And the pair proceeded to continue
their winning ways established in the World Championship rounds, with
victories at Cadwell Park, Mallory Park and Brands Hatch. They would
probably have won at Scarborough, too, had not they suffered from a
slipping clutch and been forced to retire.

Behind The Scenes

But as was to become apparent as 1966 turned into 1967, all was not well
in the Scheidegger camp. For a start, Fritz had still not finally decided
whether or not to race again, and his passenger John Robinson had returned
to Britain in the last two weeks of December sizing up the prospects of
financial support and trade backing if Fritz did decide to make up his mind
to try for the title hat-trick.

   This is what Mick Woollett wrote in the 7 January 1967 issue of *Motor
Cycling*: 'In fact, the indications are that we shall see this dynamic duo in
action again with the 500cc BMW this year – and with Scheidegger's new
700 car-engined Munich [BMW] twin in the larger-capacity British events.'

The Problems

But there were other problems of which the public were largely unaware.
Besides the fact that Fritz and John had made very little money from their
two previous seasons (1965 and 1966), even though they had been crowned
champions on both occasions, many of the pair's problems were not of a
financial nature.

For one thing Fritz had been in hospital, for operations for an abscess and a hernia, and he was due to go back into hospital before the season started to have his tonsils and adenoids removed.

Not only that, but John was scheduled to undergo an operation for cartilage trouble in his left knee. The weakness, caused when he fell off a road bike several years before, had been getting worse recently.

Mallory Park, 29 March 1967

On 29 March 1967 at Mallory Park near Leicester the 1966 world champions were having their first race of the new season and the first since the pair had been reinstated as winners of the previous year's controversial Sidecar TT.

But the meeting was clouded by tragedy on the 10th lap of the Up-to-1000cc Sidecar Race of the Year when, carving his way through the field after a slow start, Fritz went straight on at the Hairpin at high speed (it was later to be revealed that the accident had been caused through brake failure). Driver and passenger were flung from their BMW outfit (the 500cc GP machine was being used – although the new 700cc pushrod-engine model was on display in the paddock). But the race was only stopped some laps later so that an ambulance could reach the pair. Gravely injured, Fritz was rushed to the Leicester Royal Infirmary but died the same evening. John was treated at the circuit and then transferred to hospital with a broken leg and other injuries.

The author was at Mallory Park that fateful day. And the meeting had drawn a 'huge crowd' (*Motor Cycling*), with competitors and spectators buffeted by freezing winds and sleet showers. All in all it was one of the worst moments in my 50-plus year motorcycle racing career, as spectator, competitor, sponsor and team manager.

Fritz Scheidegger John Robinson, with their BMW (10) at Mallory Park, shortly before the fatal crash at the Hairpin section.

The following week Max Deubel had this to say: 'Before Scheidegger's fatal accident at Mallory Park I had decided to race again if a new BMW machine that a sponsor was building for me was good. But now I have definitely decided I will never race again.'

Max was one of the many famous racing personalities who attended Fritz Scheidegger's funeral, which was held on Saturday 4 April 1967 in his home town of Langenthal, Switzerland.

CHAPTER 14

HELMUT FATH

Helmut Fath was born on 24 May 1929, and his first motorcycle came in 1946 when, at the age of 16, he purchased a well-worn, pre-war BMW 250 single. In those days Fath was living just outside Mannheim, working at an experimental laboratory where research into high-altitude aviation was undertaken. He had begun there at the age of 14 in the dark days of 1944, when the whole of Germany was under great strain with the Allies attacking on all sides.

When the war finally came to an end in the following year, the young Fath was kept on at the plant after it was taken over by the victorious Allied forces. Serving an apprenticeship as a precision engineer, he stayed on until he was 18. By that time, Helmut had been converted to the ranks of motorcycle enthusiasts and had owned a string of machinery. This interest led him to quit the aviation industry and go to work (for less money!) in a motorcycle dealership. With his precision engineering background, Fath was soon given the more specialised jobs, such as building up BMW crank-shafts and inserting valve seats, for example.

The following year, 1949, he took part in his first competitive event. This was a trial in which he rode a twin-piston German Triumph (TWN) two-stroke.

With money in short supply, his real interest – road racing – had to wait. It was to be three long years before his ambition on this front was finally realised. This came in the shape of a standard, road-going BMW pushrod flat-twin, which was tuned and fitted with a sidecar. The effort proved two things: the machine was simply not fast enough, and neither was its pilot!

Tuning Work

For 1953, the BMW chassis was retained, but the engine was subjected to a vast amount of tuning work. Having several years of experience on this type of unit was a distinct advantage, but the problem of finance, or lack of it, remained. As he was only able to race in his holidays, Fath took part in only three meetings that year. However, a victory was taken at each of these, with the result that the name Helmut Fath joined the Senior category in German classification. This meant that although Fath could only race within the German borders, he was able to take part in international meetings.

His new status posed another problem, however – the home-tuned pushrod BMW, although quick enough to win races in the Junior class, was totally outclassed among the superior opposition which he now faced.

Therefore, taking the chance to sell his original outfit, Helmut Fath ordered one of the small batch of Rennsport BMWs that the Munich factory was building at the time. Unfortunately, a financial hiccup prevented him from obtaining his overhead-cam BMW, with the result that he did not compete in a single race during 1954.

However, in December that year, he finally managed to obtain a solo Rennsport model – one of the 1954 batch – and set about converting it to sidecar use. This included building a special frame, converting the brakes to hydraulic operation and constructing a superbly-crafted aluminium fairing.

For the next four years, it was a case of steady and ever-improving form, and in 1959 Helmut finally launched himself as a serious contender for the World Sidecar Championship when he finished the season in fifth spot, partnered by Alfred Wohlgemuth on a BMW Rennsport outfit.

World Champion

The year 1960 was full of glory, for the duo totally dominated the title series, winning four out of the five rounds, and placing second in the other, the Dutch TT.

Typical of the man behind the name, Fath not only won the Isle of Man TT, but also helped his rival, Pip Harris, to gain second place. Harris had

Fath and Wohlgemuth during their victory in the 1960 Isle of Man TT. They had made their TT debut two years earlier in 1958.

Fath and Wohlgemuth pictured during 1960, taking part in the famous Freiburg Schauinsland hill climb. Photo W. Gruber/Archiv

A lovely Wolfgang Gruber photograph of Helmut Fath (right) and passenger Alfred Wohlgemuth after winning at Hockenheim, 29 May 1960.
Photo W. Gruber/Archiv

blown his BMW engine in practice and, to his surprise, Fath had waded in and completely rebuilt the Rennsport engine, using new spares, pieces from Pip's old engine and parts from Jackie Beeton's BMW engine. The work took the best part of two days, and Helmut's only reward was Pip's second position – true sportsmanship indeed.

The following year, 1961, Fath and Wohlgemuth looked all set to retain their world title, following a runaway victory during the first round in Spain, where they lapped the entire field.

Tragedy

Then came tragedy. A week later, at the international Eifelrennen meeting over the Nürburgring circuit, the world champions crashed in appalling conditions of heavy mist and rain. This left Wohlgemuth dead and Fath badly injured. His injuries included a broken leg, ankle and hand, and they effectively sidelined Helmut for five long years.

Most men would have given up, but Helmut Fath was nothing if not determined. His burning ambition was to make a comeback – and with his own engine.

Once he had recovered from the effects of the accident that had claimed his passenger and friend, Fath set about designing, building and finally testing his own across-the-frame, four-cylinder, double-overhead-camshaft racing engine. This was known as the URS, after the village of Ursenbach where he had made his home.

The URS Design

The URS design was really a pair of side-by-side parallel twins, coupled together by a countershaft driven from the crankshaft between cylinders 1 and 2 and 3 and 4. The firing order was 1-4-2-3, and the engine featured a central timing chain. The crankshaft ran on six main bearings, with caged roller big- ends and phosphor-bronze small-ends in the titanium cogs. The lubrication system included a combined oil cooler and filter. The bore and stroke measurements of the new engine were 60 x 44mm, the ultra-short-stroke unit giving useful power between 8,000 and 13,500rpm. Even from the first prototype, the URS was a very high-revving unit, and it was a remarkable technical achievement to be able to control the valves up to 15,000rpm without a conventional two-valves-per-cylinder layout.

Credit for this went to Fath's partner, Dr Peter Kuhn (formerly a lecturer at Heidelberg University). He had designed the cam profile and valve spring rates to match – the special Swedish wire used for these springs was later supplied by Fath for use in various other engines.

The valves themselves were large in size – 34mm inlet, and 30mm exhaust – and were splayed at 67 degrees. As a result, twin 10mm sparking plugs were fitted in each cylinder and, unusually, these were mounted vertically, as otherwise there was not enough room for the valves.

Fuel was injected directly into the ports by a Bosch injector mounted between wide-angle upper frame tubes, above and behind the engine unit. The injector had come from a 1.5-litre Borgward car, and a divided cable from the twistgrip moved the single flat throttle plate to regulate the fuel supply. Although contemporary press reports claimed 80bhp for the engine, Fath laughed at this and said his dynamometer had told only him – and he was keeping it a secret!

After suffering a terrible accident at the Nürburgring in early 1961, in which Wohlgemuth was fatally injured, Helmut Fath was to sensationally return several years later. Not only did he make a comeback, but he designed and built his own engine, the four-cylinder URS.

A Sensational Comeback

Fath made his comeback in May 1966 at the West German Grand Prix, staged at Hockenheim. His reappearance five years after the Nürburgring accident, and the new engine, created a sensation. Unfortunately, he retired after just three laps when lying sixth. This was the start of a series of problems which its creator discovered with the URS engine during that first season. In fact, Helmut hardly finished a race.

Helmut Fath, pictured at home in his workshop at Ursenbach (hence the URS name).

At the beginning of 1967, it appeared to be the same story, the URS seeming not to have enough power. However, at the West German GP at Hockenheim, Fath took an instant lead from the start, but despite building up a four-second lead over Klaus Enders' BMW, he was forced out near the end with a broken gearbox selector mechanism.

Solo Use

It was also during that year that the URS engine was first considered for solo use, with the news that John Blanchard was considering racing one mounted in a frame built by Colin Seeley. At the same time, Blanchard stated: 'I think the engine may be better for a solo than a sidecar, and is now giving good power.' Unlike the sidecar power unit, the solo engine was fitted with carburettors and had magnesium-alloy, instead of aluminium, castings.

By the time of the 1967 TT, Helmut Fath's home-built, four-cylinder URS outfit was outspeeding the fastest short-stroke BMWs – no mean achievement. Furthermore, it appeared that if he could achieve reliability and improve handling, he would once again dominate the class.

It was then revealed that although the engine had repeatedly suffered from fractures of the long bolts clamping the crankcase halves to the central driving sprockets, some of Fath's engine failures had been due to the inability of the battery/coil ignition system to cope with the unorthodox crankshaft layout. Therefore, to stabilise the ignition, Helmut had reverted to magneto.

The difficulty had been due to his choice of crankpin spacing. Instead of having all four in one plane (two up, two down), Fath had spaced them like the points of a compass to achieve smoother running. This gave firing intervals of 90, 180, 270 and 360 degrees. However, at the peak power point of 14,000rpm, the 90-degree interval had given the contact-breaker

Helmut Fath (URS, 14) leads Pip Harris and Colin Seeley at Brands Hatch, 29 May 1967.

precious little time to do its job. It was hoped that the new system would solve this problem.

Visiting England

Both Fath and Dr Kuhn spent time in England with John Blanchard at the Seeley works in Belvedere, Kent. Late July saw the Seeley-framed Fath four solo racer completed, and a particularly neat effort it looked, too. Many of the cycle parts – except the full duplex cradle frame – were the same as used on the production Seeley 7R and G50 ohc single-cylinder racers.

Fath and Blanchard both appeared with their respective fours at the Hutchinson 100 at Brands Hatch on 13 August. Two weeks later, the duo appeared at Scarborough on Saturday 26 August, when Helmut and his passenger, Wolfgang Kalauch, scored an impressive win over the world champion Klaus Enders.

Blanchard, however, fell at Mere Hairpin, putting himself out of the running. There followed a row, with Blanchard being withdrawn from the Snetterton and Oulton Park meetings in the following two days of the Bank Holiday meetings. This followed a stormy exchange between Seeley and Blanchard at Snetterton over the bike being fitted with a Lockheed disc brake before Scarborough, without Seeley's permission. The result was that Blanchard was dropped as development rider and would not be allowed to ride the machine any more that season.

A couple of weeks later, following discussions between Seeley and Fath, the prospects of work continuing on their four-cylinder solo racer brightened. However, Helmut had elected to leave all decisions concerning the project to his partner in the design and development of the URS, Dr Kuhn.

The Rickman Brothers

In any case, the Seeley-Fath co-operation did not last beyond the end of the season, and for the future the Fath team chose to use the Metisse chassis made by the Rickman brothers of New Milton in Hampshire. John Blanchard returned to ride the URS-Metisse solo – and in a supreme irony, it was fitted with the very Lockheed disc brake set-up that had caused the rift between him and Seeley.

Blanchard gave the machine its first outing at Brands Hatch in January 1968, when he was principally concerned with testing the brakes and suspension, watched by Derek Rickman and Mike Vaughn of Lockheed. Afterwards, all decided that they were very happy with the machine's performance, but thought that a little more experimentation was needed to sort out the rear suspension.

More tests were carried out before Blanchard and the URS-Metisse were entered in the season's first classic, the West German GP at the Nürburgring. This was anything but a successful debut, as Blanchard crashed *twice*. The machine was then offered to John Hartle, who rode it at Hockenheim on 12 May.

A Grand Prix Victory

If the solo plans didn't proceed as intended, Fath's own racing efforts certainly did. At the Nürburgring, he and Wolfgang Kalauch took the flag at the front of the field – Fath's first Grand Prix victory since his win in Spain in April 1961. What a sweet taste of success it was for a man who had not only made a successful comeback, but built the engine of his machine into the bargain!

Then came the Isle of Man TT and a fourth followed by a fifth in the Dutch TT, a retirement in Belgium and then a couple of victories in Belgium and the final round at Hockenheim. The last event was to have taken place at the Italian GP at Monza, but as the sidecar event was cancelled, by FIM decree, it was contested at Hockenheim, with the final of the German National Championship in October.

A Desperate Gamble

Before Hockenheim, both Fath and Georg Auerbacher had gained 21 points each, while TT winner Siegfried Schauzu was four points astern, but still in with a chance. With so much at stake, Fath took a desperate gamble after official race practice finished. Dissatisfied with his engine, he fitted a completely new short-stroke unit, which had not been raced before, but which had been showing promising results on the test-bed. Would it last the race? Fath commented grimly before the start: 'The only way to find out is to use it.'

The gamble paid off. Before the first corner Fath and passenger Wolfgang Kalauch already had a tremendous lead, and even the super-fast BMW of ex-world champion Enders was unable to get a tow in the slipstream of the flying URS. A wet and slippery track failed to deter a determined Fath, then 39 years old, and at the end of the second lap his lead was 6.6 seconds. This doubled in the next two circuits to take him out of reach of everyone – a lead which was maintained until the end. The 15-lap, 63.15-mile (101.60km) race was won at an average speed of 98.55mph (158.56km/h), with a fastest lap (by Fath) of 100.72mph (162.05km/h), breaking Enders' previous record.

Making History

Helmut Fath made history because, up to that time, nobody had ever won a World Championship on a home-built machine. Strangely, when defending

During 1968 Helmut Fath (passengered by Wolfgang Kalauch) became world champion for the second time. He is pictured here (again with Kalauch) during the 1969 TT. His speed trap reading of 134.8mph was a full 10mph quicker than the fastest BMW!

the title in the following year, the results turned out almost in reverse, with wins in France, Holland and Belgium, a third in the Isle of Man, and a retirement in Germany. With two rounds to go and leading the Championship, he crashed in Finland, preventing his participation in the final round in Ulster – Klaus Enders took the title for BMW.

For 1969, Fath built a larger version of his four – initially for British short circuits, where it was popular to race larger-capacity outfits. The 68 x 51.5mm bore and stroke gave 748cc, compared with the smaller unit's 60 x 44mm. Much longer con-rods were used, together with different cylinders to produce an engine with tremendous low-down punch, rather than power at high revs, and Fath hoped that a four-speed gearbox would be adequate. In this he was proved wrong, as like the 500, the 750 needed at least five speeds.

The 500 Solo Racer

At long last, however, the 500 solo racer began to shine. Ridden by veteran Karl Hoppe, the URS-Metisse dominated many of the early-season Continental internationals. Perhaps his finest performance came just a week after his first victory – the Eifelrennen at the end of April – when Hoppe won the 500 class of the non-Championship Austrian GP at Salzburg. Under ideal racing conditions, in front of a crowd of 28,000 spectators, no one could keep up with Hoppe, who shot away from the start and won as he pleased. Not only was his race speed a record, but he also shaved 0.7 seconds off Giacomo Agostini's lap record, which had been set on an MV four in 1967.

Then, to prove that his early form was no fluke, Hoppe finished a fine second in the West German GP at Hockenheim, behind Agostini's MV. Sadly, however, Hoppe did not contest the remainder of the classics. This was a great pity, as except for MV, 1969 saw the URS emerge as the most serious World Championship contender in the 500cc solo class.

Although there were several URS engines in existence, there were still only two machines: Fath's own outfit and the Metisse solo ridden by Hoppe. Fath had also received help from several British companies, including Reynolds Tubes, Automotive Products, Renold Chain, Duckhams Oil (the main sponsor) and Dunlop, who had developed a special 4.00 x 12 tyre for the outfit. Both types of the URS engine were now giving useful power between 9,000 and 13,000rpm, and transmission was via a Norton box with a six-speed Schafleitner cluster.

The Bosch Fuel Injection

The Bosch fuel injection on the sidecar engine now had twin air intakes instead of the single intake previously used. Moreover, a final solution had been found to beat the ignition problems which had remained, despite the adoption of a fully transistorised system. The answer was found by fitting a separate coil for each cylinder and making a special contact-breaker with four sets of points spaced at 45, 90, 135 and 180 degrees. Since each cylinder had two spark plugs, the coils were double-ended to furnish pairs of sparks simultaneously.

Things looked bright, indeed, but then Fath sustained a broken leg in Finland on 12 August. While he was recuperating, towards the end of the month, there came the news that the Fath team had been purchased by Friedl Münch with American backing. The Münch/Fath tie-up eventually took place in May 1970, and because all of his machinery had been taken over, it was not until much later that Helmut resumed manufacturing. During 1970–71, he was strictly a tuner, although during 1971 he was said to be one of the top Yamaha tuners around – even the 250 world champion was a customer.

A Brand New Design

In the middle of 1973 came the first news that Fath, then aged 43, was thinking of a possible comeback. At his forest hideout near Heidelberg, Helmut was busy constructing a brand-new four-cylinder outfit. Furthermore, not only did he have plans for a racing return himself, but he hoped to have a spare engine for Billie Nelson to race in solo events.

This time, his design was for a water-cooled, disc-valve, two-stroke flat-four, which many wrongly considered at the time to be a development of the König. In fact, any resemblance to the König began and ended with the flat-four cylinder layout. In any case, in the early 1960s Fath's original scheme had been to build a water-cooled flat-four (albeit a four-stroke) before ultimately opting for the across-the-frame layout of the URS. The reason he had not built the original design was said to be the reluctance of BMW to provide certain parts, notably the transmission, on which the design depended.

Unlike the König, Fath's two-stroke had a longitudinal position for the crankshaft and an integral six-speed gearbox with the clutch at the rear of the crankcase, in a similar manner to the BMW design – but with a pair of bevel gears coupling the output shaft to the left-hand side-mounted sprocket for the chain final drive, turning it through an angle of 90 degrees. Another departure from König practice was the oil supply to the big-end which, on the Berlin company's engine was by a direct shower of petroil. Fath devised a belt-driven pump, controlled by the throttle, which dribbled a supply of straight oil to the big-ends, main bearings and disc bearings. Caged needle rollers were used for both the big- and small-ends.

With a capacity of 495cc (56 x 50mm), the Fath four had aluminium-alloy cylinders with Nickasil bores. Originally, Yamaha pistons were used, but these were soon replaced by purpose-built units, carrying only a single ring each.

A Unique Feature

A unique feature of the Fath design was that each cylinder casting incorporated half the crankcase, so that the crank chambers themselves were also water-cooled. There was no water pump of the type fitted to many water-cooled 'strokers', but as on Bultacos and MZ, the thermo-siphon system was used, water entering the underside of the cylinders and leaving them at the top.

Fuel was supplied by a quartet of separate carburettors – 34mm Japanese Mikunis. Because Helmut used four carburettors, this called for four small disc valves instead of the König's one, but like the König, the drive to these was by toothed rubber belt. But unlike the König, the Fath design used four separate expansion chambers in an attempt to extract the maximum possible power output – 112bhp at 12,200rpm. The exhausts ran from the top of the engine and back under the rider's legs. To prevent him from being burned, they were coated with a baked-on finish, and as Billie Nelson was to remark: 'It's really amazing. You can touch them and not get burned even after a long race.'

At first, the ignition was by a Bosch flywheel magneto, with the generator incorporating a pair of ignition coils, two pulse coils and three more for the water pump, fuel pump and tachometer. However, this system proved too heavy, and thereafter a battery was installed for current, and only a pulse unit was fitted to the front of the crankshaft.

The Debut

At 44 Helmut Fath was not sure if he would race again, but May 1974 saw Fath's new four in action for the first time, at the West German GP at Hockenheim in solo trim with Billie Nelson up. Ready to race, but without fuel, the Fath weighed only 130kg (286lb), some 25kg (55lb) less than the comparable Yamaha or Suzuki 500 fours – but there were problems.

The power proved exceptional, but not so the handling. The frame had been constructed in only 10 days, after the original builder failed to come up with the goods, and Fath freely admitted that he was not a frame specialist. The problems centred around the swinging arm, which was whipping so badly at Hockenheim that it caused Nelson's ultimate retirement. There were also early problems with the transmission system.

The Isle of Man TT was given a miss, and the machine's next outing was at the international meeting at Raalte in Holland, where again it showed a tremendous turn of speed. However, trouble with the throttle linkage slowed Nelson in the race, although he kept going to finish fourth.

The next race was the Dutch TT at Assen where, in the 350cc race, Nelson clocked up a fourth on his Yamaha. At the start of the 500cc race, however, the Fath four oiled a plug. By the time it had been changed and Nelson got started, the leaders had already come round to complete one lap. He followed them down the straight, and, to his amazement, caught them up easily. He said afterwards that he could have passed them easily, but for

One of the Fath 500 two-stroke engines receiving attention in the paddock during the mid-1970s.

two things. Firstly, he was not totally confident in the machine's handling on the very fast curve towards the end of the straight, and secondly he himself hated people who indulged in what he called: 'Dicing with me when I am lapping them.' The riders whom Billie Nelson was in danger of catching in this way were none other than the trio of Barry Sheene (Suzuki), Giacomo Agostini (Yamaha) and Phil Read (MV Agusta)!

Besides the evident speed, Nelson was impressed by the smoothness of the engine, describing it as: 'Just like a big electric motor.' He thought the wide spread of useable power from 8,000 to 13,000rpm was particularly impressive, and development continued apace through the summer of 1974, with an excellent understanding existing between builder and rider.

Billie Nelson's Death

However, on Sunday 8 September, all this shattered. Billie Nelson, the man who had once been known as 'Mr Consistency' on the Grand Prix circuit, died after he crashed during the 250cc race at Opatija in the Yugoslav Grand Prix. He crashed on a 125mph (201km/h) left-hander at one of the highest points of the closed road circuit on the Adriatic coast. The Yamaha went onto the crowd and a spectator was seriously injured, while Nelson suffered severe chest injuries and died after an operation in hospital at nearby Rijeka.

The 33-year-old Nelson, from Eckington, Derbyshire, had begun racing in 1958 and made his Continental debut six years later in West Germany.

He combined solo racing and sidecar passengering for several years. It was a crash while racing as passenger with Fath in 1969, during the Finnish GP, which ruined not only Fath's chances of retaining his world title, but also Nelson's hopes of taking the Bill Hannah-sponsored Paton twin to second place in the 500cc World Championship behind Agostini.

Fath and Nelson had been firm friends as well as colleagues, and his death was a cruel blow. Following the accident, Fath decided to make a return to the sidecar scene, the engine from Nelson's solo being built into a special three-wheeler for Siegfried Schauzu. However, Helmut was far from happy with the outfit (it was not of his design) and, in May 1975, said: 'It is far too big and the width of the sidecar alone loses me 10–15bhp.'

By then, Fath had almost completed a new engine which he said would produce even more horsepower, and he hoped that the rest of the outfit would be modified. Early results were far from impressive, however, with only one placing in the top 10 at any of the Grands Prix that year, when the ARO-Fath finished at Hockenheim.

For 1976, the sidecar team consisted of two pairings: Schauzu and Kalauch, plus newcomer Heinz Schilling partnered by passenger Rolf Gundel. In the very first round at Le Mans, in France, Schilling managed a third place, with Schauzu coming home eighth. At the Salzburgring, in Austria, Schauzu came in third, although Schilling had to retire.

Improved Reliability

Displaying their greatly-improved reliability, both crews finished the punishing Isle of Man TT, Schauzu in fourth and Schilling in sixth place. Then, in Holland, Schilling was fifth, with Schauzu in 10th place, while on the following weekend, in Belgium, the ARO-Fath teams made it third and fourth – Schilling and Schauzu. Neither team competed in the Czech GP at Brno, and the season ended with a ninth for Schauzu at the Nürburgring. As a result, Schauzu and Kalauch came fifth overall in the year's Championship table.

In the same year, Alex George, the Scottish solo racer, then based in Holland, rode Helmut Fath's four-cylinder 'stroker' solo in the Czech Grand Prix. George's Suzuki four had been sidelined with a broken idler gear, so he took over the Fath bike, the chassis of which remained untouched since Billie Nelson last raced it. He found the machine to be around 10mph (16km/h) slower than the all-conquering (but at that time, none too reliable) Suzukis, and a match for them on acceleration. He led for most of the first lap, but gradually dropped back and retired when he grounded one of the plug caps.

Werner Schwärzel

For 1977, the ARO team was again reorganised. Schauzu left to race his own Yamaha, while Schilling was provided with a new ARO-Yamaha. Then, after the season had started, Werner Schwärzel (second in 1976 on a König) was brought into the team with passenger Huber and took over one of the vacant ARO-Fath outfits.

Schwärzel's first finish was at the Dutch TT, with a third, following which he demonstrated his own superb skill and the potential of the Fath engine to the full by winning the next round in Belgium on the super-fast spa Francorchamps circuit. He then retired in Czechoslovakia, but won the final round at Silverstone to finish third in the world series. This was an amazing result when you consider that the team had only finished in three of the seven rounds.

This result was to prove the pinnacle of achievement by Fath's flat-four, even though it did not appear so at the time, and the man himself was still interested in both the sidecar and solo classes at world level.

At the end of 1977, South African Jon Ekerold, later to be World 350cc Champion in 1980 on a Bimota-Yamaha, was tipped to be rider of a new machine powered by a Fath flat-four. Fath had been so impressed with Ekerold's riding ability, when he saw him in action at the end-of-season Nürburgring international, that he offered to let him have one of his 500cc engine and also to prepare Ekerold's 250 and 350 Yamaha power units.

Ekerold soon had a Nico Bakker frame with monoshock suspension constructed to house the Fath four, but in the end he decided to concentrate on riding his Yamahas. The Fath four was shelved, this time never to reappear. With the speed and reliability of the new breed of Japanese four-cylinder 'strokers', a private effort, even with as gifted a tuner as Fath, simply could not compete.

More Disappointment

In the 1978 world sidecar series, Fath was to suffer yet more disappointment. Schwärzel still proved almost unbeatable, but his two victories at Assen and the Nürburgring, with a second a Mugello, in Italy, and a sixth in Nogaro, France, simply were not enough to stop Rolf Biland and his passenger, Englishman Kenny Williams, from taking the title with their Yamaha-powered BEO machine. What a machine it was too – quite simply the most radical interpretation of the sidecar construction rules that had ever been seen.

It appeared to be a perfectly natural development of a line that began earlier in the mid 1970s. Parallelogram suspension had appeared when

Helmut Fath pictured at
Hockenheim in 1991.
(© Courtesy of Jim Blanchard)

sidecar racing constructors started using racing-car suspension and wheels on conventional, short wheelbase outfits. However, this line of development, as racing outfits grew steadily more like three-wheeled racing cars, was speedily terminated when Biland produced his BEO *tricar*, which was so radical that it forced the FIM into creating *two* world sidecar classes for 1979: the B–2–A for conventional outfits, and the B–2–B for the new breed.

Regulations were hastily redrafted to outlaw racing-car suspensions and steering systems, and this meant a total reappraisal for everyone connected with the three-wheel racing fraternity. The result was a new breed of long-wheelbase, fully-enclosed racing three-wheelers – now commonly referred to as *worms*.

The Last Straw

This was the last straw for Fath, who by now had not only given up the idea of making a return himself, but with the split of the Championship in 1979 had finally decided to call it a day in his bid to be a combination of world champion and one-man motorcycle manufacturer.

It was the end of an era that had spanned 20 years, during which he had been world champion in 1960, fought back from serious injury to win back the Championship in 1968 with his own four-cylinder dohc engine, then had everything taken from him in the Münch deal in 1970, before coming back *again* with a completely new design to join the contest once more. In the process, some of his closest friends and racing partners had lost their lives through accidents, and it is unlikely that any other man in the history of motorcycle sport has ever suffered such peaks of triumph and depths of despair as Helmut Fath. In overcoming the setbacks, his character can be summed up in one word: fighter.

Helmut Fath died on 19 June 1993.

CHAPTER 15
KLAUS ENDERS

Until the advent of first Rolf Biland, and later Steve Webster, Klaus Enders had been the most successful sidecar racer with a total of 27 Grand Prix victories and six World Championship titles to his credit.

Klaus Enders was born in the market town of Giessen, near Frankfurt, on 2 May 1937. In the mid-1950s he began his motorcycling career on a diminutive 50cc Mars two-stroke – little more than a moped. Next came an Austrian Puch split-single with a 125cc engine and later still, inevitably, a flat-twin BMW. It was with the latter bike that he first considered racing and assisted by some pals – at the time Klaus was working in the Leica camera factory – he shoe-horned his BMW engine into a supposedly superior-handling Horex chassis and entered the solo 500cc class at the Noris Ring races at the Nürburgring circuit, aged 23 in 1960. But his solo outing turned out to be a dismal affair, as he crashed out early in the race. However, help was at hand thanks to friend Kurt Meixner who lent Klaus his BMW sidecar racing outfit – and the name Klaus Enders appeared for the first time on a results sheet, in fourth position.

Friedl Münch
Then in 1961, Klaus Enders's big break arrived in the shape of Friedl Münch, who sponsored him on a solo – a 499cc Manx Norton. Soon he was right up at the front of the field, including a class win at the Nürburgring. Münch was, at the time, deeply involved with the Horex twin-cylinder engine, and it was with one of these that Klaus resumed his sidecar activities.

German Junior Champion
The next major step in his career came in 1963 when he was crowned German Junior Champion. But it was to be in the Sidecar class

The most successful sidecar racer of the late 1960s and early 1970s, Klaus Enders, won six world titles (1967, 1969, 1970, 1972, 1973, and 1974) and 27 Grand Prix victories.
Photo W. Gruber/Archiv

where Klaus Enders really shone and, more importantly, enjoyed his racing. His best result on three wheels during that year was finishing fourth on his Horex outfit, behind no less a trio than Max Deubel, Florian Camathias and Georg Auerbacher (all with BMWs).

The Rennsport Engine

Next, at the end of 1964, Klaus began his drive to the very top, helped by being able to purchase Ludwig Hahn's spare BMW Rennsport engine – as Hahn was retiring. Dieter Büsch, the renowned tuner of the Munich-made twin-cylinder engine, breathed his magic on the motor, resulting in several top placings and the purchase of a brand-new chassis on the proceeds.

The Championship Trial

1966 saw Klaus enter the World Championship arena, a highlight coming with his Isle of Man TT debut. He and passenger Ralf Engelhardt covered over 500 miles (800km), learning the ultra-demanding Mountain course by sports car. But this paid off handsomely when they not only finished fourth, but also won the Overseas Newcomers' award. That year there were only five rounds in the Championship series and Enders also finished fourth in the final race, the Belgian Grand Prix at Spa Francorchamps.

In that first year contesting the World Championship series Klaus and passenger Reinhold Mannischeff finished fifth in the points table, which was a truly remarkable performance, with the promise of even better results to come. And, this, in fact, was just what was to transpire the following year.

Enders leading Georg
Auerbacher at La Source,
Belgian Grand Prix.
Photo W. Gruber/Archiv

Klaus Enders was the most successful sidecar racer of his era, with a total of 27 Grand Prix victories and six World Championship titles to his credit.

1967 – The Year Of Change

Fritz Scheidegger's death and Max Deubel's retirement was to benefit Klaus Enders and his new passenger, Ralf Englehardt, during the 1967 season.

In fact, they won five of the eight events counting towards the Championship, and quite simply no one else was in a position to really worry them. The other GP victors that year being Georg Auerbacher (wins in the first and last rounds: Barcelona and Monza respectively) and Siegfried Schauzu (winner of the Isle of Man TT).

Klaus Enders and Ralf Engelhardt during the 1967 Dutch TT.
Photo W. Gruber/Archiv

Siegfried Schauzu

Siegfried Schauzu was born on 21 September 1939 in Passendorf, Germany, and although never a world champion he did score no less than nine Grand Prix victories, being particularly successful in the Isle of Man TT, including breaking the lap record on more than one occasion.

An engineering background meant that 'Siggi' was someone who put pride into his machinery. He had made his racing debut, on a two-stroke Adler solo machine, on grass, during 1959. He quickly moved on to the tarmac, however, and in 1963 became the new German nation Junior champion.

He first made an impression in international sidecar racing during the 1965 West German Grand Prix, staged at the Nürburgring. This was the first GP of the year and was staged in truly awful conditions of freezing cold rain. But for young Schauzu it was a blessing because, piloting an outfit with an ancient push-rod BMW engine, he and his passenger, Horst Schneider, held on to the ultimate race winner (and 1965–66 World Champion) Fritz Scheidigger, after almost half of the field had dropped out.

The following year, 1966, saw Siggi purchase a second-hand BMW Rennsport motor from a retiring competitor. In June that year he and passenger Horst Schneider made their first foray to the Isle of Man TT, where they came home an impressive seventh. But at the next round in the Championship series, the Dutch TT over the Assen circuit, the pair bettered with a fifth – behind the race winner Scheidigger, Max Deubel, Otto Kolle and Georg Auerbacher – one place in front of another newcomer, a certain Klaus Enders, the latter destined to become a six-times world champion (see Chapter 15).

During 1967 Schauzu and Schneider not only won their first GP event, the Isle of Man TT, but scored points in each of the eight-round series except one,

Siegfried Schauzu and
Horst Schneider, 492cc
BMW at Mallory Park,
18 June 1967.

The 1971 500cc Isle of Man race winners Siegfried Schauzu and passenger Wolfgang Kalauch. Left to right: Jusof Huber, Arsenius Butscher, Kalauch, Schauzu, Hermann Hahn and Georg Auchbacher.

the Finnish GP at Imatra, finishing the season third in the points table behind Klaus Enders/Ralf Englehardt and Georg Auerbacher/Edward Dein. The pair won their second TT the following year and also repeated their previous year's World Championship position of third in the points table.

In 1969 Schauzu and Schneider won the 750cc TT and were runners-up in the 500cc GP event. In the World Championship series, overall the duo finished fourth. The next year, 1970, saw the Isle of Man TT results exactly as in 1969: 750cc first, 500cc second; however, with two other seconds (Finland and Ulster) and two thirds (France and Holland), Schauzu and Schneider finished third in the points table (behind champions Klaus Enders/Wolfgang KalAuer and the runners-up Georg Auerbacher/Helmut Hahn).

Then in 1971, with a new passenger (Wolfgang Kalauch), Siggi led the 500cc TT from start to finish and followed this up with his first Continental European Grand Prix victory at the super-quick Spa Francorchamps circuit in Belgium. After another victory in the next race, the Czech GP at Brno, Schauzu could almost smell the Championship title. But it was not to be, as the URS/Munich outfit of Horst Owesle/Peter Ruterford won the final two races, while Schauzu retired in Finland and came home runner-up in the final round, the Ulster GP.

The following year, 1972, Siggi began in fine form with victory in West Germany, second in France, while on the Isle of Man he became the first man to score a sidecar TT double. But after such a great start he could not maintain his winning style and could only manage thirds and fourths. So yet again the world title eluded him, his final position in the points table being third. In 1973 he was third again, but without winning a single Grand Prix.

In France, Siggi began his 1974 season well, with a last-bend victory over Werner Schwärzel at Clermont Ferrand. He also won at the Salzburgring in Austria. And as he took to the Isle of Man he led the title race, and although favourite for a win he was sidelined by engine trouble, but he did add another 750cc win to his TT tally. By the season's end Schauzu had scored more points than his rivals; however, under the prevailing points system (which saw only the top five positions of each driver to count) he only made third place in the rankings.

In 1975 Siggi, along with the majority of other leading sidecar competitors, finally ditched their four-stroke BMW Rennsport engines in favour of a new breed of two-stroke, including König, ARO and Yamaha. Schauzu chose the ARO. But it was not to be a happy marriage, his ARO-Fath machine having only one GP top-10 finish all season. In the Isle of Man TT he was destined to retire on the first lap; however, the bigger BMW twin he had retained for the 750cc class events gave him not only victory, but a new sidecar TT lap record of 99.31mph (159.78km/h).

In 1976 his overall performance was little better with the ARO, but he did gain a third position in the Austrian GP, while he set a new 500cc sidecar lap record in the Isle of Man TT, with a speed of 97.50mph (156.87km/h), this coming after a slow start, and he eventually finished fourth of 36 starters. He followed this with runners'-up spot (on his 750cc BMW) in the bigger sidecar event.

Using the ARO engine in the early rounds, he later switched to Yamaha power in the GPs in 1977, his best result being a runner-up in the Czech round at Brno. But in many other races when using the ARO he did not show very well. Then for 1978 another switch was made to a Schmitt outfit with that make of engine. But again the results were not forthcoming, and mid-season saw Schauzu on a Yamaha-engined Busch machine; gaining seventh in Czechoslovakia and ninth in the British GP at Silverstone.

For the 1979 GP season the FIM introduced a two-class sidecar Championship: B–2–A and B–2–B. In the former Siggi at last got back to something like his old form. At the first round, at the Salzburgring in Austria, he was second to Guy Brondin, gaining the same result at the next round at Hockenheim (this time behind Rolf Steinhausen). But later results did not match the early-season promise, with only a pair of fourth places in Belgium and Czechoslovakia and seventh in the British round at Silverstone to show for his efforts; leaving him fourth in the title stakes.

This really was his final effort and 'Sideways Sid', as his British fans had dubbed Siegfried Schauzu, finally departed the scene.

Siegfried Schauzu with his ARO Fath outfit, Isle of Man TT, June 1976.

The Five Victories

The Enders and Englehardt partnership won five rounds and they were crowned world champions of 1967. Their victories came in round two at Hockenheim, round three Clermont-Ferrand, round five Assen, round six Spa Francorchamps, and round seven Imatra. They were also second in Barcelona and the Isle of Man.

Runners-up in the Championship were Auerbacher/Dein and in third place Schauzu/Schneider. But the champions had a clear lead in the final points tally.

A Brand New Outfit

In 1968, with a brand new outfit, still BMW powered, the pair did not win a single round of the Championship. Originally, there was scheduled to be an Italian round at Monza. However, the sidecar event was cancelled, by governmental decree; it was in fact contested at Hockenheim, with the final of the German national Championship that October. 1968 was the year when Helmut Fath dominated with his home-built URS outfit.

Also in 1968, the pair set a new Isle of Man TT sidecar lap record at 94.32mph (151.76km/h), only to have the crankshaft break on the final lap while they were well into the lead; even so, they coasted in with a silent engine to secure eighth position.

Fellow German Georg Auerbacher was one of Klaus Enders's main rivals, winning a total of six Grand Prix between 1967 and 1971. Photo W. Gruber/Archiv

1969

The year 1969 saw a second title for Enders and Englehardt, although some could say they were assisted by the fact that the 1968 champion Helmut Fath suffered a forced retirement. By now they were effectively racing a works BMW-engined machine and had little difficulty in beating everyone with the exception of Fath with his four-cylinder URS outfit.

Klaus and Ralf had wins at Hockenheim, the Isle of Man, Imatra and in Ulster. Although by now they were fast becoming invincible all over Continental Europe, it was their TT performances which really stood out. In 1969, they had led the 500cc Sidecar TT from start to finish (setting a new race record of 92.48mph – 148.89km/h) with Schauzu runner-up and Fath third.

Another Championship – Another TT Victory

For the 1970 season Klaus had a new passenger, in the shape of Wolfgang Kalauch. And he carried off his third title, with five victories in the eight-round title chase. With victories in France (Le Mans), Isle of Man, Czechoslovakia (Brno), Finland (Imatra) and Ulster (Dundrod).

Klaus also scored his second TT victory, yet again setting a new race record, this time with a speed of 92.93mph (149.52km/h). He also broke the 750cc sidecar lap record before being forced to retire.

Retirement

Then at the end of 1970 came the shock announcement that Klaus Enders had decided to retire, at 33, and was going to try his hand on four wheels. However, his car racing (still with BMW) career was to be short-lived – only lasting a single season and Klaus, by now running his own tuning business, made a return to his first love for the 1972 GP season.

Klaus did not achieve the success he had hoped for on four wheels. And considering himself to be too young to leave the racing game, he made the decision to don his leathers once more.

In addition there is no doubt that BMW encouraged him to return to the sidecar fold, as the company needed a title challenger after Horst Oswele had won the world crown with the powerful URS four-cylinder in Enders' absence during 1971. And as Englishman Chris Vincent was taking over the URS for 1972, the Munich firm feared that without Enders they would be beaten once more.

Dominating Once More

As it was, both Vincent and Enders did not get off to the best of starts, neither finishing in the top six at the first two rounds (at the Nürburgring

A dejected Klaus Enders and passenger Ralf Engelhardt after being forced to retire at Ramsey, when a tyre punctured in the 1972 Isle of Man TT.

and Clermont-Ferrand). Then at round three, the Austrian GP at the Salzburgring, Enders partnered again by Englehardt won, at an average speed of 97.32mph (156.63km/h). Next came the Isle of Man, where after again leading they were forced to retire, with, of all things, a flat tyre!

The next three rounds, at Assen, Spa and Brno, Klaus and Ralf won. The best Chris Vincent could do was finish runner-up at Assen. The final round that year was the Finnish Grand Prix at Imatra. Here, at last, Vincent was able to bring the URS home in front of the BMW outfit.

In fact when the author interviewed Chris Vincent while compiling this book, he told me that of all the sidecar men he had raced against, it was Klaus Enders whom he most respected. In fact he went as far as saying that with Enders he felt a special bond, being able to follow him more closely as his control was 'inch perfect'.

A New Monocoque-framed Outfit

For 1973, Enders had a brand-new monocoque-framed BMW outfit which cost the then high price of £6,000 (in today's value getting on for £100,000). This weighed in, complete with engine and transmission, on 375lb (170kg), while the Busch-tuned motor put out nearly 70bhp. However, BMW were by then beginning to come under pressure from the new breed of two-stroke-engined outfits, notably the König liquid-cooled flat-four. The König was very fast, but also, at this stage, equally unreliable.

The Czech Grand Prix at Brno in 1973 saw yet another victory for Enders and Engelhardt and their rapid Busch-tuned BMW outfit.

Klaus and Ralf during the 1973 Isle of Man TT. That year they won all seven races in which they took part counting towards the world title.

BMW Reliability

The double-overhead camshaft BMW twin cylinder engine had ruled the roost at the highest level for some two decades. And still had its great smoothness **and** reliability. When, in those days, the two-strokes were largely untried and thus inclined to either slow as the race progressed, or break down entirely.

And so, with its supreme reliability, BMW and Enders won yet another Championship title – his fifth.

In fact, 1973 was the most impressive of all his crowns thus far, as he won no fewer than seven of the eight rounds: Le Castellet, France; Salzburgring, Austria; Hockenheim, West Germany; Isle of Man; Assen, Holland; Spa Francorchamps, Belgium; Brno, Czechoslovakia.

In fact, in the final round at Imatra in Finland (the eighth in the series), Klaus Enders, together with all the other established sidecar stars, did not make the journey north, and so the race was made up entirely of local competitors. In reality, Klaus had won every race against his competitors that year!

1974 A Year of Challenge

In 1974 Klaus Enders and Ralf Englehardt took their sixth and fifth world titles respectively. Accustomed to taking the lead virtually from the beginning of the year, they were forced in 1974 to await the outcome of the last round before winning the title. Problems with the preparation and tuning of their new Busch-tuned engine, as well as the ever-increasing competition from the König drivers, caused extremely stiff and difficult races. In fact, in the author's opinion, only Klaus's supreme skills were able to save the day. As proof of this is that of the eight rounds contested Enders and Englehardt only won two races: the Italian GP at Imola and the Dutch TT at Assen. Other winners were: Schauzu (2), Schwärzel (2), Lüthringhauser (1) and Steinhausen (1). The two-stroke pack was closing in…

Difficulties

And so Klaus Enders's final World Championship had come in 1974, but by then he was having increasing difficulties with sponsors and mechanical reliability. Previously, the twin-cylinder BMW had been unbeatable. But by 1974, with the arrival of the König this was not so, the BMW, now pushed to the very limit of its reliability to keep up with the flying 'strokers, often hit a mechanical problem and thus failed to finish.

But *when* the BMW had kept going, it and Klaus Enders were potentially still an unbeatable combination; particularly over the ultra-demanding 37.73-mile (60.70km) Isle of Man Mountain circuit. Although he had been an early retirement in 1974, Klaus Enders had broken the race and lap records for the 500cc Sidecar race the year before. And his record lap of 95.22mph (153.20km/h) was not bettered until two years later.

The *Motor Cycle* dated 23 November 1974 carried the following news: 'Klaus Enders, the 37-year-old ex-camera mechanic from Wetzlar, home of the famous Leica company, has decided to quit following a long disagreement with sponsor Gerhard Heukerot and with Dieter Busch, the man who built the outfits and prepared the special BMW engines he used.'

Past Glories

1975 saw little of Klaus Enders, while a final attempt to relive past glories came at the beginning of the 1976 season, when he piloted a four-cylinder Yamaha outfit in the opening round at Le Mans in France. However, the transition from four-stroke to two-stroke was not a success. And after disagreeing with his new sponsor, Klaus quit the sport for good.

Rumours of another return rumbled on for many months, but he never graced the Grand Prix circuits of Europe again. But his immaculate style and superb skill, however, combined with Ralf Engelhard's nimble, neat ability as a passenger, will be long remembered by all those enthusiasts who saw them at their unbeatable best.

Truly, Klaus Enders was one of the most brilliant of all Sidecar Champions, if not the greatest of them all.

CHAPTER 16

HORST OWESLE

Horst Owesle is today one of the least-remembered ex-holders of the World Sidecar Championship title, which he won in 1971, driving a Münch URS (read Fath!) double overhead camshaft four-cylinder outfit.

Born on 14 November 1938 in Weiher, Germany, Horst was a skilled engineer who, like Helmut Fath, was very much responsible for his own success on the track, due to his mechanical skills off it.

The Back-room Boys

Together with Dr Peter Kuhn and Paul Smetner, Horst Owesle was one of the original members of Helmut Fath URS development team, prior to the break up which is described below. And as thus he had intimate knowledge of the engine's design and subsequent development.

Double world champion Helmut Fath (see Chapter 14) had won his second title, driving the four-cylinder URS in 1968.

Friedl Münch

Friedl Münch had sprung to world-wide fame back in the mid-1960s when he had built the first Mammoth, this being powered by the air-cooled NSU Prinz 1000 'superbike'. The success of this venture brought in his first business partner, the veteran American publisher, Floyd Clymer. This was to enable Münch to move from his existing cramped, stable-like premises to a purpose-built factory unit at Ossenheim, which opened in September 1967. Clymer, a former Indian works rider, had a dream not only of assisting Münch build his Mammoth superbikes, but of also relaunching the Indian brand, having purchased the manufacturing rights to the American machine when the original factory went out of business in 1953.

However, Clymer's health was to deteriorate, resulting with his decision to retire from the project in May 1969. It was also a well-founded rumour, at the time, that he had sold his entire interest in the Münch operation to an unidentified source, represented by the Chase Manhattan Bank of Frankfurt. Later, it transpired that this mystery backer was an American millionaire's son, George Bell, himself a Münch Mammoth owner.

Racing Rather Than Production

Although, initially, Bell stated that he had intended increasing the production tempo and putting the company on a sound financial footing, it transpired that he saw the Münch enterprise very much as a means of acting the playboy in the Grand Prix racing arena. Soon, he had Münch working on racing projects rather than production roadsters. The proof came in September 1969 with press headlines proclaiming: 'Fath-Münch Tie-up!'

Helmut Fath

The story behind the headlines was the joining up of two of Germany's greatest-ever special builders – Helmut Fath and Friedl Münch. The man behind this marriage of engineering expertise was George Bell, who wanted the two men to combine in the design and development of racing and record-breaking machinery. Bell saw this as a quick route to success – Münch was already building a potential record breaker, while Fath had the URS Grand Prix racing engine.

The Fath-URS Team

At the start of this collaboration with Bell and Münch, Fath together with his right-hand man Dr Peter Kuhn and Horst Owesle (development engineer) and Paul Smetner (test rider) would continue to operate from their existing premises in the village or Ursenbach (hence the URS wording). However, it was planned that a brand-new facility, scheduled for completion the following spring, would be constructed at Altenstadt, near the existing Münch works at Ossenheim. When this was completed, all Münch and Fath interests would be centralised there, and both men would co-operate on racing and roadster projects.

The Daytona 'Bomb'

The first project to be completed by the new team, during the winter of 1969–70, was a larger displacement version of the NSU-engined Mammoth, this being intended for an attack on the existing One-hour world speed record – held by Mike Hailwood and MV Agusta at 145mph (233km/h).

Built in the short space of six weeks, the new machine was intended to provide valuable press coverage for the Münch street bikes. With a capacity of 1370cc this put out an impressive 125bhp at 8,600rpm. And when tests began around the Daytona speedbowl it achieved a highly impressive 178mph (286km/h)! But there were snags .. major snags. These centred around the tyres. Quite simply after three laps (around nine miles) the rear tyre would cry 'enough' and start shedding great chunks of rubber. And no tyre tried improved the situation. As for the bike itself, this was destined to languish in a Miami warehouse for the next 11 years, under a court order taken out by one of the project's American backers in lieu of payment. But that's another story.

Back In Germany

Back in Germany the team returned to their respective tasks. For Fath, Kuhn and Owesle this meant getting the Münch-URS solo and sidecar racing venture off the ground.

But at the first round of the World Championship series (in which only the 500cc solo actually took part), tensions which had existed, almost from the very start of the Bell-Münch-Fath partnership, came to a head. During practice, Münch had insisted that Fath (who was still an active competitor at that time) should race the new low-line Münch-URS sidecar outfit.

However, Helmut objected to this, wanting instead to use his own non-Münch machine. When Münch disagreed with him, Fath announced that he was quitting the team altogether.

The Break-up

When Helmut Fath had originally agreed to join the team, Bell had, in effect, bought out the entire Fath racing equipé. This meant that even though Fath had not moved all his machinery to the Münch operation in Ossenheim, he was no longer the legal owner of the remaining hardware. This was to result in considerable ill-feeling: 'I was cleared out', stated an upset Helmut Fath afterwards, when he was left with an empty workshop. 'They came with a pantechnicon and cleared out every engine I had.'

Even though Fath (and solo rider Ferdinand Kaczor) had quit, Horst Owesle and Dr Peter Kuhn stayed with the Münch organisation. Although the new partnership did not have any real hope of 500cc solo class honours, Kuhn did develop a 750cc four-cylinder version and, more importantly to *Sidecar Champions Since 1923*, with the help of Horst Owesle, went on to garner some famous victories on three wheels.

German National Junior Sidecar Champion

Horst Owesle had been German National Junior Sidecar Champion in 1969 on a BMW flat-twin. And George Bell had been astute enough to sign up Horst as his team's reserve sidecar racer when he first took over the Münch-Fath enterprise. With Helmut now departed, Horst Owesle was quickly promoted to the number-one spot. And as events were to prove, his faith was fully justified.

The 1971 World Championship Campaign

Not a single pundit predicted just how much of a threat Horst Owesle would be at the highest level. And armed with the latest development of the URS four-cylinder engine, and partnered first by Julius Kremer and from the Dutch TT onwards by Englishman Peter Rutherford, the combination of Owesle and the URS created a great shock to the sidecar racing world by carrying off the title at their very first attempt. However, it was not to be an instant success story because, in the eight-round series, it was not until the final five races that Owesle, with Rutherford in the chair, suddenly emerged as title challenger with three victories and a couple of runner-up spots.

Before this, the best the original pairing of Owesle and Kremer could achieve was a fifth in the opening round at the Salzburgring in Austria. In fairness, these first few events were more about striking the right mixture between racing and sorting out the technical aspect of the sidecar outfit itself. For example, at the Isle of Man TT (in which both Owesle and Kremer were beginners) the pair did not complete either the 500cc World Championship race or the 750cc event (the latter with the new seven-fifty motor).

Engineer, mechanic and driver Horst Owesle working on the four-cylinder Münch URS during his 1971 Championship-winning season. Photo W. Gruber/Archiv

Success Starts To Come

Success began to come from the end of June onwards.

First, at the Dutch TT, in front of over 100,000 spectators Horst, with Peter Rutherford in the chair for the first time, took an impressive victory in truly awful wet conditions after several of the BMW stars retired for various reasons.

The Dutch result was followed eight days later with runner-up spot (to Schauzu/Kalauch – BMW) at the Belgian Grand Prix. It was the same result a couple of weeks later at Brno, the scene of the Czech GP behind the Iron Curtain.

A Second Victory

The pair's second victory came at the 3.7-mile (6km) Imatra circuit, the home of the Finnish Grand Prix at the very end of July. The race was run through fields and pine woods within a few miles of the Russian border. Roughly square and with a few fast curves, the course placed the emphasis on acceleration and braking.

Conditions for the competitors were basic to say the least – and this was probably why the lavatory block in the centre of the paddock was burnt to the ground...

Anyway, the 37,000 crowd did see some good racing, with the solo race victories going to Giacomo Agostini (350 and 500cc), Rod Gould (250cc) and Barry Sheene (125cc) joined by Horst Owesle and Peter Rutherford in the sidecar event on their Münch-URS outfit.

Clinching The Title

The Anglo-German pairing were again victorious at the eighth and final round, at Dundrod in Ulster during mid-August. With the 7.4-mile circuit awash after two days and nights of continual rain, a smaller crowd than usual came to watch, not helped by the result of the ongoing civil strife in nearby Belfast.

Their victory was, said *Motor Cycle*: 'Clear-cut' with Klaus Enders's (BMW) lap and race records falling to the Münch team.

Motor Cycle's front-page headline read: 'Ulster's Mystery Men'. This was in response to not only Horst Owesle's victory, but also that of Ray McCullough's 250cc win – the first Irish rider to win the Ulster GP since Dick Creith had shocked the aces in the 500cc class on a Norton in 1965.

This is how the newspaper saw the Münch world champion: 'Even among sidecar men, who usually have a longer racing career than their solo counterparts, 30 is a late age to start competing. But it isn't too late, decided Horst Owesle, and he proved it at Saturday's Ulster Grand Prix by clinching the World Sidecar Championship in his first full season of international competition, aged 33.'

Mention here should be made of the Münch team manager and former solo racer, John Blanchard. And it was to be John who lined up the German squad to contest some of the top end-of-season British short-circuit events.

Heinz Luthringshauser (BMW) at Braddan Bridge in front of Horst Owesle (URS), 1971 Isle of Man TT.
Photo W. Gruber/Archiv

Silverstone

The first of these came a week later, following the Ulster GP, at Silverstone. And the famous Northamptonshire circuit had seen nothing like it since the great days of the early 1950s, when Geoff Duke (solo) and Eric Oliver (sidecar) reigned supreme on works Nortons. Every road to the 2.9 mile (4.6km) circuit was jammed two hours before the meeting was due to start and programmes were sold out before racing got under way. Why? Well, there were several reasons, including a return by Mike Hailwood and the fact that this was the first major motorcycle promotion at Silverstone for six years.

In the two sidecar races (500cc and 750cc), 'New sidecar world champion Horst Owesle put on a fantastic display overcoming the very real disadvantage of a right-hand sidecar at Silverstone to win both the 500 and 750cc races on his four-cylinder Münch' (*Motor Cycle*, 25 August 1971).

Later the Münch pair competed at Mallory Park (Race of the Year meeting), Cadwell Park and Brands Hatch.

Horst Owesle and Peter Rutherford (Münch URS) winning the final round – and thus the Championship – at the Ulster Grand Prix in August 1971.

Retirement

In fact the Brands Hatch meeting on 3 October marked the last race in their racing careers of both Horst Owesle and Peter Rutherford; Horst going on to assist Englishman Chris Vincent (see Chapter 11) in his (unsuccessful) pursuit for the 1972 title with a URS-engined machine.

Credit must be given to Owesle for his technical expertise. Once Helmut Fath had left, it was he who not only put on his leathers (for the 1971 season), but also overalls to become the team's technical wizard.

The 1971 Championship-winning engine was bench-tested at 86bhp, using a quartet of Japanese Keihin carburettors, higher lift camshafts and dry-sump lubrication.

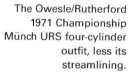

The Owesle/Rutherford 1971 Championship Münch URS four-cylinder outfit, less its streamlining.

During his time with the Münch team (which ended later in 1972) Horst had not only been responsible for the sidecar engines (in both 500 and 750cc sizes) but also the solo machines which were occasionally raced during the time, notably by Tony Jefferies at certain British short circuit meetings in the latter half of 1971.

The Cost

Racing was to prove the centre of the Bell-funded Münch company's problems. Despite warnings from Fried Münch himself, George

Mallory Park 1992, after
the Münch URS bikes,
spares, etc, had finally
been sold.

Bell sank over half-a-million deutschmarks into the 1971 racing programme alone, and although Horst Owesle and Peter Rutherford had emerged as champions, the factory itself was in dire financial straits. With creditors pressing from all sides, George Bell quickly departed the scene and returned to America, leaving Münch to solve his own problems. This he ultimately did, thanks to a succession of other backers.

During the 1980s, Horst Owesle established his own company, Owesle-Motorräder GmBH becoming an authorised Suzuki dealership in Mörlenbach-Weiher.

On 5 August 1994, after a year-long stay in hospital, Horst passed away, aged only 56.

As for the Münch-URS race team, this was rescued thanks to John Blanchard which involved the actual Championship outfit and also a number of engines – as was witnessed by the help provided to Chris Vincent during 1972 – and also the technical assistance which Chris was to receive from Horst Owesle.

Later still in the late 1980s and early 1990s the URS racing venture was to be reborn thanks to not only John Blanchard, but also work put in by others including Steve Collins (given the nickname Crazyman by Helmut Fath), Horst Owesle, Jeff Dobberson, Steve Hayman and Paul Smetner. There was even the return of Helmut Fath himself!

A final point of interest is that none of the URS engines were numbered; instead they were given names such as 'Emil', 'Gustav' and 'Heinrich' – each derived from World War Two Messerschmitt 109 fighter aircraft.

CHAPTER 17
ROLF STEINHAUSEN

Rolf Steinhausen was born on 27 July 1943 at Numbrecht, near Cologne, Germany, and was destined to become a double world champion and win 10 Grand Prix races. But for two serious accidents, both resulting in long periods in hospital, he might have added to these totals quite significantly, in the author's opinion.

But strangely, neither of these injuries was sustained in sidecar racing. The first came at the Nürburgring circuit when Rolf, then just 18 years of age, was making his racing debut aboard a BMW solo. Unfortunately, he crashed heavily, and was rushed to hospital with serious facial injuries. His jaw was broken, teeth shattered and his nose damaged. In fact, it was to be many months before surgeons could rebuild Rolf's face – using plastic to replace the broken bones. Even so, he eventually recovered and his love of speed only temporarily dimmed.

Then, several years later he was to be the victim of another major accident, but this time it was sustained while skiing. On a fast downhill run, his ski hit a hidden rock. The result was a badly broken leg – this was so bad in fact that doctors feared he would lose the leg. But after many months in hospital, several operations later and a skin graft to his right hip, Rolf was to make a return to life outside the hospital grounds.

But the skiing accident left a permanent legacy, as now Rolf's left leg was much thinner than the right one – and also had limited ankle movement.

Rolf Steinhausen had graduated as an electrical engineer after leaving school. And because of the two accidents already described, he did not begin his sidecar racing career until the age of 24. In fact Rolf's interest in three-wheels had been sparked by his fellow countryman four times world champion Max Deubel, who also happened to be a member of the same Bilstein motorcycle club.

Rolf had also found time to get married, to Ursula, the couple having two sons, Maik, who was born in 1968, and Jorg, who arrived two years later.

Rolf's first dabble at chair racing came with a home-brewed outfit powered by a push-rod BMW roadster engine, prepared in his own workshop. Later he moved on with a BMW overhead-cam Rennsport motor. With this he rapidly improved, winning the 1970 German Sidecar national Championship title.

That same year Rolf Steinhausen became a full-time professional racer. But he soon found it a hard struggle, with his biggest problem being the high costs of campaigning one of the by now aging Rennsport engines. And it was to be the staggering costs of running the BMW, which saw Rolf make a switch for the 1972 season to a König two-stroke.

The König

Meanwhile, back in 1969, Dipl. Ing. Dieter König, managing director and chief engineer of the König firm, had decided to build a 500cc-class solo racing motorcycle.

Based in West Berlin, the König factory had already built up a name during the 1960s, but not for motorcycles, instead as a manufacturer of a successful range of multi-cylinder, two-stroke engines for powerboat racing. It was one of these modified production boat engines, a horizontally-opposed, water-cooled, four-cylinder two-stroke, which formed the basis of the bike engine.

In effect, the engine comprised a pair of flat-twins mounted side-by-side in a common crankcase. The pressed-up, three-bearing, single-crankshaft ran across the frame. Bore and stroke dimensions of the four cylinders were classic two-stroke, 54 x 54mm, while each Mahle piston featured a single Dykes-type ring. A belt-driven pump circulated under the engine via a small radiator and a reservoir under the engine.

For bike racing, the boat engine had been fitted with a pair of East German BVF carburettors to improve acceleration. Each of these supplied petroil mixture to one pair of fore-and-aft cylinders, which fired at the same time, while induction was controlled by a single disc valve situated on top of the crankcase. The exhausts from the front and rear pairs of cylinders were siamesed and ran into a massive expansion chamber over the (separate) gearbox.

Development Work

Although much of the early development work on the König was carried out in the solo class (500cc), notably by New Zealander Kim Newcombe (tragically killed on the machine at the British GP at Silverstone in August 1974), it was in the sidecar class that König was to have its major successes – and with Rolf Steinhausen at the controls in 1975 and 1976, earning him the title 'King of the Königs'.

In the winter of 1971–72, a major redesign of the König engine took place. For the first time, the original square engine dimensions were dispensed with, to be replaced by four cylinders with the short-stroke of 50mm and a wider bore of 56mm, giving 492.6cc, as against the original 493.4cc size. The crankshaft was redesigned with two main bearings on the drive side, one at the opposite end, and a fourth in the middle. Lubrication was still by petroil (at a ratio of 16:1), and because the mixture was directed straight at the caged-roller big-ends, there was no need for the usual two-stroke slots in the con-rod eyes, providing additional strength. Another major change was a 45mm twin choke Solex carburettor, still controlled by a single inlet disc.

In 1972, a 680cc version of the König had been introduced and, as well as the solo racers, both the new engines (500 and 680cc) had debuted in sidecar events. In fact, it was Rolf who gave König its first sidecar GP top 10 finish, at the second round of the 1972 World Championship series, at Clermont-Ferrand in France, followed at the next round with a fourth in Austria at the Salzburgring.

To start with, reliability was something of an issue, but over the months Rolf sorted out the teething troubles with the König and by 1973 he was finishing far more races.

The 1973 Season

There were eight rounds of the 1973 Championship: France, Austria, West Germany, Isle of Man, Holland, Belgium, Czechoslovakia and Finland. However, the final round at Imatra was to only be contested by locals.

The first race took place at Le Castellet; here Steinhausen finished back in fifth place behind Enders, Gawley, Schwärzel and Wenger.

Next came the Salzburgring where another fifth was recorded. But at the third round (Hockenheim) only Klaus Enders and his super-quick BMW finished in front of Rolf. Then came the ultimate test of machine and man, the Isle of Man TT over the fearsome 37.73-mile (60.70km) Mountain circuit.

A magnificent third was scored in the Island, with Enders victorious and fellow König driver Gerry Boret runner-up. More places were to follow in Holland (sixth) and Czechoslovakia (fifth).

In essence, the reliability had improved greatly, but now more speed and better handling were needed to enable further progress to be made.

Dieter Busch

Over the winter of 1973–74 Rolf persuaded the highly rated Dieter Busch to construct a special chassis to house the flat-four. And with this new outfit Steinhausen was at last armed with a truly competitive machine. However, it was not to be an immediate success, with only two finishes in the first five races: Nürburgring (fourth) and Imola (third).

Then came Assen, with Rolf finishing runner-up to Enders – his best GP finish to date.

A First Victory

After Assen came the Belgium round at Spa Francorchamps. And it was here that Rolf Steinhausen scored his first ever Grand Prix victory, finally beating multi-world champion, Klaus Enders. Interestingly, Enders also used a Busch outfit, albeit powered by a works-supported BMW engine.

And so Rolf finished fourth in the world ranking at the end of the 1974 season. This coming after he had switched passengers midway through the season. His crewman earlier in the year had been Karl Scheurer, but they eventually split and Rolf talked Sepp Huber out of retirement to team up with him.

The 1975 Championship Season

With five König engines, the Busch outfit and Sepp Huber as his passenger, Rolf Steinhausen had a brilliant year in 1975, not only winning three rounds of the Championship series, but also the Championship title itself.

The pair began the campaign with a fourth in the French round at Le Castellet. Next came victory at the Salzburgring in Austria, followed by a third at Hockenheim. But the highlight for Rolf was round four, the Isle of Man TT. Here every facet of racing came into play, not just skill but stamina too, likewise for the machine – speed being of no use without reliability on such a demanding course.

The final three rounds saw mixed fortunes for the pairing of Steinhausen and Huber. First, in the Dutch TT at Assen, came a retirement, followed by victory a week later in Belgium; finally they finished runner-up to Werner Schwärzel/Andreas Huber (also König mounted).

And this was the final positions in the Championship: Steinhausen/Huber as Champions, Schwärzel/Huber as runners-up. Rolf Biland (Yamaha-Seymaz) was third; but Rolf used more than one passenger that year.

Champions Again

The defence of the Championship did not get off too well at the first round of the new 1976 season, at Le Mans in France, Rolf (still with the same passenger) with a retirement. They were immediately successful second time out at the Salzburgring in Austria, with a victory from Schwärzel/Huber and Schauzu/Lorentz.

And this was followed by a second victory in the Isle of Man TT, this time from British opposition in the form of Dick Greasley/Cliff Holland and Mac Hobson/Mick Burns, who gained second and third places respectively. Siegfried Schauzu/Wolfgang Kalauch (driving an ARO-Fath) came home fourth.

Rolf Steinhausen and Josef Huber (König), world champions and TT winners in 1976. This photograph shows them during the TT that year.

Then in the Dutch TT the pairing could only manage a lowly eighth, but they then bounced back with a third successive Belgian Grand Prix victory, were runner-up in Czechoslovakia, before winning once more at the home round (staged over the Nürburgring), this being the final round of that year's series.

As in their first Championship year, the pair had Schwärzel/Huber as their nearest rivals. Sadly, a tragic road accident in the close season meant that Sepp Huber's racing career was over.

1977 Year of Change

The arrival of the four-cylinder Yamaha engine into Grand Prix sidecar racing had seen the König power unit become obsolete almost overnight. So Rolf was forced to abandon his beloved König in favour of the Yamaha after

Steinhausen competing in the Dutch TT at Assen circa 1974. Photo W. Gruber/Archiv

the early rounds, campaigning one of the Japanese units mounted in the proven Busch chassis. Another problem was the role of passenger; Rolf having several before, mid-season, linking up with the highly experienced Wolfgang Kalauch.

And the final three rounds saw Rolf and Wolfgang back to top form, with a victory in the Czech GP at Brno and two runner-up positions in Belgium and the final round, the British GP at Silverstone. So had Rolf begun the season with

Steinhausen (with passenger Wolfgang Kalauch) with their Busch-König outfit negotiating Ramsey Hairpin during the 1977 Isle of Man TT, in which they finished runners-up.

Rolf Steinhausen's outfit pictured prior to the start of the 1978 Isle of Man TT.

Yamaha power he might just have made it three titles in a row. As it was, the consistent British pairing of George O'Dell and Kenny Arthur became the 1977 world champions (see Chapter 18); without, it has to be said, actually winning a single round!

1978 was quite simply an awful year. Armed with the old Busch outfit, and a new Seymaz featuring sidecar wheel steering, nothing seemed to go right and their only finish in the top 10 was at Spa Francorchamps, Belgium, where they finished fourth. Rolf also became disillusioned with organisers, feeling that sidecar racers were treated as: 'Second-class citizens.' And he could not agree terms to race in the Isle of Man.

1979: The Year of Controversy

The Swiss engineer/driver Rolf Biland had put the cat among the pigeons by winning the 1978 Championship with a machine which embodied some pretty controversial ideas (see Chapter 19).

So, for 1979, the sport governing body, the FIM, created two sidecar categories: B–2–A and B–2–B.

With the number-one plate of world champion, Rolf Steinhausen during the Austrian Grand Prix at Salzburg. Photo W. Gruber/Archiv

This spurred Rolf to recreate at least some of his past glories, with two victories in the B–2–A class, at Hockenheim (round two) and Spa Francorchamps (round four); these, plus a third at the Salzburgring (round one), runner-up at Assen (round three) and fifth at Silverstone (round six) saw Rolf, together with new passenger, Englishman Kenny Arthur, finish runner-up to Biland/Waltisberg in the Championship table.

Swansong

In 1980 the title chase saw only a single class. And the Yamaha-powered KSA outfit of the previous year exchanged for a Yam-Bartol machine, but

The British Grand Prix at Silverstone, August 1981. Rolf Steinhausen and Gerhardt Willmann (FKN).

Steinhausen and Willmann with their 496cc FKN at the Gooseneck during the 1981 TT.

still with Kenny Arthur as passenger. However, success was to be strictly limited: a fifth in the opening round in France and a seventh in the Belgian GP (round four).

1981 did not get any better, with a ninth in the first round (Salzburgring) and a sixth (Hockenheim) in round two.

After that there were occasional appearances during 1983; Rolf then called it a day. However, he could look back on his achievements with considerable pride, and of course, two World Championship titles.

As one commentator put it: 'A thorough professional, Rolf has been a credit to the sport.'

Finally, Rolf Steinhausen was the last man to use a right-handed sidecar layout in Grand Prix history.

Later, Rolf's younger son Jorg continued the family tradition of being a top-line sidecar competitor, when he and passenger Trevor Hopkinson ended the 2002 season runners-up in the World Championship.

CHAPTER 18

GEORGE O'DELL

George O'Dell was nothing if not controversial. In 1977 he became the first Britain to win the World Sidecar Championship title since Eric Oliver back in 1953. But he achieved this feat without winning a single race in the series!

Only four years later, following domestic problems, an armed siege resulted in a house fire in which George lost his life. He was just 35 years old.

The 'Rocker' Sidecar Champ

O'Dell was born in Hemel Hempstead, Hertfordshire, in November 1945. Journalist, and friend of the author, Nigel Clark described George O'Dell as the 'rocker sidecar champ'. This was a pretty accurate description as in his youth George had been well known for not only a quick temper, but his contempt of any form of authority. In fact Ian Beacham, in the 1978 book *Sidecar Championship* (written in conjunction with George) says: 'George O'Dell was a tempestuous youth, with a poker-hot temper and a disregard of most forms of authority which led him into constant trouble, sometimes towards the verge of delinquency.'

George was the eldest son of a wood machinist and a waitress who resided in a small two-bedroomed cottage in Hemel Hempstead.

The following is how George described his schooldays: 'For much of the time, I hated lessons. It was perhaps the feeling of being cooped up inside a room. I loved to be going out and about.'

One of his few real interests was two wheels – at first it was pedal cycles, then motorcycles. And George was only 10 years old when he acquired an ancient pre-war single-cylinder Francis-Barnett two-stroke. Although far from complete he set to and stripped the machine and rebuilt it, something he was to do with other bikes in his back garden at home. But he soon came to the attention of the local police when he rode them on the public highway! George again: 'I was a tearaway, there's no denying it. But I reckon the bikes helped to keep me out of serious trouble.'

The Other George

But there was another side of the young O'Dell. He loved birds (the ones with wings!) and as his father shared the same passion, father and son would often spend hours together at their aviary. They successfully bred budgerigars and kept a large collection, but would also attend to an injured or sick bird in the local area.

Another love was model aircraft.

Next came his 'legal' motorcycling. He passed his driving test with an Excelsior Talisman (a twin cylinder 250cc two-stroke) and soon became a rocker – most evenings he could be found at such well-known hangouts as the Busy Bee or Ace cafes; centres of activity during the 1960s for the leather jacket brigade.

The BSA Gold Star

With money saved up from his first paid job as an apprentice printer, George bought a BSA Gold Star from Streamline Motorcycles of Dulwich. However, as George was later to recall: 'A month to the day I was in hospital. I ran into the back of a police car.' Continuing: 'They did me for dangerous driving.' He broke his right leg, and some fingers, damaging his kidneys and vertebrae and was in hospital for several weeks.

Eventually, after leaving the printing trade he found that his mechanical skills were far more to his liking, and with the benefit of a further education course behind him became a foreman in a local brush factory.

He was then 22 and had just begun his sidecar racing career. This move came after the chance appearance of a racing sidecar outfit outside a local garage. After talking to the owner, George found himself watching the outfit at a Mallory Park meeting the following weekend.

George described what happened next: 'My mate Alan Gosling had a Gold Star but he crashed it and bent the forks on the way to Mallory. He really fancied having a go as a passenger.' George also admitted: 'I fancied being the driver, so that was that. It seemed like a challenge. I didn't imagine it would be any different from riding a solo just because it had a third wheel.'

A Racing Debut

Within a couple of weeks they had purchased a six-fifty Triumph-engined sidecar outfit and on this the intrepid pair made their racing debut at a Racing 50 Club meeting at Snetterton on 4 March 1967.

The first race yielded a third place – the George O'Dell band wagon was rolling. The outfit was, said George: 'An amazing contraption. It had a sawn-down Manx Norton frame, a pair of Manx Norton spoked wheels 16 inch in diameter, while the third wheel had seen better days on an original Watsonian chair. Running costs were shared fifty-fifty.'

Club Champions

The next year, 1968, George and Alan Gosling won the final race to clinch the Southern 67 Club Championship at Thruxton. The pair beat the likes of the Boret brothers and Arthur Teasdale. Not only that, but the win had come on an engine borrowed from another competitor who had finished last in the previous race. It was then that George knew 'he had something' and 'I pressed on hard to be a success.'

The Engineer

By carrying out all his own tuning and chassis building, George was becoming more and more the engineer, not just the driver.

A TT Debut

Alan Gosling quit after a disagreement, to be replaced by Peter Stockdale, a young Hemel Hempstead printer. The new pairing decided to enter the 1970 Isle of Man TT. They had two rides. In the first, their race ended at the Gooseneck when the contact breaker points fell out of the magneto while they were lying 16th. In the other race they were halted for 25 minutes while repairing an oil pipe. George later explained what transpired: 'A spectator lent me his penknife so that I could cut off a length of pipe to stick in the tube. We then had to replace the lost oil by draining his BSA's oil tank into a sandwich bag and pouring it into ours.' But George and Peter still managed to get a finisher's award.

The 1971 TT Crash

The difficulties of the 1970 TT were as nothing compared to what happened a year later. The front wheel disintegrated in practice at Greeba Bridge. As George later described: 'We ploughed straight into the bridge, through a fence and into someone's garden. We finished up with the outfit up side down back on the road.'

George broke two fingers, his right foot and nose, while Peter Stockdale broke both ankles and immediately quit racing for good. As for the outfit, this was a complete write-off.

The next passenger was Bill Boldison (a toolmaker from Abbots Langley), while in his search for more power George created a twin-engined (two Triumph 500cc) layout, which was then raced for two seasons with reasonable success, including winning every Lydden Hill sidecar event during 1971.

Switching to BSA Power

During the early 1970s the engine to have for most British sidecar short-circuit racing was the BSA unit twin. And so a deal was agreed with the widow of racer Pat Sheridan in a West Bromwich pub car park resulting in a 750cc works BSA motor for the princely sum of £70. As Nigel Clark commented in an issue of *Classic Racer*: 'All the favoured BSA men were curious about the identity of the 'insider' who had sold him the engine, but George always remained tight lipped.'

Making the History Books

George O'Dell's name went into history books in 1972 when he took the last-ever race victory at the South London Crystal Palace circuit, with the BSA outfit. Also that year had seen the oil giant BP assisting the team.

Then in 1973, with the BSA fast coming to the end of its competitive life, O'Dell transferred to an 8-valve 700cc Westlake. However, this suffered such serious vibration that it triggered frame breakages within a couple of meetings!

Going Two-stroke

So reluctantly, he purchased a two-stroke 500cc German König water-cooled flat-four engine from Jeff Gawley who was retiring. Although it cost £500 it was money well spent as immediately the König garnered some excellent results. This included finishing runner-up to the German pairing of Heinz Lüthringhauser and Hermann Hahn (BMW) in the 500cc Isle of Man TT.

The liquid-cooled German König two-stroke with which George O'Dell and passenger Bill Boldison finished runner-up in the 1974 Isle of Man TT.

As one of George O'Dell's three targets in sidecar racing was getting on a TT rostrum, this left two more ambitions as yet unfilled: a TT victory and then to win the world title.

A Bigger König

The prize money won at the TT helped O'Dell most of the way to purchasing a 680cc König, which would allow him to take part in the big sidecar class at British meetings. In addition the 12 points scored at the TT would allow him to gain access into the following year's World Championship series, as it also meant 12th place in the final World Championship table.

Next Bill Boldison decided to quit racing due to family commitments and Alan Gosling made a return as passenger, with a new Renwick-built hub centre steering 'wedge' outfit. George O'Dell was sad to see Bill go and their parting was an amicable one.

Hard Work

George and Alan had high hopes for the 1975 season. However, they soon realised that GP racing was hard work. Instant disappointment came when at the first round in France they could finish no higher than a lowly 16th. The next round was at the Salzburgring and here George and Alan finished sixth, just behind the Boret brothers on another König. But the next two rounds – West Germany (at Hockenheim) and the Isle of Man the pairing just could not get going or were to suffer mechanical problems. In fact George O'Dell came very near to quitting. And if it had not been for commentator Chris Carter he probably would have done just that. But after being told by Chris that perhaps he had not the staying power for long races, this fired up George and the team took in the next round of the Championship; the Dutch TT at Assen.

The 1975 Dutch TT

The 1975 Dutch TT was a turning point in George O'Dell's international racing career, with a fourth place behind the likes of Werner Schwärzel (the winner) and Rolf Biland. This was not only because of the result but by the arrival of Eric May, a Windsor, Berkshire, businessman with a welding company, who was destined to become his entrant-cum-sponsor from then on.

This is how George explained what happened later: 'The day before the Dutch TT the König had seized and I had repaired it by working through the night. Eric had come on a Tee-Mill trip and, because I had done some work for him back home, he looked out for me. It turned out he spent the night, keeping me awake with a non-stop supply of coffee.'

And so the May-O'Dell link was forged; the following day Eric offered to buy George a new Yamaha engine, which was something he had 'longed for.' A TZ700 Yamaha engine was obtained and the Swiss importer and Eric footed the £1,600 bill.

A 100mph Silverstone Lap

Second time out on the Yamaha and George O'Dell not only became the first sidecar driver to complete a 100mph (161km/h) lap at Silverstone, but also won the race. George told reporters: 'I made a good start, then had a bit of a dust-up with Werner Schwärzel but his König couldn't stand the pace.'

Then the *Motor Cycle* Sidecar Championship, a Lydden Hill race record which was to remain unbeaten for several years and the first 90mph (145km/h) Brands Hatch GP sidecar circuit lap rounded off a more than reasonable year. But it was the help of Eric May which had made all of it possible.

The 1976 Season

The Renwick was not out for the 1976 season. Instead a new outfit with a frame designed by Terry Windle was the one on which George O'Dell would fight for honours that year. But as he explained after winning the world title in 1977: 'To be honest, I made a mess of selling my Renwick. A Dutch guy offered me a lot of money for it and, as I needed cash to buy two motors for the coming season, I took it. I thought I would be able to build my own hub-centre steering outfit in the time available but I just never got around to finishing it. So I had to buy a Windle chassis to keep going racing.'

Crankshaft Problems

For almost three months of the new 1976 season, George was plagued with crankshafts breaking or else bearings would 'run'. In fact, until just after the TT he managed to only finish one race. When it came to the Mallory Park Post TT meeting and yet another breakdown he decided on a new course of action. As well as obtaining his Yamaha bearings from a different supplier, he switched to a thicker grade of oil.

The next outing was the Dutch TT at Assen which was staged in front of 150,000 spectators. It was also a record for high temperatures at the event. As George recalled later: 'I felt I could cope at the start. But I had forgotten about protection for my hands. The fantastic heat from the exhaust pipes, which were only a foot away, built up in the fairing and I had blisters on my hands the size of 50 pence pieces. I had no option but to retire.'

George O'Dell with the ex-Rolf Biland Seymaz after purchase in early 1977.

A New Passenger

For the Dutch, there was yet another fresh young man in the chair, Kenny Arthur. This was because Alan Gosling had been injured after clipping a wall in the Isle of Man TT earlier that month.

The new pairing then went on to score points in the remaining three rounds of the World Series; sixth in Belgium, fifth in Czechoslovakia and third at the final round in West Germany. This gave O'Dell 21 points and eighth place in the title rankings.

Switching to Shell

Shell offered George a better deal than BP for the 1977 season and yellow livery replaced the former green. Rolf Biland, who had finished fourth in 1976 on the superbly crafted Seymaz outfit ran into financial problems and was forced to sell it (less engine) for £5,000. Seeing his chance, George O'Dell re-mortgaged the house and with further assistance from Eric May acquired the ex Biland Seymaz.

On paper the Seymaz should have been superior to the Windle. With its aluminium construction, it was 55lb (25kg) lighter for a start. However, it would not prove a good buy for George. First time out at Cadwell Park, passenger Kenny Arthur fell out of the 'chair' on the Mountain section and the Seymaz somersaulted no less than three times, almost destroying itself. Eric May had it flown back to Switzerland to be repaired. And the old Windle was wheeled out for the first GP of the season, at the Salzburgring in Austria.

More Problems

But more problems were to rear their ugly heads. On the drive across Europe, a Calor gas bottle exploded in the back of the van, blowing open the doors and scattering clothing and components all over the motorway. Then four studs sheared off the van's double rear wheel hub allowing the tyre to rub on the bodywork and eventually puncture. Thereafter, the overworked second tyre kept overheating, forcing the team to make lengthy stops to allow it to cool.

Nearly a Win

Despite the exhausting journey, George and Kenny assumed an immediate lead at the Salzburgring. In fact, they led for 17 laps on the Windle, before Biland (with a Yamaha-powered Schmid) moved in front to take the victory; even so the British team had 12 points. A good start.

Next, at Hockenheim they gained 10 points for third, behind Biland and Max Venus (König). But to get anywhere near Biland the return of the Seymaz was vital.

Repair Work

George O'Dell's total commitment to his 1977 Championship campaign is vividly illustrated by the fact that he and mechanic Ken Upton worked solidly for seven days and seven nights with a mere five hours' sleep, such was the repair work needed to get the Seymaz back on the track.

However, the human body can only take so much, and the combination of a poor diet and lack of sleep eventually took its toll, with George suffering with severe stomach pains. Even so, somehow, the team made it to Le Castellet in France for round three. Despite being less than fully fit, George and Kenny came home second, behind winner Alain Michel, Biland having retired with a broken gear pedal. The 12 points scored meant that George O'Dell was leading the world Championship for the first time.

The 1977 TT

The 1977 Isle of Man TT was the first without World Championship status, and so the team decided to use the Windle rather than the Seymaz. Even so George and Kenny screamed round to an unofficial first 100mph (161km/h) sidecar lap during practice with a speed of 101.3mph (162.99km/h).

In the race Dick Greasley set the first official 100mph lap at 100.59mph (162.4km/h) but in beating him by 50 seconds, George raised the record to 102.8mph (165.4km/h). And the second ambition had been achieved.

Cliff Holland Arrives

Following the TT, Kenny Arthur left, to be replaced by Cliff Holland.

Rolf Biland had earlier warned George that the Yamaha engine had a tendency to drop into gear while being warmed up. Biland always warmed up on blocks. As the O'Dell squad warmed up the Yamaha for the Dutch TT it did just as Biland had forecast – and at 7,000rpm. The sudden catapult forward twisted the suspension leg of the Seymaz and the subsequent hasty repair failed during the race. With Rolf Biland and Alain Michel finishing first and second, these two both overtook George in the points table.

Spa Francorchamps

With the Belgian GP at Spa Francorchamps taking place the following weekend and with the handling issues of the Seymaz, the team decided it was back to the Windle. After making a poor start, George worked his way up the field to finish third behind the winner Werner Schwärzel and the runner-up Rolf Steinhausen. It was Biland and Michel who were both to suffer retirements in this outing. And so with an additional 10 points gained O'Dell climbed up to second in the title race.

Brno

Next came the 6.8-mile (10.9km) public road course in Czechoslovakia, this being the penultimate round in the 1977 Championship trail. During practice Bruno Holzer spun his Yamaha-LCR outfit, hit the Armco barrier and headed against the flow of traffic. George was first around the blind corner and the resulting collision once again put the jinxed Seymaz out of action. The battered O'Dell team could only make ninth fastest and a fourth row starting position. But for once luck was on the British pairing and they were elevated from seventh to third place as one after another of their rivals were forced to retire. Biland had stopped to tighten a battery connection but fought back from 10th to fourth. Following this, the O'Dell team still led the Championship table by a single point, with just the final round at Silverstone to go.

Customs

O'Dell and Holland had been given air tickets by Eric May to fly home from Prague, to provide them with an additional day's rest before what was to be the most important race of their lives. But because they wanted to bring a quantity of vital chassis components for the broken Seymaz for instant repairs they had to endure a maze of Czech customs formalities. The shapes of certain parts were even drawn on their visas by helpful race officials at Brno to facilitate passage through customs.

Silverstone

The O'Dell squad was still one of the last to arrive for practice at Silverstone, after working continuously for two days on the Seymaz in a last desperate attempt to sort out the handling gremlins. But in the end the decision was made to use the slower Windle. George commenting: 'I had rushed the work so much. To rely on the outfit to win the World Championship after all the damage done to it would have been silly.'

Meanwhile, Cliff Holland had worked on the Windle outfit, paying particular attention to the exhausts. Yamaha silencers being fitted which it was hoped would provide increased power.

Fitting a larger front wheel and special forks, O'Dell made third fastest in practice in 1 min 43.02s as Biland went round fastest at 1 min 39.9s. Then came disaster during the final practice lap. George had revved the Yamaha up to

George pictured after winning the 1977 world title, with a collection of his trophies, including a TT silver replica.

11,000rpm and cut the motor for a 'plug chop'. But the engine locked solid with a broken big-end which took with it the crankshaft, barrels and cylinder head.

The team then worked flat out until 5 o'clock in the morning of race day to build the replacement engine but woke up a couple of hours later – it was raining – and they had no wet tyres to fit the larger front wheel!

Twenty minutes before the start of the race the entire front end was replaced with the smaller original.

Then their luck changed. Rolf Biland could not remove his slick-clad wheels having employed an extra strong locking compound on the wheel studs.

The Race

The race was staged in truly appalling conditions. Werner Schwärzel cleared off, never to be headed. Rolf Steinhausen finished runner-up, while George drove a steady consistent race to come home third. Alain Michel lost a visor which ended his slim hopes of glory.

Slipping and sliding on slicks, Biland eventually finished ninth – good enough to have clinched the title if O'Dell had failed to score. But as it was, the Englishman lapped his big rival and took the 1977 world crown by eight points. He did not win a Grand Prix during that season, but the ecstatic home crowd did not care. The world champion was British.

Celebrity Status

George was to finish second to Barry Sheene in the *Motor Cycle News* 'Man of the Year' contest. Then he went on an all-expenses-paid trip to the States, taking in Leguna Seca to promote sidecar racing. Unfortunately, this proved something he probably wished he had not undertaken as he crashed the Windle outfit when the rear brake locked. In this incident he broke his thigh and damaged arteries, and a pin 17 inches (430mm) long was inserted into the bone.

George campaigned in 1978 with this Yamaha-engined outfit that had a Windle chassis.

Anti-climax

The following season, 1978, proved an anti-climax as not only was Biland in unbeatable form, but George was forced to sit out the final two rounds after breaking his leg again at the TT.

George O'Dell pictured by Jan Barszczynski at Cadwell Park during 1980.

The team finished the season on 23 points and eighth in the rankings.

The following season saw one final attack on the world series, but O'Dell was eighth again, a third at Silverstone being the best result.

At the beginning of 1981 George was advised to quit the sport on medical grounds, having lost the feeling and partial paralysis in his arms, a neurological legacy of damaged discs from too many crashes.

The Final Twist

Then came the final chapter of the George O'Dell saga in March of 1981. A domestic argument with his second wife of six months got out of hand.

George followed her to the Hemel Hempstead home of her foster parents armed with a shotgun. His wife was shot in the leg and her father in the back.

In the ensuing siege which was to last over six hours, George soaked the house and himself in paint thinners.

Police negotiators succeeded in getting the injured parties away from the house and to hospital, but George died in the fire which engulfed the house shortly afterwards. A truly sad end for a man who had given so much to the sport he loved.

George with Kenny Williams in the chair during the British Grand Prix at Silverstone in August 1980; the pair came home third.

CHAPTER 19

ROLF BILAND

Born on 1 April 1951, in Baden, Switzerland, Rolf Biland not only radically changed the development of sidecar racing, but he also became the most successful three-wheel racer of all time, with no less than 81 Grand Prix victories between his first in the German round at Hockenheim in 1975, and his last at the Catalan GP in Spain during 1996, some 21 years later.

No Easy Route

Certainly Rolf Biland was very much a self-made man. And although his father was a successful car dealer, Rolf received no financial help from that direction. His father being of the opinion that his son should make his own way in life – as a car mechanic – once his apprenticeship had ended.

So how did Rolf get into sidecar racing? Well, as an enthusiastic teenager he had become passenger to Fritz Hänzi. And during a practice day at Switzerland's only circuit, at Lignieres, Rolf had asked Fritz if he could pilot the 500cc Linto outfit himself.

As Fritz was not keen on being a passenger, one of Rolf's young friends volunteered. At first everyone thought Rolf would soon find driving was more difficult than passengering. However, after a dozen or so laps, these same onlookers were amazed when Rolf and his passenger were only a second slower than the lap record!

The Switch

After the end of the practice session, Rolf exited the Linto, and it was immediately evident to everyone that he would never again be content to act as passenger. Quite simply, Rolf Biland had that day made the switch which was to kick-start his drive to stardom in the sidecar racing world. But even he could never have dreamed of just how successful in both racing and development work he was to become in later years.

The Outfit

During the closed season of 1971–72 Rolf constructed a conventional tubular-framed sidecar outfit featuring 10-inch wheels and hydraulic suspension. To provide the motive power he purchased a 492cc Suzuki

T500-based twin-cylinder two-stroke engine, an assembly then widely used by several Swiss competitors at that time.

During the 1972 racing season the by now 21-year-old Rolf simply cleaned up in local races and hill-climbs. By season's end, the name Biland was becoming the byword for success, with not only a string of hill-climb victories, but runner-up spot in the Swiss Junior Championship series.

Continuing with the same Suzuki outfit the following year, Rolf went one better and was the 1973 Swiss national Champion.

Going International
Without financial support from his father, Rolf's finances were limited to say the least, so intending to make the switch to international events during 1974, he worked the previous winter months for the well-known sidecar racer Rudi Kurth. His job included not only testing the Swedish Crescent two-stroke engines used by Rudi, but also working on moulds for his employer's CATVAN race transporter. In return Rolf was provided with a specially constructed CAT frame and into this fitted a 3-cylinder Crescent engine.

Joining The Grand Prix Circus
And so Rolf Biland joined the Grand Prix circus, together with passenger Fredy Freiburghaus and, at the third round of the 1974 World Championship series secured his first top 10 finish at this level, with an eighth at the Austrian round at the Salzburgring.

That year the series was staged over eight rounds. And at the fourth, the Italian Grand Prix at Imola, he shook the sidecar racing world by finishing runner-up to the multi-world champion Klaus Enders (BMW). This really was an incredible result as behind the young Swiss driver were many established stars including Rolf Steinhausen, Siegfried Schauzu and Heinz Lüthringhauser.

Mechanical Gremlins
But after the Italian Grand Prix, the Crescent engine 'went on strike' (*Motorcycle Racing*) with the result that Rolf was unable to finish in any of the remaining GPs that year. Even so, the seeds of success had been sown and for the first time people had begun to take notice of the newcomer. And as for Rolf himself, fired with a new passion and determination he was already planning to construct an entirely new outfit for 1975.

Eric Vuagnat
Rolf spent the winter of 1974–75 in Geneva with Eric Vuagnat, then a well-known Formula 1 car constructor. Slowly details of an entirely new sidecar

racing machine began to leak out. The all-enveloping red-and-white bodywork was very similar to the latest Formula 1 car practice, while the suspension used hub centre steering at the front and the entire machine was ultra-low.

The Television Interview

Before anyone could officially see his new device, Rolf contacted Swiss television and as *Motorcycle Racing* magazine were later to report: 'Practically demanded that they interview him.' During the subsequent 10-minute programme, Rolf calmly stated that he was going to win the world title.

This was to cause great controversy among the large number of Swiss sidecar racing fans. Typical of the comments at the time were remarks such as: 'You can't say things like that on TV.' But Rolf's reply to this was simple and in two words: 'I can.'

A First GP Victory

For 1975 the new outfit was called the Yam-Seymaz. In more detail the power unit was one of the four-cylinder Yamaha two-strokes which were just coming into Grand Prix racing in the 500cc solo class, while the chassis was a Seymaz, the latter the work of Eric Vuagnat and was of aluminium construction to save weight.

It was at the third round, at Hockenheim, the scene of the German GP, that Rolf and passenger Fredy Freiburghaus scored their first Grand Prix victory (at an average speed of 96.99mph – 156.086km/h). Werner Schwärzel was second, Rolf Steinhausen third and Siegfried Schauzu fourth.

The Mettet Crash

The German GP win was followed by a bad crash at the non-Championship meeting at Mettet, Belgium. This was not caused by an error, but a broken suspension arm. In the accident passenger Fredy Freiburghaus suffered a broken leg, but as for Rolf himself he escaped injury. But the same could not be said of the outfit. For starters the fairing was shattered into no fewer than 35 separate pieces. However, these were painstakingly collected together, and returned home to Switzerland where Dane Rowe (Rudi Kurth's English passenger) fibreglassed the red jigsaw back into one piece; a remarkable achievement.

The other component needing major work was the frame. However, Rolf took this to Geneva and got it successfully straightened.

A Dutch Return

The fourth round of the Championship series was in the Isle of Man and the crash had ruled this out, so a return was not made until the end of June at the Dutch TT. And at Assen Rolf, with new passenger Bernd Grube, immediately proved that he had lost none of his skill, or for that matter nerve, by coming home in second spot behind Werner Schwärzel and passenger Josef Huber.

But this result hid an interesting fact and one which displayed not only the sheer determination of the man, but also his ruthless nature when it came to racing. His original passenger for the race was Freddy Stuaffer. However, during a practice run, the latter missed a hand-hold, fell from the sidecar and landed unconscious in a drainage ditch three feet deep with water.

Rolf stopped, looked behind, saw that his passenger was no longer in the sidecar and rode back to the start-line to pick up another passenger (Bernd Grube) who was waiting for a trial run! Maybe, at the time, Rolf did not realise exactly what had happened, but even so many others would at least have investigated further; Rolf Biland seemed more interested in himself than his unfortunate passenger that day…

Obviously, everyone has two sides and in Rolf's case off the track, at home or in his workshop, he was a much more humane person. But as his record proves, on the track he was entirely determined, selfish almost, for success; focused only in the desire to succeed at his given profession.

After Assen, Rolf was not to score any further points in the 1975 Championship series. Even so, he was still to finish third in the points table, behind the winner Steinhausen and runner-up Schwärzel (both with König powered outfits).

The 1976 Season

For the 1976 season Rolf had Englishman Kenny Williams in the chair. And the new pairing made a brilliant start to their GP campaign by winning at Le Mans in France. But using the same Yamaha-powered Seymaz outfit as Biland had raced the previous season they were dogged with a host of non-finishes after the French result. In fact, they did not record a finish until the final two races, at Brno in Czechoslovakia (third) and Germany at the Nürburgring (fourth).

Financial Problems

The run of non-finishes and expensive repair bills was by now taking its toll on Rolf Biland's finances. And after the season had ended, in October 1976, matters came to a head. The Yamaha engines and spares consumed during the season had not yet been paid for, and to make matters worse, the tax-man was sending Rolf threatening letters. The result was that to pay his debts he was forced to sell the Seymaz chassis (without engine) to fellow competitor George O'Dell. This raised some £5,000 (the cost of a small house at that time!).

Hermann Schmid

So what was Rolf Biland to do for the forthcoming 1977 Grand Prix racing season?

With very little money available – and with no machine – Rolf effectively went into partnership to form a team with fellow Swiss driver/constructor Hermann Schmid and the then largely unknown Trachsel.

The Yamaha-powered Schmid outfit was more of a conventional outfit, and quite unlike the quite revolutionary Seymaz. Even so, Rolf soon showed his skill, when he comfortably won the opening round (still with Kenny Williams in the chair) in Austria, at the Salzburgring), with Englishman George O'Dell second and Frenchman Alain Michel third. And he followed this up with another victory in the second round, the German GP at Hockenheim. Round three in France saw Biland retire after suffering a broken gear change pedal (caused through incorrect suspension settings made after practice). Then in round four at Assen Rolf stormed back to take another victory. But then, seemingly with the Championship title in the bag,

Rolf Biland and English passenger Kenny Williams on the way to victory in the 1977 Dutch TT at Assen. The outfit is a Yamaha-engined Schmid.

the Biland steamroller came off the tracks. In Belgium Rolf's red-and-white outfit ended up stationary just before the high-speed Masta Straight. Then, with one round to go Biland and Williams came home fourth in the Czech GP at Brno, with their main title challenger George O'Dell with Cliff Holland one place in front, third.

The 1977 Championship was thus to be finally decided at the British round at Silverstone (the Isle of Man having lost its right to a World Championship venue at the end of the previous year).

Wheels And Tyres Lose The Title
In the end it all came down to the weather and the fact that Rolf was forced to slither around Silverstone on slick tyres in what turned out to be a very wet race. The result of this was O'Dell came home third and was crowned champion, even though he had never won a race, while Biland was down in eighth and thus finished the season runner-up. This was the case, even though the Swiss star had won three of the seven races!

World Champion At Last
Strangely, the following season, 1978, Rolf and passenger Kenny Williams won the title; even though they only managed to win three races in a Championship which had been extended to eight rounds – Austria, France, Italy, Holland, Belgium, Great Britain, Germany and Czechoslovakia (in that order).

Changing Machinery
At the first round, at the Salzburgring, Rolf and Kenny used a Yamaha-engined TTM outfit. The pair won from Mac Hobson/Kenny Birch (Yam-Seymaz) and Alain Michel/Stu Collins (also Yam-Seymaz mounted). At the next round at the French Nogaro circuit the pair repeated the victory, but this time Michel/Collins were runners-up, with Hobson/Birch third.

Sadly, Mac Hobson was to lose his life in the Isle of Man, whereas at the third round at Mugello, Italy, Rolf and Kenny emerged victorious yet again. The wins in France and Italy had both been secured driving the ground-breaking car-like BEO outfit (again Yamaha powered).

Then came the protests, other competitors claiming the BEO device was outside the rules. And Rolf thus used the TTM chassis for some races. Although, at the sixth round (Silverstone) he finished runner-up (to Alain Michel). With a third place in Belgium and a second at the final round in Czechoslovakia, at last Rolf Biland had proved his earlier prediction of becoming world champion to be true.

Bruno Holzer

Bruno Holzer's claim to fame was that he and passenger Charly Meierhans were Sidecar World Champions in the one-year-only B–2–B series staged over six rounds in 1979.

Bruno had been born at Neukirch, Switzerland on 9 February 1947 and began sidecar racing with a Honda outfit in 1973. Next, in 1975, Bruno became Swiss champion. The following year, 1976, saw Bruno Holzer (LCR-Yamaha) and passenger Charly Meierhans enter the world stage, beginning with a fourth place in the opening GP, the French at Le Mans; behind Rolf Biland, Alain Michel and Hans Schilling.

The only other top-10 GP finish that year came at the seventh and final round, at the Nürburgring in Germany, with a fifth, behind Werner Schwärzel, Rolf Steinhausen, George O'Dell and Rolf Biland.

Into 1977 and Holzer/Meierhans, still with the LCR-Yamaha, scored a seventh at the opening round in Austria. Next came the German GP at the ultra-fast Hockenheim circuit where the Swiss pairing came home fourth. At the Dutch TT they were fifth.

But it was really the following year, 1978, when Bruno and Charly really began to show their potential, with a series of excellent results which saw them finish the season third in the Championship points table.

In the eight-round series, they scored points in six of the eight rounds:

Austrian GP (Salzburgring) fifth
French GP (Nogaro) fifth
Italian GP (Mugello) fifth
Dutch TT (Assen) fourth
Belgian GP (Spa Francorchamps) first
German GP (Nürburgring) fourth

Bruno Holzer, the 1979 B-2-B Series sidecar world champion, with his LCR outfit at Le Mans that year.

> Then came 1979, the year of the two Championships, B–2–A and B–2–B. Bruno Holzer and Charly Meierhans elected to contest the latter series, which was staged over six rounds – Austria, Swiss (750cc), Britain, Germany, France and Holland (750cc).
>
> As with George O'Dell in 1977, the Swiss pairing did not win a single race; however they did finish runners-up in all six events. And even though Rolf Biland had won four races and Alain Michel the other two, Bruno Holzer and passenger Charly Meierhans were declared the victors, as they had assembled the most points.
>
> After this, it was very much a rapidly declining situation, with their best places in 1980 a couple of thirds (Finland and Czechoslovakia). Other top 10 results that year being: fifth Germany, sixth France and eighth Holland.
>
> By 1981 they had left the GP scene.

1979 – The Year Of Two Championships

For the 1979 season the FIM sanctioned two separate sidecar World Championships – B–2–A for conventional outfits, B–2–B for outfits like the BEO design. Actually, except for engine sizes the two categories are very similar to the Formula 1 (worm-type) and Formula 2 (conventional) outfits of today.

Most of the usual GP crowd chose the B–2–A series, including Schauzu, Steinhausen, Schwärzel, O'Dell, Jock Taylor and Dick Greesley among others. While the new technology outfits included Alain Michel, Bruno Holzer and Rolf Biland. In fact, Biland competed in both categories (which were separate races that year), winning the B–2–A title and finishing runner-up (to fellow Swiss, Bruno Holzer) in the B–2–B category. In the 'A' class Rolf (now passengered by Kurt Waltisperg) won three GPs (in Holland,

Rolf Biland with the revolutionary car-like BEO device during the 1978 Isle of Man Sidecar TT, in which the Swiss driver set a new lap record.

This 1978 view of Biland and Waltisperg shows their machine to be definitely more car-like than bike-like. Photo W. Gruber/Archiv

Great Britain and Czechoslovakia). While in the 'B' series he won four rounds (Austria, Switzerland – but actually held at Le Castellet, France – Germany and France). Actually, as with George O'Dell the previous season, Bruno Holzer (with passenger Charly Meierhans) did not win a single GP, instead Holzer came home runner-up in each of the six rounds.

1980 – A One Series Championship Again

For the 1980 season the FIM reverted to a single sidecar series. And although Rolf and Kurt Waltisperg won the first two rounds (in France and Yugoslavia), the Scot Jock Taylor and his passenger, the Swede Benga Johansson, emerged as Champions with four victories, against the Swiss pair's three (the other being in Czechoslovakia).

Biland and Williams in vivid kerb-lifting action circa 1980. Photo W. Gruber/Archiv

This all-action shot of Biland and Waltisperg was taken by sidecar racing enthusiast Jan Barszczynski at the 1981 British Grand Prix.

A Third Title

Then in 1981, Rolf Biland won his third world title (and Kurt Waltisperg his second). In an extended Championship series (there were no less than 10 rounds), the pair dominated proceedings with seven wins, in fact in the final five meetings Biland and Waltisperg cleaned up with five victories. Their main rivals that year were Taylor/Johansson (who won the first round) and Alain Michel/Michael Burkard (who won the remaining two events).

The 1982 Season

In 1982 there were nine rounds and amazingly although Biland and Waltisperg won six of these, it was Werner Schwärzel and his passenger Andreas Huber who won the title – even though, like George O'Dell in 1977 – Schwärzel did not win a race!

Rolf and Kurt took their wins in Austria, Holland, Belgium, Sweden, Finland (where only 75% of the race was completed due to a fatal accident suffered by the 1980 world champion, Jock Taylor) and Germany.

1983 – Champions Again

For the 1983 season the Championship series was reduced to eight rounds (Imatra having been axed from the calendar). Rolf and Kurt winning six of these, in France, Austria, Holland, Belgium, Sweden and San Marino.

But following this success was to come a long period where Rolf Biland and Kurt Waltisperg, although scoring several Grand Prix victories, did not actually become champions again until 1992.

I have listed below the years and victories of the 1984 – 1991 period:

1984 French GP, Dutch TT, Swedish GP
1985 Austrian GP, Dutch TT
1986 None
1987 Austrian GP, French GP, Swedish GP, Czech GP
1988 Portuguese GP, German GP, Austrian GP, Dutch TT, Belgian GP, French GP
1989 Austrian GP, French GP, Swedish GP
1990 Italian GP
1991 French GP, British GP, Czech GP, Le Mans GP

A Trio Of Championship Titles

Then came what can only be described as an amazing trio of World Championship titles in 1992, 1993 and, finally, in 1994 – the last of a ground-breaking career.

The 1992 title was gained with victories at Assen (Dutch TT), Hungaroring (Hungarian GP), Magny-Cours (French GP) and Donington (British GP).

The following year, 1993, the Swiss team took six victories: Hockenheim (German GP), Assen (Dutch TT), Brno (Czech Republic GP) 18 July, Donington (British GP), Brno (Czech Republic GP) 22 August, Jarama (FIM GP).

The 1994 title was achieved with five wins: Hockenheim (German GP), Assen (Dutch TT) 25 June, Donington (British GP), Brno (Czech Republic GP), Assen (Dutch TT) 11 September.

The Run-down

After the trio of titles in 1992, 1993 and 1994, Rolf and Kurt continued for a further two seasons, 1995 and 1996. In the former they won four races – at Les Mans (French GP), Donington (British GP), Brno (Czech Republic GP) and Catalunya (European GP).

Then in 1996, in what was to be their final season, Rolf and Kurt had two victories – Brno (Czech Republic GP) and Catalunya (Catalan GP).

The Machinery

For someone who effectively changed the whole evolution of sidecar racing itself, the machinery is a vital part of the Rolf Biland story. His first two victories (1975 German GP and 1976 French GP) were won using Yamaha-powered Seymaz.

Biland's LCR as it was during 1983 and 1984.

Rolf Biland/Kurt Waltisperg (Yamaha-LCR), the 1981 world champions; pictured winning the British Grand Prix at Silverstone that year.

Then, after selling the Seymaz chassis to rival George O'Dell for financial reasons, Rolf used a more conventional Schmid-Yamaha for the 1977 season. Into 1978 he campaigned a TTM-Yamaha and the controversial BEO-Yamaha.

In the 1979 season there were two distinct classes, in the B2A series he raced a Schmid-Yamaha, while the B2B category saw him aboard an LCR-Yamaha – LCR standing for Louis Christian Racing.

And Rolf was to race the LCR-Yamaha from then until the end of the 1984 season. But after this although the chassis remained an LCR, the power unit was now a German Krauser unit; the man behind the new engine being Mike Krauser, who had first risen to fame in the motorcycle world as a luggage manufacturer!

This view (again from Silverstone 1981) shows just how radical Biland's Yamaha-LCR was – more Formula 1 car technology than motorcycle.

Then, for the 1991 season only, a switch was made to an ADM engine, before for 1992 a return to the Krauser. For 1994 Biland used a Swissauto, before, finally in 1995 and 1996 a BRM. But right from the B2B series of 1979, the chassis was always an LCR.

And the LCR was to become the choice of other champions, including Steve Webster, Alain Michel and Egbert Streuer.

The Man

So what of the man, the real Rolf Biland? As one journalist was to remark: 'His career has been influenced by many things, not least his determination which sometimes borders on ruthlessness. He is selfish about his racing, without being big-headed, and he can be very, very hard.' That meant that he was not racing for his homeland Switzerland, not for a manufacturer or sponsor, not for his fans, but for himself.

Certainly, he was never to be a 'fan's favourite', as for example Jock Taylor or, in earlier days, Florian Camathias.

But what you did get from Rolf Biland was a win at all costs regime, in which the hunger to succeed was the priority. And this shows in his record of 81 Grand Prix victories, unsurpassed by any other sidecar racer.

This photograph shows Rolf Biland at the 1985 British Grand Prix at Silverstone, when the Swiss multi-champion decided not to race because of the 'dangerous' spray caused by torrential rain on race day.

Loyalty

Strangely, considering the episode already described during practice for the 1975 Dutch TT and the unconscious passenger, Rolf showed that, actually, he could also be very loyal, having the same passenger, Kurt Waltisperg, from 1979 until his final race in 1996, a period of some 18 years. The same could be said of Rolf's association with Louis Christian and the use of LCR chassis – again this spanning the period 1979–96.

CHAPTER 20

JOCK TAYLOR

John Robert (but universally known as Jock) Taylor was born in the Vert hospital, Haddington a few miles south-east of the Scottish capital, Edinburgh, on 9 March 1954.

His parents, Jackie and Peggy could never have imagined that their son would rise to become not only the 1980 World Sidecar Champion, but also one of the very best-loved motorcycle competitors of all time.

The BSA Outfit

Jock's racing career began in 1974 at the age of 20, when he purchased a Windrick (built by Terry Windle and John Crick) BSA outfit, less engine. This was ex-Mac Hobson and Jock teamed up with Kenny Andrews who supplied a Triumph 650 engine and gearbox. Kenny drove and Jock passengered for the full season.

Next, during the winter of 1974–75, his friend Lewis Ward (born 18 June 1955) told Jock that he would not only purchase a BSA engine, but also passenger for him. As Lewis related to the author recently: 'We went down on a train from Edinburgh to London, my brother picked us up and drove us to Newmarket, in Suffolk, to test a sidecar owned by Alex Harper which had an A70 specification engine fitted.' Lewis continued: 'We tested the bike around a local housing estate, paid £230, removed the engine and exhaust system, put them in a box and drove back to London; then loaded the box into the guards-carriage and headed back to Edinburgh.'

The First Race

The first race with the BSA engine came at Silloth, Cumbria, where in their heat Jock and Lewis finished second to Colin Jacobs. In the final they were fourth or fifth after a good start.

As Lewis says: 'Jock quickly perfected the style of high-speed, full sideway sliding. We also bought a blown up Devimead seven-fifty engine and Jock also had an A65 road bike, so we ended up with a long-stroke A75-based engine with good torque and an A65 short-stroke which we kept as a spare engine and used a couple of times that year.' The pair spent the 1975 season trying to beat their main rivals Alastair Lewis and Jimmy Law. As Lewis recalls: 'Jock studied Alastair's driving technique and tactics to

Jock Taylor and Lewis Ward at Knockhill in 1975 with the BSA 750 outfit.

great effect, while I attempted to copy Jimmy's great technique and timing which I never quite managed. Looking back, Jimmy was probably the best passenger I have ever seen.' Jimmy Law later passengered for Jock in a couple of GPs.

At the last meeting of the 1975 season at East Fortune the BSA engine blew up in a big way and the outfit was sold with the damaged engine and enough parts to rebuild it.

Moving Into 1976

During the winter of 1975–76, the duo dispensed with the ex-Mac Hobson outfit. Jock and Lewis purchased a second-hand Hartwell Imp engine and Norton gearbox for £800, and then ordered a new chassis from John Crick. It was also around the same time that Jock suffered a road accident on a 250 Suzuki, breaking his right leg above the knee in three places, and was laid up in hospital in traction for several weeks (see photograph). Behind his hospital bed was a large window with secondary glazing which was crammed with cans of beer; Jock's bedside table was full of spirits and glasses, so when people came to visit they could all have a drink. On New Year's Eve Jock and the rest of the patients had a party, Jock got so drunk he fell out of bed and was left hanging by traction!

Winter 1975 – Jock's stay in hospital, described in the main text. From left to right: Ian 'Mose' Hutchison, Tom Dickie, two nurses, Jock, Lewis, Jock's mother Peggy, Jock's girlfriend Alison, Ian Dickie.

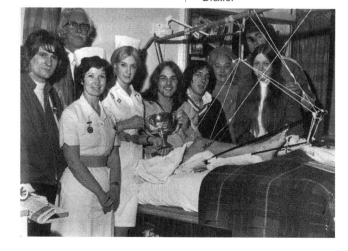

The Hospital Presentation

During this period Lewis and Jock were presented with awards won during the past season from the Melville Club (East Fortune). These were officially handed over at a presentation in the hospital; but Jock's doctor told him that he would not be able to race during the 1976 season. However, Lewis, together with their mechanic Charlie Swanson, rebuilt the Imp outfit anyway.

After Jock's release from hospital – and when he was fit enough to kneel his injured leg, as Lewis says: 'We tried to fit him into the bike but to do this we had to pivot the kneeling tray some 45 degrees. During the first part of the season we slowly moved the kneeling tray back until his leg was straight.'

During 1976, Jock and Lewis 'kept trying to improve'. And at the end of the season they entered a national meeting at Croft, where all the top British sidecar teams were taking part. Lewis commenting: 'During the race we had a puncture and pulled up at the chicane and watched the rest of the race from there, we were amazed at the speeds the top boys were doing on their TZ750 Yamahas; it looked a different world – little did we know that the following year we would be doing the same.'

The Next Step

At the end off 1976 the Imp outfit was sold to north-east racer Dave Mallon of Morpeth, and Jock and Lewis went in search of a two-stroke for the 1977 season. They travelled down to the Racing Show in London and had a good look at the flat-four Kholer engine (like a König). As Lewis Ward says: 'We were seriously thinking about it when an Ireson TZ700 came up for sale in Chippenham, owned by Spike Hughes and raced by Dave Lawrence, so we drove down to look at the bike. We tested it around the local industrial estate, liked the machine so we both took out loans and bought it for £2,700; my parents bought the spares, which included two 350 top-ends for £300.'

Advice From Jock Findlay

Scottish solo champion Jock Findlay offered to show the pair how to strip and rebuild the TZ engine, so they accepted this kind offer and took their assembly to his Bonyrigg workshop.

As Lewis told the author: 'We didn't like the sidecar wheel arch, so we made our own one, copied from the Biland-Seymaz. With the outfit fully rebuilt and resprayed Robbie Allen offered us a free stand at the Scottish Motorcycle Show in Glasgow. Jock took the outfit to the show on a trailer, but travelling along the M8 motorway from Edinburgh to Glasgow he got into a large skid which took up all the lanes of the motorway. Luckily, he managed to regain control, so we nearly lost the machine before we started.'

Their first race meeting of 1977 came at a national (at Croft), which was used as a 'shakedown' (Lewis's words). Everything went well and they won their races. Next came the Easter Transatlantic races. One of their sponsors, Spike Hughes, was a friend of race commentator Fred Clark – and this helped get entries for Brands Hatch and Oulton Park.

Brands Hatch

And so came Jock and Lewis's first sight of Brands Hatch. Lewis takes up the story: 'We set off on the Thursday teatime in a newly acquired Ford Transit van our sponsor Jimmy Mitchell had purchased, towing a trailer. At Scotch Corner the engine blew up just at the exit slip road. Jimmy's son Richard arrived around 2am the next morning with a car and we towed the van the wrong way up the slip road and left it in the nearest garage with a note. We then hooked up the trailer, piled everyone plus spares into the car and set off for Brands.'

Although they arrived too late for their official practice, they somehow managed to still get the required three laps in to qualify. As for the race itself, Lewis recalls again: 'The race started and all the outfits flew down the hill towards the Hairpin; they all lined up for the corner leaving a large gap on the inside, so Jock just stuffed it up the inside which took us into third place behind George O'Dell [destined to become world champion that year]. Later, after the meeting they telephoned Spike Hughes as pre-arranged, and when I read the Brands results without a pause he suddenly stopped me and asked me to repeat who was third. He was truly amazed and phoned back later telling us to meet him on Sunday at a "posh country hotel" near Oulton where all seven of us were put up complete with large evening meal free of charge.'

Unfortunately, it was not to be another fairy-tale ending as, while lying third in the race, their fuel pump failed.

Racing At Knockhill

When Jock and Lewis competed at Knockhill the last race 'was a handicap event, run by the Kirkcaldy club; they would always hold us to last on the grid. The first outfit would be coming out of the Hairpin before we were flagged away but we always won, it must have been good for the spectators to watch as we went flat out through the pack.'

The Ulster GP

Travelling to the Ulster Grand Prix for the first time in August 1977: 'We stripped the engine to find out that all the pistons were cracked [too much tuning].' So the 350 top-ends were fitted while four new pistons were located from solo rider, the late Billy Guthrie. These were modified and fitted for race day. After lots of problems (including their van being vandalised!) Jock and Lewis made fourth place. The organisers later promoted the Scottish pair to third position, as they had been held on a red flag after a serious accident by another team during the race.

International Scarborough

The following month, September 1977, and our men were at Oliver's Mount, Scarborough, for the International Gold Cup meeting. This attracted many foreign stars, including Rolf Biland and Werner Schwärzel. Biland suffered engine trouble, Schwärzel won, but Jock and Lewis finished second ahead of George O'Dell. Later, in the invitation event their engine seized.

Next came Cadwell Park (another international meeting). Unfortunately the pair were to suffer a serious accident. The following night they drove straight to Trevor Ireson's workshop in Swindon. There they stripped down the outfit. A week later their mechanic Charlie Swanson went to Trevor's and picked up the repaired frame with new, wider forks, which allowed the use of a wider 10in tyre. Trevor donated a new fairing and Jock, Lewis and Charlie re-built the outfit and raced it at East Fortune the following weekend.

The First International Victory

The final Oulton Park meeting of 1977 saw Jock and Lewis record their first-ever international victory (again beating George O'Dell, who was by now the new world champion). Then came meetings at Mallory Park and finally Brands Hatch. The pair finished the year as Scottish Champions, second in the British Championships and third in the *Motor Cycle* international series.

The Grovewood Awards

Jock and Lewis were nominated for the Grovewood Award (for the most outstanding newcomers) and asked to appear on the *Motor Cycle News* stand at the London Earls Court Show. Journalist Chris Carter organised everything for the boys. The highlight being meeting Mike Hailwood at the awards ceremony. However the pair were to return from the Show still without sponsorship for the 1978 season – as Lewis told the author: 'We desperately wanted to do the World Championship series in 1978.'

Sponsorship

But soon things began to change. First Castrol contacted them to say they were interested in a deal. Next Centurian helmets came forward with another deal. Then Chris Carter attempted to broach a major deal with Rae Hamilton of Ham-Yam Racing. As Lewis recalled recently: 'We drove down to his shop in Chester-Le-Street, Durham for talks. He offered us a new Dieter Busch outfit complete with 500 Yamaha engine. But the proposed deal came with too many clauses, it was like a business deal not a sponsorship, it would have cost us too much, so we scrapped the idea.'

Dennis Trollope

In early 1978 Dennis Trollope heard of the problem – previously he had thought the team was fully sponsored by the names on their fairings in 1977. When Jock told Dennis what little real sponsorship we had 'he came to our rescue' (Lewis Ward).

Lewis again: 'Jock, Charlie and myself drove down to Bristol as arranged and met Dennis and his wife Ann, Dennis then started to hand over the counter all these engine parts, a complete 500 top-end, four 250 exhaust pipes, a spare ignition kit and so many engine internals. It was mind blowing, you name it, we had it, everything any racer could dream of and more. We signed on the dotted line and drove home. Dennis had no hidden clauses; we kept our sponsorship and prize money. He also loaned us an TZ750F exhaust pipe, the one which gave the most brake horsepower. We took this pipe to a company in Glasgow who e-rayed it, this providing us with the crucial dimensions of the last cone joining the silencer.'

Dennis Trollope recalls the start of this relationship: 'Jock and I first became involved when he had the use of a TZ750 motor that had been used

At East Fortune Raceway with the Crick Hartwell Imp outfit, which Jock and Lewis raced during 1976.

SACU (Scottish Auto Cycle Union) dinner/dance 1977. Jock Taylor and Lewis Ward collecting the haul of trophies.

by my solo rider Clive Watts. Clive had decided to retire from riding and Jock became my first sponsored sider racer.' And later remembered Jock in the following manner: 'Jock was a lovely person. We all seemed to grow up together. We were all young and he was like part of the family when we were all travelling the Grand Prix scene.'

1978

As Lewis recalls: 'We started to prepare our outfit for the 1978 season by fitting a new sidecar wheel arch incorporating the radiator. The fuel tank was modified so it would hold more fuel to last the GPs and TT. The carbs were bored out to 35.5mm as recommended by ex-Yamaha works mechanic Ian McKay, who also supplied us with phosphor bronze water and oil pump gears. Bill Simpson helped with a lot of these modifications. We used Dennis' engine as a 500, we had stuffer plates manufactured and fitted onto the crankshaft flywheels to raise the primary compression. We cut up the standard 250 pipes and fitted them on with pipes one and two now running along the front where the radiator used to be. The bike was then painted in Team Castrol colours.'

Jock Taylor and Lewis Ward racing at Beveridge Park, Kirkcaldy in 1977.

After competing in the three Easter Transatlantic meetings (Brands Hatch, Mallory Park and Oulton Park), and with the help, says Lewis: 'Of my Aunty and Grannies pension savings, we hired a small (very small) 4-berth caravan for four weeks.'

Tom Kinnard

The day prior to setting off, the pair visited Knockhill for a final test session of the 500 package. During this they had problems with fuel delivery to the carburettors and suction pipe was too soft. On loading the outfit to leave, Tom Kinnard, owner of Knockhill, arrived for a chat. Finding out that they were leaving the next day for the GPs, he opened his wallet and said: 'Whatever is here is yours.'

And so Jock, Charlie and Lewis and the latter's father Harry, described by Lewis as: 'Head cook and bottle washer', set off for Continental Europe.

The Austrian Grand Prix

The journey to the first GP, the Austrian at the Salzburgring, was fraught with mechanical problems – the van first going on three cylinders (an exhaust valve had melted) and then on reaching Austria the fuel pump packed in.

In the Salzburgring paddock the Scottish team set up camp next to Alain Michel and Stu Collins. The latter gave them some fuel pipe for the fuel pump which sorted out that particular problem, while Lewis rebuilt the head and re-fitted to the van.

A Steep Learning Curve

Then came what Lewis describes as a: 'Steep learning curve.' This included being supplied, free of charge, with Champion race plugs. As Lewis says: 'We had previously always bought NGK. We fitted the Champions for the race, but when it started the engine would only fire on three cylinders. We pitted on the first lap, removed the Champions and fitted NGKs. This cured the problem. But after a few laps the air temperature hot the water temperature went to max on the gauge. This obviously slowed things up.' And as Lewis says: 'Surprisingly, we finished 12th.'

After the Austrian round, a visit was organised to go with Hermann Schmit back to his workshops in Switzerland and modify the cooling system.

The French Grand Prix

Next it was the French GP at Nogaro, where Jock and Lewis finished seventh. Then it was on to Mugello in Italy for the third round in the Championship, where an eighth was gained.

Then it was off back home to Scotland. They had arranged to stop off at Terry Windle's workshop and inspect a new rolling chassis. On arriving home, Lewis says: 'I arranged a team meeting for the following night where I announced that I was quitting. Since we had started the GPs, the team's strong tight working bond had started to change. I had stopped enjoying it all so it was time to pack it in.' Lewis continued: 'Looking back it was the biggest favour I did for Jock because he had to look for a new passenger, especially for the TT. Luckily to choose Kenny Arthur who had vast Isle of Man experience.' Jock and Kenny worked out a signalling system which allowed Jock to trust Kenny's experience in getting quick lap times which gave them overall victory in the two-race 1978 TT.

Although Lewis Ward had parted company with Jock, this most certainly was not the end of his involvement with racing and this continues to the present time, when as this book was being compiled he had joined forces with Richard Tracey to assist in the re-manufacture of Armstrong 250/350 works updated bikes and engines; he lives in the Isle of Man.

James Neil

Jock's next regular passenger was James Neil (born Edinburgh, 21 September 1960), who was only 17 years of age at the time when he joined up with Jock in June 1978. James had first met Jock at the inaugural event at the newly opened Knockhill race circuit, back in 1974.

After a couple of British short circuit meetings Jock and James took in their first Grand Prix together, the Belgian at Spa Francorchamps. And a

In early 1978 Dennis Trollope became involved with the Jock Taylor racing effort. This was to result in a 500cc Yamaha four (and also a 750TZ engine for British events). Also not long after that year's Grand Prix season began Lewis Ward quit, to be replaced by the 17-year-old James Neil in June that year.

pretty successful debut it was too, as they finished sixth behind a host of top names, including the winner Bruno Holzer, Michel, Biland, Steinhausen and Hodgkins.

On The Podium

The undoubted highlight of the 1978 season, as far as Jock and James were concerned, came at the British Grand Prix at Silverstone. This, the sixth round of the series, saw them come home third behind the winner Alain Michel (passengered by Stu Collins) and Rolf Biland (passengered by Kenny Williams). The 1977 world champion George O'Dell was fifth.

Round seven was staged over the fearsome long Nürburgring circuit. Laid out in 1927, the original course was not only the pride of German racing, but also the most tortuous and demanding of circuits which one can imagine. In many ways it was an even more hazardous venue then the legendary Isle of Man Mountain lap.

The magnificence of the Nürburgring's setting and the concentration of its hazards were truly awe-inspiring. The tarmac surfaced road wound and dipped, in a confusing sequence of blind bends and undulations, over the beautifully wooded slopes of the Eifel mountains. In its 14.165-mile (22.791km) lap, the road fell and climbed nearly 1,000ft.

Jetting Problems

The very nature of the Nürburgring could cause problems with carburettor jetting on highly-tuned two-stroke engines. And this is precisely what Jock and Jamie soon discovered. Then, on the warm-up lap, an expansion chamber fell off. Jamie thought this would be the end of their race, but no, they eventually sorted things out. But the race started without them. This was to result in Jock being left several miles behind the field. Jamie described their position: 'Everyone else had cleared off and it became very silent. We finally got going. Jock rode out of his skin, setting a succession of lap records on a circuit he had never seen before; it was incredible. Towards the end we suddenly began to overtake several other outfits. I'm sure if the race had gone on for another lap we would have been up with the leaders!'

The final round of 1978 was the Czech Grand Prix at Brno. Here the Scottish pairing came fourth, behind Alain Michel, Rolf Biland and Dick Greasley.

Mixed Fortunes

Then it was into the 1979 season – the year of the two Championships, A and B. Jock chose the former. The Scottish team failed to score any points in the first round, the Austrian GP at the Salzburgring. Next came the German round at Hockenheim, where Jock and Jamie finished fifth; behind Steinhausen, the winner, Siegfried Schauzu, Dick Greasley and George O'Dell. Then came another podium finish in the Dutch TT at Assen. The previous year the pair could not gain an entry for this event!

However, the pressure was beginning to tell on young James. One has to remember that he had only just turned 18. And this pressure was to lead to a parting of the ways, his reign as Jock's passenger having lasted just over 12 months since he had replaced Lewis Ward. When asked by the author to give his views of Jock he simply described him as 'magical and wonderful.' He also described how: 'Jock had a way of becoming very friendly with important people.' To illustrate this he provides the story of how Jock befriended Kenny Roberts, the American Yamaha ace giving the Scottish team a set of Lectron carburettors for their Yamaha engine.

Today, James Neil is still involved with sidecar racing, campaigning his TWR (Taylor Wrine Racing) Yamaha R1 outfit in Scottish events, with passenger Graham Whitehill and with backing from Charles Johnson. Not only that, but another member of the team is Stewart Taylor – a cousin of Jock's!

Benga Johansson

Benga Johansson (or to give him his full name, Bengt-Göran Johansson) arrived on the scene in July 1979. It was while the Swede was at Snetterton, contesting the 125 and 250cc solo races, that fate intervened. As Benga was to recall later: 'I was parked next to Jock in the paddock and I could tell by

The Swede Benga Johansson arrived as Jock's passenger in July 1979, after meeting each other at Snetterton, where Benga was contesting the 125 and 250cc solo classes. This photograph shows the pair racing a Fowler Yamaha in 1980 TT.

his attitude that something was wrong. As practice time arrived I realised what it was. Passenger James Neil had not arrived. Jock asked me if I was interested to help out and I said I could be. When Dennis [Trollope] arrived he quickly gave permission for me to take over, saying if I didn't passenger he would have to and that he was not over keen on the idea.'

The Race Debut

As *Motorcycle Racer* magazine was to comment: 'The inexperienced Benga took to his new task like a duck to water.' And I can certainly agree with this statement as I was spectating at my local circuit that day. In fact Benga and Jock looked set for a dream first-time-out victory when their machine broke down. Benga takes up the story: 'We were in the lead at the time and had already broken the lap record, so it was not too bad.'

A First Grand Prix Victory

After Snetterton it was a journey to Benga's homeland and the Swedish Grand Prix at Karlsoga, and also the first GP victory for Jock. The pair took their Yamaha-engined Windle to a popular win, averaging 77.408mph (124.571km/h), with Werner Schwärzel second and Rolf Biland third, Dick Greasley fourth and Egbert Streuer fifth.

As Jock's best previous GP finish had been a third, he asked Benga to stay on for the rest of the season.

The partnership went from strength to strength and at the end of the year, Benga decided to quit solo racing and become a full-time passenger with Jock in 1980.

During the close season the friendship between the two strengthened, with Jock spending three months at Benga's home in Sweden. But it was far from a holiday, as the pair were working on the outfit for much of the time.

The first two rounds of the 1980 World Championship were won by Rolf Biland, with Jock and Benga runners-up at the first race, the French GP at Le Castellet. Then at round two, the Yugoslav GP at Rijeka they finished third (Alain Michel was second).

The 1980 Isle of Man TT

Next came the Isle of Man TT, which although no longer counting towards World Championship points was still a popular and prestigious event in the sidecar racing calendar.

Trevor Ireson won his third Sidecar TT in succession with a start-to-finish victory, but with wet roads around the circuit no records were broken. Jock and Benga, from fifth in the first lap, rode brilliantly to finish second in the three-lap 113.19 mile (182.12km) race and set a fastest lap of 106.08mph (170.68km/h). In addition Jock and Benga were declared the overall winners of the two-race contest.

For the TT, Jock switched back to the previous year's outfit. At the time he said: 'That is one trouble with racing in the Isle of Man, you have to have two machines, one for the GPs, the other a rough and ready one. Anyway we run a 750cc Yamaha engine in the Island and the new outfit will only take a 500cc motor.'

Despite this, Jock liked the TT, commenting: 'It's a difficult place where you have to race with your brain more than anything else.' He continued: 'I enjoy it there mainly because of the atmosphere that simply cannot be found anywhere else.'

Jock also said: 'At the end of the day Benga and myself came away from the Island much wiser men. He can figure out just about everything he wants to know about passengering the machine and I have found the best techniques to handle the machine properly.'

He continued: 'Another good thing is that there's so much testing during the TT period without the pressures of a Grand Prix. Then there is the relaxation as well because we go there for two weeks, practice for the best part of four or five days and then race twice.'

In 1980 Jock and Benga became sidecar world champions – with the Yamaha-powered Fowler Yamaha.

The Grand Prix Trail

After the Isle of Man came the Dutch TT at Assen. Here Jock and Benga scored their second World Championship race victory, with Alain Michel runner-up and Derek Jones third. Other notable finishers included Egbert Streuer (fourth), Werner Schwärzel (fifth), Bruno Holzer (eighth) and George O'Dell (ninth).

For the Belgian GP a week later the venue had switched from Spa to Zolder. Here Jock and Benga won again, from Michel, Rolf Biland and Jones.

A third consecutive victory was gained in the Finnish GP at Imatra, this time from Schwärzel, Holzer and Biland.

Next came the home round at Silverstone, where Derek Jones (passengered by Brian Ayers) won, from Jock and Benga, with George O'Dell and Kenny Williams third.

With Rolf Biland winning the Czech GP at Brno, it all came down to the final round in Germany.

World Champions

At the Nürburgring, Jock and Benga took their Yamaha-Windle outfit to victory and secured the World Championship title. Their only challenger, Rolf Biland, did not score any points.

So the final Championship table read:

A happy-looking Jock Taylor (astride a Yamaha TY250 trials bike) after being crowned 1980 world champion.

Taylor/Johansson
Biland/Waltisperg
Michel/Burkhardt
Streuer/van der Kaap
Schwärzel/Huber

As for costs, the British-made Windle chassis cost some £2,500 – less than half the price of the European opposition. The Seymaz used by Frenchman Alain Michel cost £6,500, while Swiss Rolf Biland's LCR (Louis Christian Racing) cost £5,500.

The conventional British design had been developed by Yorkshireman Terry Windle during the previous 15 years.

Ride With A Champion

I had been around the circuits with my camera for a few years and got to know most of the sidecar crews fairly well as I supplied them with photographs which they found difficult to obtain from the press or other sources. At the end of the 1980 season I was approached by Jock Taylor's sponsor and asked to supply photographs of Jock and Benga, which I did.

To my surprise and delight at the Alexandra Palace Road Race Show the following spring I found Jock's bus adorned with posters proclaiming 'Jock Taylor and Benga Johansson 1980 Sidecar World Champions', complete with my signature as a photograph credit in the bottom-left-hand corner (an autographed copy of which hangs in my front room today). On meeting Jock he commented: 'Well now I've made you a famous photographer I suppose you want lots of money.' 'No thanks, I'd rather have a ride in the chair' I replied, never dreaming that that could happen!

'All right' came the reply, and true to his word a letter came in the summer inviting me to Donington to have a ride in practice at the European Sidecar Championship round. So off I went on the big day, complete with leathers, Jock Taylor's replica helmet and better half and soon found Jock's bus. Jock and Benga took the outfit out on the circuit for a few laps while I waited in eager anticipation in the pit lane for my turn.

After seven or eight laps they pulled into the pit lane, Benga dismounted and Jock said 'Lie in the chair and then I'll take you round.' 'Not likely, I want to do this properly' I replied, so after a few basic instructions from Benga we set off down the pit lane. First lap Jock went fairly slowly, keeping an eye on my movement in the chair, and as he seemed happy with that the next three laps fairly flew by. According to the stopwatches in the pit lane, lap three was within 0.1 of a second of Jock's lap record.

The ride of a lifetime for sidecar racing fan Jan Barszczyuski, with world champion Jock Taylor; European Championship round, Donington Park July 1981.

Down the start straight, move right for Redgate, stay right then move left for the kink in Craner Curves, right for The Old Hairpin at the bottom of the hill, right again at Coppice, tuck in down the straight under Dunlop Bridge then right and left at the chicane and back to the start.

The thrill of a lifetime and much cherished memories. Those four laps are as fresh in my mind today as if they had only happened yesterday. Sadly Jock was taken from us soon afterwards and is still missed today, not just because he was a world champion and would undoubtedly have been again, but because he was such a thoroughly decent, likeable person.

Thanks for the ride, champ!

Jan Barszczynski

The following is what Jock told *Motor Cycle News* magazine during his 1980 Championship year:

'Biland and Michel have to make too many experiments to be successful. Too many experiments have to be made to adjust the chassis for testing them – suspension heights have to be altered as with a racing car. The engineering qualities of the LCR and Seymaz are excellent for that they are, but they are actually cars. They're Formula One three-wheelers.'

Also in 1980 Jock was awarded the *Motor Cycle News* 'Man of the Year Award.'

The 1981 Isle of Man TT

Quite simply Jock and Benga dominated the 1981 Isle of Man Sidecar TT, winning both races. In the first leg they set a new lap record of 108.12mph (173.96km/h), with a race average of 107.02mph (172.19km/h); the latter quicker than the fastest lap the previous year.

Afterward Jock told reporters: 'I've been so relaxed at the TT this year. In fact, when I was waiting for the starts I was never more so.'

There is no doubt that the speed achieved astounded the pair of them, Jock commenting: 'In practice we did not seem to be going all that fast and I couldn't believe it when Dennis Trollope pointed out that we had done a lap at around 107mph. We just do not seem to be going that fast.'

The 1981 Grand Prix Season

As for the 1981 GP season, Jock and Benga began the defence of their title in great style with victory in the first round at the Salzburgring in Austria. The pair won with an average speed of 106.824mph (171.91km/h), in process showing the likes of Biland, Michel and Schwärzel the way home.

At round two, the German GP at Hockenheim, the pair finished runners-up to Alain Michel, with Werner Schwärzel third and Mick Boddice fourth; Biland was a non-finisher.

Round three saw another second place, this time to Rolf Biland, at the French Grand Prix which was staged at the Le Castellet circuit; Michel was third. Then at Jarama in Spain the pair finished ninth and last after experiencing problems; Biland won again. Round five, the Dutch TT at Assen, and Jock was runner-up to Alain Michel. It was turning out to be a close fought battle for title honours, with the three main contenders clearly marked out: Biland, Michel and Jock.

Next came the Belgian GP at Spa, this saw Biland victorious, Jock second and Michel third. However, the final four rounds saw Rolf Biland win every race and thus clinch the Championship.

The final 1981 Championship table looked like this:

Biland/Waltisperg
Michel/Burkhardt
Taylor/Johansson
Jones/Ayres
Schwärzel/Huber

The Wedding

In November 1981 Jock married Kate Stewart at Pencaitland, East Lothian. News also leaked out that he was, together with Terry Windle, Benga and Windle's right-hand man and former passenger Stu Collins, working on: 'Something completely different as far as outfits are concerned.'

As the December 1981 issue of *Motorcycle Racer* said: 'chassis king Terry Windle knew what Jock was up against when he saw the rivals on LCR and Seymaz machinery at the Belgian GP this year.'

So Stu Collins was promptly employed by Windle for his valuable construction experience. Collins was ex-passenger for Alain Michel and had been working in Geneva for Seymaz boss Eric Vaugnat, having quit racing in July 1980.

He spent the winter in Vaugnat's factory, but said: 'But because of permit problems I had to leave the country for two months every year. This was ok when I was racing.' He continued: Then while on holiday in Malta, I rang up Terry and asked about job prospects in the UK. He said come over, and promptly offered me a job.'

Wobbly-Wheeler

The new chassis was basically constructed of 18 gauge aircraft aluminium, which it was claimed was four to five times more expensive than conventional steel tubing, and held together by aircraft rivets 'out of necessity' said Terry Windle and 'I'm using hub steering.'

The press labelled the new project 'wobbly-wheeler', and the monocoque outfit was clearly intended to take in the best features of the Seymaz and LCR principles.

But Terry Windle still had reservations, saying: 'Jock is a full-time professional but many riders may not have the time to set up the geometry of a wobbly wheeler such as this. They would be better off with a conventional outfit. All they've got to worry about is the engine. That's why I have not been in favour of wobbly-wheelers up until now. If they are set up wrong it does not do them any good...and it does not do me any good.'

In February 1982 came news that the coming season would almost certainly be the last for the sidecar World Championship-winning team of Jock Taylor and Benga Johansson. The latter revealing that he had decided to make a career in car racing and that it seemed likely to take up all of his time in 1983.

Interviewed by *Motorcycle Racer*, Jock emphasised that there was no suggestion of a break-up of their friendship. Going on to say: 'Benga has always been keen to get into motor racing and he has been testing a lot in a Formula Three car. I say good luck to him, he is just the right age to get into the sport and I wish I had done the same or gone solo racing when I was a bit younger.'

Sponsorship

The early 1980s were a time of recession, and this was evident when the former world champions lost their Centurian helmet tie-up at the beginning of 1982. However, they did manage to secure a deal with the Wrangler jeans

Sidecar race at Mallory Park on 11 April 1982, Jock and Benga with their 750cc Fowler Yamaha. Then came that fateful day at the Finnish Grand Prix, 15 August that year, when in a rain-lashed race Jock was to crash and be fatally injured. The sidecar world had lost one of its most popular competitors.

company. However, as Jock pointed out: 'Wrangler are with us only for the TT this time, but I hope we can justify the cash they have given us and hopefully see them backing the bike in the GPs next year.'

The 1982 TT

Again the Sidecar TT in the Isle of Man was a two-leg affair. In the first, Jock hit trouble on the first lap, stopping to make adjustments at Alpine Cottage, and reaching the pits for a long stop. Rejoining the race, he eventually finished 18th. But in the second leg after early leader Mick Boddice retired Jock turned up the heat setting a new lap record of 108.29mph (174.23km/h) to comfortably secure victory.

The Fatal GP Trail

And so to the GPs. Certainly, in 1982, Jock and Benga seemed less competitive than previous years. In the first five rounds the best they could achieve were a couple of third places (Belgium and Sweden).

Then came that fateful day on 15 August 1982, the Finnish Grand Prix at Imatra, and the accident which robbed the racing world of one of its most loved characters. Ironically, Jock's tragic death during a rain-lashed race came after several drivers had pressed for the race to be cancelled.

But Jock was not one of them – he wanted the show to go on – as journalist John Brown was to say in a tribute published in the September 1982 issues of *Motorcycle Racer*: 'That was the determined character he was. He never wanted to give in however hard the challenge.'

Tim Reeves and Gregory Cluze with the Jock Taylor Trophy at his memorial in Beveridge Park, Kirkcaldy, 15 August 2010. This memorial was erected by the Kirkcaldy and District Motorcycle Club to Jock and other Scottish racers who have died on circuit.

In fact, Jock was a lover of the closed roads circuits like the one where his death occurred after his new Windle outfit aqua-planned into a road-side pole.

John McComisky of *Bike Sport News* had this reaction to news of Jock's death: 'Seldom before has the sport had such a likeable and respected ambassador who was so universally admired by everyone.' But the last word must go to John Brown, who concluded his tribute back in 1982 by saying: 'A truly great rider who called a spade a spade and who had one of the most likeable personalities in the game, Jock Taylor is a great loss to the sport in general, not just as a superb sidecar competitor.'

CHAPTER 21

WERNER SCHWÄRZEL

Werner Schwärzel was born in the German town of Meissenheim on 6 September 1948.

And besides scoring 10 Grand Prix victories, Werner won the world sidecar Championship title in 1982. He also finished runner-up four years running in 1973, 1974, 1975 and 1976.

His first GP victory came in Germany at the Nürburgring in 1974; his last over 11 years later, again at the German GP, but this time at the Hockenheim circuit.

Although Werner Schwärzel began his racing career, like most of his countrymen, equipped with a BMW, he was one of the very first sidecar men, along with arch rival Rolf Steinhausen, to enjoy international success with the water-cooled flat-four König two-stroke.

Junior Champion

In 1970 Werner had been the West German Junior Champion, but it was not until 1973 that he made his presence felt on the world stage. That year had seen a handful of König drivers cause severe problems for the previously dominant BMW Rennsport double-overhead camshaft flat twins. In the first round of the Championship, at Le Castellet, France, Werner was third, and in the next round, at the Salzburgring in Austria, he was fifth, but even better was to come at the third round, on home soil (or should that be tarmac!) at Hockenheim when he took his outfit to second place behind world champion Klaus Enders. Then came third places at Assen (Holland) and Brno (Czechoslovakia), meaning that Werner and his passenger Karl Kleis took runner-up berth in that year's World Sidecar Championship table. Certainly one of the most impressive GP debut seasons ever.

The 1974 Season

Into 1974 and a new passenger – Andreas Huber. Werner was leading the opening round in France (this time held at Clermont-Ferrand in the middle of the country), until his machine was slowed with engine problems on the last lap, letting Siegfried Schauzu through to an unexpected victory. In their next outing, at the Nürburgring, Werner led from start to finish and was never approached by either Enders or Schauzu. In Austria, the result was the same as it had been in France, with Werner taking second place behind Schauzu. But Enders was back in form at the Italian GP (held that year at Imola). The result was that Schwärzel and Enders battled at the front, when just two laps from the finish Werner's König engine went sick once more, but this time he failed to score points.

Disaster in the Isle of Man

Then came disaster at the Isle of Man TT, when he crashed in practice. Although not seriously injured, the experience had dampened his enthusiasm of racing over the Mountain road course.

Then, at the next round, at Assen, he struck engine trouble once more, again when leading the race. However, after making a pit stop he was able to finish, eventually crossing the line in fifth position. Next came Belgium where he was third, before winning the final Championship race, the Czech GP at Brno. That year Werner Schwärzel and his passenger Andreas Huber took in some end of season British international meetings where they were victorious at Brands Hatch, Scarborough and Silverstone, using a larger displacement 680cc König engine in the 1000cc sidecar events.

1975

1975 once again saw the start of the sidecar Grand Prix season in France, this time at the Paul Ricard circuit. This race saw the virtually unknown Swiss driver Hermann Schmid score a first GP victory, with Schwärzel/Huber runners-up. Then after failing to score in Austria, the German pairing were second again, this time at Hockenheim, behind Rolf Biland.

But Werner did not contest the TT – put off by the experience the previous year. The next round was in Holland. After the TT (which Steinhausen had won), Schwärzel was 24 points adrift of his similarly mounted fellow countryman. But he closed the gap after winning the race, while it was his rivals turn not to score any points. Then at the Belgian GP it was Werner's turn to retire.

And although he won the final GP of the year, at Brno, he was still 13 points adrift in second position in the title chart once again.

Non-Championship Racing

In non-Championship racing Werner gained considerable success, particularly in Britain, with more wins at Brands Hatch and Silverstone.

Then during the 1976 season the main competition for top spot was still between the two German König drivers, although neither got off to a good start at round one in France. However, from round two onwards both really began to motor, with the two rivals battling it out in a great race at the Austrian Salzburgring. But bad luck intervened and Werner Schwärzel slowed and was forced to accept the runner-up spot once again. Then, with no points from the Isle of Man TT, he had to make up ground on Steinhausen at the Dutch TT which followed – a repeat of the situation of the previous year. But drama was to ensue, when after heatwave conditions, which caused the leading driver to suffer a heart attack, Schwärzel came home in fourth position.

The weather, a week later, was also very hot indeed for the Belgian GP. But this time Schwärzel and Steinhausen were clear ahead of the pack, with the decision going to the former by a mere 0.4 seconds. In the Czech GP Werner looked set to win, but was passed by Schmid. And although Steinhausen was back in fourth spot he won the title for the second year running. As had happened the previous year Werner won the final GP – this time in Germany – but that was only enough to make sure of runner-up spot in the Championship for the fourth time in a row.

1977

For the 1977 season Werner was equipped with an ARO-sponsored, Fath-powered (a flat-four two-stroke) outfit, prepared by the ex-world champion himself, Helmut Fath. At the first round, staged over the Salzburgring, he was fifth. But in both the next rounds (Hockenheim, Germany and Le Castellet, France) fuel starvation and unscheduled pit stops saw the ARO-Fath entry unplaced. Then things began to improve when, at Assen for the Dutch round, a rostrum position was achieved for the first time with the new machine: when Schwärzel/Huber posted a third place.

The Final Three Rounds

Then came the final three rounds of the 1977 Championship – and two victories at the Belgian (Spa Francorchamps) and British GP (Silverstone).

A Silverstone Victory

At Silverstone, his victory was particularly hard won, because in a rain-swept race he had put in a tremendous performance of determination and skill; leading from start to finish. It should also be remembered that at the other round (between Belgium and Britain), the Czech GP at Brno, he had again been leading, but after four laps his gearbox packed up, this retirement meaning that he only scored 46 points and was lower in the Championship table than his driving deserved. There is absolutely no doubt that, had the ARO-Fath been more reliable, Werner Schwärzel would have been the 1977 champion instead of George O'Dell.

And so Schwärzel, partnered as usual by Andreas Huber, actually finished third in the Championship; behind O'Dell and the Swiss star, Rolf Biland.

Although 1978 saw Schwärzel score impressive victories in the Dutch round at Assen and on home ground at the Nürburgring, plus a second at Mugello in Italy, the remainder of his GP season was a disaster. His only other finish being a fifth at Nogaro in France. And so the title went to Rolf Biland who scored all his victories in the first three races; Werner Schwärzel finishing the season fourth in the points table.

1979

For 1979, with a two-series sidecar Championship (B–2–A and B–2–B) Werner Schwärzel made the switch to Yamaha power, having become disillusioned with the on-going gremlins suffered with the ARO-Fath. Unfortunately, this switch did not start to work until after halfway through the 7-round series. The final three rounds seeing finishes in each race, in stark contrast to the first four! The Swedish GP at Karlskoga saw Werner finish runner-up to Scotland's Jock Taylor. Then came the British GP at Silverstone, were a fourth place was recorded, followed at the final round, the Czech GP at Brno, with a third. Biland was again Champion but Werner was back outside the top six table as regards points scored in the 1979 B–2–A world positions.

In 1980 and 1981 Werner Schwärzel could do no better than sixth in the Championship; both years using Yamaha power, but not adding to his Grand Prix victory tally.

World Champion At Last

Then came 1982. And what an amazing year it turned out to be for Werner and his long-running passenger Andreas Huber.

First their Yamaha-powered Seymaz outfit finished every single race in the nine-round Championship with the following results:

Austria	3rd
Holland	3rd
Belgium	4th
Britain	2nd
Sweden	2nd
Finland	3rd
Czechoslovakia	2nd
San Marino	2nd
West Germany	6th

Werner Schwärzel was world champion in 1982. The German is seen here during the British Grand Prix at Silverstone the previous year.

Controversially, Rolf Biland was to finish runner-up in the Championship – even though he had won no less than six of the rounds, whereas Werner Schwärzel had not won a single GP that year!

The 1984 Season

The 1984 season kicked off at Le Mans in France, Schwärzel and Huber coming home third with the Yamaha-Seymaz outfit, behind the winners Biland/Waltisburg and surprise package Mick Barton/Simon Birchall. No points were scored at the next round (Hockenheim), then at the

Werner Schwärzel and passenger Andres Huber (Seymaz-Yamaha), their 1984 outfit.

British driver Derek Bayley (12) leads Werner Schwärzel out of the chicane during the 1984 Dutch TT at Assen.

Salzburgring Werner and Andreas brought their Yamaha-Seymaz home second behind Biland and Waltisburg. Another runner-up spot came at the next round (Assen), followed by a fourth in Belgium, sixth at Silverstone for the British GP, third in Sweden and finally another third in the last round at Imola.

But in truth although the 1980s had at last seen Werner Schwärzel crowned champion, it was the 1970s which had been his real glory period.

One Last Twist

There was one last twist to Werner's sidecar racing career. And this came shortly before his retirement from the sport in which he had been a major figure for over a decade, with his final German GP victory at Hockenheim in 1985.

A special mention should also be made of his passenger Andreas Huber, who had been at his side almost exclusively throughout Werner's long GP career.

A 1985 podium photograph of the Swedish Grand Prix at Anderstorp, Werner Schwärzel finished second. From left to right: Fritz Buck, Werner Schwärzel, winners Bernard Schnieders, Egbert Streuer, Tony Hewitt and Steve Webster.

CHAPTER 22

EGBERT STREUER

Egbert Streuer was born in Assen, Holland, on 1 February 1954 and was not only to be the victor of 22 Grand Prix races, but also a triple world champion, winning the title in 1984, 1985 and 1986.

Assen – The Home of Dutch Racing

Although not the only racing circuit in Holland, Assen is certainly the most famous. And Egbert Streuer was to grow up closer to racing than the great majority of other youngsters, certainly in his homeland.

So what of Assen's history as the home of the Dutch TT? This all began on 14 May 1925, when the local Assen and District Motor Club, barely three years old, caused a major stir by announcing that it planned to provide Holland with its very first motorcycle road race. A major reason for the uproar which followed was at that time there was a speed restriction on Dutch roads of 12mph (19km/h), and a ban on open-road speed competitions meant that racing in the country at that time was limited to grass-track events.

The KNMV

The passing of a new Motoring and Cycling Act in 1924 meant that the government on The Hague were able to give permission for the KNMV, the motor sports' governing body in Holland, to at last consider motorcycle road racing. And eventually Assen in the north of the country was chosen as a suitable venue, with a triangular circuit of just over 17 miles (27.4km) was utilised with Rolde, Borger and Schooloo at its corners. After much red tape had been negotiated, on Saturday 11 June 1925, 27 competitors (all solos) lined up for the start, comprising two riders of 250cc machines, 13 350cc and 11 500cc. British machines won all three classes; BSA, New Imperial and Norton respectively.

An Expanded Programme

The 1926 programme was expanded to include 750cc and 1000cc machines with separate categories in each race for amateurs, seniors and professionals. Not only this, but car parks and grandstands had been constructed.

By 1927 the Dutch TT had become well enough established to attract foreign riders, a notable entry being the Irish star, Stanley Woods. And it was Stanley who was to emerge the winner, riding a factory Norton.

By the following year Norton, AJS and Rudge all sent works machines and riders. While the year 1930 saw the Dutch TT officially recognised as part of the European (the forerunner of the World) Championship series, together with the Isle of Man TT, French, German and Belgian GPs.

The 1934 meeting attracted a then record attendance of some 60,000 spectators and 120 entries. 1937 saw track improvements which had a big effect on speeds, the German Karl Gall (BMW) improving Jimmy Guthrie's 1936 lap record by 11 seconds, with a speed of 92.22mph (148.38km/h).

With war clouds gathering the last Dutch TT before the outbreak of World War Two occurred in late June 1939. And although racing returned to Assen in 1946, and some 80,000 spectators attended, there were only local riders taking part. But by 1947 the Dutch TT had become fully international again and saw the return of the factory teams, including Norton and Velocette.

World Championships

The Dutch TT was part of the World Championship calendar right from the start in 1949, but the sidecars were not introduced until 1955, a year after Egbert Streuer had been born. It was then to become a regular venue for the three-wheelers – and very popular both with spectators and the sidecar crews themselves.

With all the top names of international motorcycle racing taking part, the circuit and Assen town itself became a byword for racing in Holland and throughout Europe.

A new venue, the Circuit Van Drenthe, had been opened to mark the jubilee year in 1955. This was, at 4.78 miles (7.69km) considerably shorter than the old public roads course, and is very much the Assen we know today. The first ever Dutch Sidecar TT was won by BMW factory start Willi Faust (see Chapter 6) that same year.

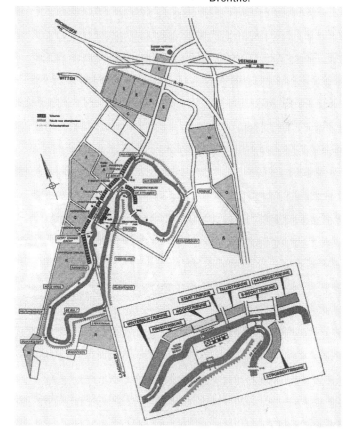

The Assen circuit Van Drenthe.

With all the above one can more easily understand how the young Egbert Streuer's imagination and dedication to motorcycle racing should occur. And Egbert was not only to become his country's first ever sidecar world champion, but he was also to win a trio of titles in 1984, 1985 and 1986.

How It All Started

Egbert Streuer began sidecar racing back in 1975 with a BMW outfit with passenger Johan van der Kaap. By 1978, now with a two-stroke König outfit the pair won the Dutch National Sidecar Championship title.

It was also in 1978 that Streuer and van der Kaap joined the Grand Prix circus, their best position that season coming in Czechoslovakia at Brno, when the Dutch pairing finished 10th on their recently acquired Yamaha-powered Schmid outfit.

Into 1979, and the FIM sanctioned two Sidecar Championships, B–2–A and B–2–B; the latter in an attempt to accommodate the new technology pioneered by Rolf Biland's controversial BEO outfit employing F1 car principles.

Egbert Streuer and passenger Johan van der Kaap took their more conventional Yamaha-Schmid to sixth place on home ground at Assen, the third round of the Championship. They finished behind Rolf Biland (the winner), Rolf Steinhausen, Jock Taylor, Dick Greasley and Guy Brodin. Another future Champion, Frenchman Alain Michel was 10th. In round five the Dutch pair came home fifth, repeating the performance in the seventh and final round, the Czech GP at Brno.

The Big Breakthrough

Egbert Streuer's big breakthrough came the following year, 1980, when with a string of decent results he was to finish the season fourth in the Championship table. The Yamaha-Schmid outfit had been replaced by a new Yamaha-LCR.

Round one was at Le Castellet in France, and here Egbert caused a stir by not only coming home fourth (behind Biland, Taylor and Schwärzel), but also finishing in front of Rolf Steinhausen, Bruno Holzer and Alain Michel.

Then, in round two at the Yugoslav GP, the Dutchman repeated this result, behind Biland, Michel and Taylor. And again in round three (Assen) to Taylor, Michel and Derek Jones.

However, in round five (Finnish GP) the Dutch team were non-finishers. Then in round six, the British GP at Silverstone, Streuer and van der Kaap were sixth. It was back to yet another fourth (the fifth of the season) at round seven (Czech GP). But the best was to come at the eighth and final round, the German Grand Prix at the Nürburgring, where they finally got on the rostrum with a third place behind the winner Jock Taylor and runner-up Alain Michel.

Yes, 1980 had really seen Egbert Streuer make his mark at the highest level. And gave an indication of his future potential.

Passengers

1980 was to be the final year with Johan van der Kaap as passenger. In fact, during 1981 Egbert was forced to miss the first two rounds. Then at round three, the French GP at Le Castellet, he appeared with fellow countryman Bernhard Schnieders in the chair. They finished fourth (to Biland, Taylor and Michel).

The next GP in which Egbert Streuer featured in the results came at round six, the Belgian at Spa Francorchamps, with an eighth (with Schnieders again in the chair). Round seven was the British Grand Prix at Silverstone, and with Englishman Kenny Williams as passenger Egbert finished fifth.

There was no Streuer in the results at the next, but at round nine, the Swedish GP at Anderstorp, Egbert had another passenger, the Finn Topen Leppänen; the pairing finished ninth. And in round 10, the last in the 1981 series, with yet another passenger, Dutchman Cees Vroegop, Egbert came home sixth.

Bernhard Schnieders

From the beginning of the 1982 season Bernhard Schnieders became more of a fixture in the Streuer team. And this immediately paid dividends as it created a more settled approach to Egbert's track efforts. To start with the pair scored their first Grand Prix victory, the British round at Silverstone. Added to this were second positions in Belgium and Germany. The only other top 10 positions were a fifth in Holland and a sixth in Finland. However, what was needed now was being able to compete and finish in more rounds. Even so, Egbert had managed to replicate his 1980 fourth-place Championship result.

A delighted Egbert Streuer (left, with beard) and his passenger Bernard Schnieders after their victory at the 1982 British Grand Prix at Silverstone.

The start of the 1982 German Grand Prix at the Nürburgring. Egbert Streuer (2) is seen on the front row between Alain Michel (4) and Rolf Biland (1).

The sidecar grid lines up in front of the vast crowd for the 1984 Dutch TT at Assen. Local hero Egbert Streuer (2) is next to the eventual event winner, Rolf Biland (1).

Championship Runners-up

In 1983 not only did Egbert and Bernhard finish runners-up in the Championship (to Rolf Biland and Kurt Waltisperg), but they also won two GPs – at Hockenheim and Silverstone. Added to these were second placings at Spa Francorchamps and Anderstorp, plus a fourth at Imola (San Marino GP).

The Start of Something Big

This was the start of something big. With Streuer and Schnieders dominating the sidecar world scene for the three seasons spanning 1984, 1985 and 1986. During these years the Dutch pair won 11 GPs, achieved with the LRC chassis and four-cylinder Yamaha two-stroke engine.

1984	Austrian GP (Salzburgring)
	German GP (Nürburgring)
	British GP (Silverstone)
1985	Belgian GP (Spa Francorchamps)
	French GP (Le Mans)
	Swedish GP (Anderstorp)
1986	German GP 25 May (Nürburgring)
	Austrian GP (Salzburgring)
	French GP (Paul Ricard)

British GP (Silverstone)

German GP 28 September (Hockenheim)

At the end of this period Egbert Streuer and Bernhard Schnieders were firmly established as not only triple world champions, but respected by other teams, the press and public alike.

More Grand Prix Success

Even though they were not destined to win another world title, Egbert and Bernhard went on to win a further eight Grand Prix races, these are listed below:

1987   Dutch TT (Assen)
1989   Belgian GP (Spa Francorchamps)
         Czech GP (Brno)
1990   Austrian GP (Salzburgring)
         Belgian GP (Spa Francorchamps)
         British GP (Donington Park)
1991   Dutch TT (Assen)
1992   Dutch TT (Assen)

Team Lucky Strike Streuer

During the late 1980s Egbert Streuer was largely responsible for creating Team Lucky Strike Streuer.

Streuer and Schnieders with their Lucky Strike-sponsored machine.
Photo W. Gruber/Archiv

The 1988 Lucky Strike
Team Streuer.

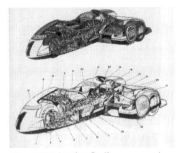

The 1988 Lucky Strike
Yamaha-LCR outfit
reproduced from the team
booklet.

An extract from the 1988
Lucky Strike team booklet
showing Bernard
Schnieders and Egbert
Streuer.

Besides Bernhard Schnieders and himself, this comprised another driver, Theo van Kempen, and his passenger, Englishman Simon Birchall. Plus Lee van Dam (team manager), Harry Poelman (driver) and four mechanics (Rinus van Kasteren, Johan van der Kaap (Egbert's original passenger), Frits Goris and Geral de Haas).

Both drivers used the latest Yamaha-LCR outfits, finished in the striking Lucky Strike livery of red, white and black.

Besides main sponsors Lucky Strike, there were also AS (Audio Sonic) and Valvoline.

It is also important to mention that Lucky Strike's involvement with the motorcycle Grand Prix world at this time also included Team Lucky Strike Roberts; with former 500cc world champion Kenny Roberts as team manager and riders American Wayne Rainey and Australian Kevin Magee.

An Insiders View

When the author spoke to Simon Birchall in the spring of 2010, Simon said that Egbert Streuer was 'a very calm and collected' person, 'laid back' even. But there is also no doubt that once on the track, with his race brain in gear, Egbert was true World Championship material – and his three titles prove just that. He was also someone who could handle the pressure of not only being a top-line competitor, but an equally effective team manager. And Egbert Streuer is certainly his country's most successful ever motorcyclist – albeit on three wheels rather than two – so has carved a special place in the history of motorcycle sport in the Netherlands.

CHAPTER 23
STEVE WEBSTER

Stephen (Steve) Webster was born in York, England on 7 January 1960. And was destined to become Sidecar Champion of the World on no less than 10 occasions, runner-up four times, third three times and fourth twice. Then in 2004 he achieved a unique triple by winning the World, European and British Championship titles in one season, the only time such a feat has been recorded. And with 60 victories Steve is second only to Rolf Biland in the all-time Sidecar Grand Prix victory chart.

Background

Steve would be the first to admit that his parents, Mick and Ann, played a major role in his racing career. His father being a three-times (1966, 1967 and 1968) British grass-track Sidecar Champion (driving a Triumph-powered outfit). And during Steve's own career was later to become the mechanic, mentor, van-driver of the team – in fact, the guy who took many of the decisions and was the driving force behind his son's early successes.

During 1987, after winning his first world title, this is how Steve described his father: 'He's my dad, but he's also my best mate.'

Steve's own competitive career began when he was 14, in a grass-track car, and as he grew up it was almost taken for granted he'd progress to some other form of motor sport.

As we know, father Mick had been a top man and multi-British grass-track Sidecar racing Champion, but had also competed in road racing, scrambling (moto-cross) and trials. So young Steve had been around motorcycles since he could walk. Mick had even built Steve and older brother (by 20 months or so) Kevin a miniature sidecar outfit for them to play with. This was powered by a 50cc German Ilo two-stroke engine. And starting as he meant to go on, Steve was usually the driver.

Steve Webster as a passenger to his brother Kevin in 1966 in their back garden. They are on a German 50cc Ilo two-stroke-engined miniature outfit built by their dad Mick, who is proudly stood behind the brothers.

When he reached his late teens, Steve decided he wanted to do some serious racing. Mick attempted to get him onto four wheels, having the Formula Ford series in mind. This was simply because he had been around racing long enough to realise that financial rewards and publicity did not happen overnight, and he considered it might be an easier task for his son to progress in the four wheel world, where sponsorship and press coverage were likely to be greater.

Three Wheels

As Mick was later to reveal: 'When he insisted on a bike, I managed to talk him into sidecars – I didn't want him to hurt himself on a solo, and there were so many people racing solos anyway. They are very expensive if you want to be competitive. You could spend a lot of money and find you were no good.'

So Webster senior took the bull by the horns and set out to construct his son's first outfit – the basis of this being a Fiddaman chassis with a twin cylinder air-cooled Suzuki Cobra (T500) engine. Mick Webster, when interviewed in late 1987 commented: 'I put Steve in the chair and drove off gunning up through the gears thinking "Mmm....This doesn't go badly at all." I looked across at Steve and he looked really scared.'

The following is how Steve himself saw that first outing: 'that was my first and last time as passenger'. And so Steve began racing, with his brother Kevin as the passenger. Soon the 500cc twin Suzuki motor was replaced by a liquid-cooled three-cylinder GT 750 from the same manufacturer.

Next came a John Derbyshire chassis, again Suzuki-powered; before going to a 750TZ Yamaha four-cylinder engine in a Windle chassis – the best chassis

Elvington circuit, some five miles east of York, 1980. This was Steve's second bike, a Suzuki 750 triple with his brother Kevin as passenger.

at the time, still with brother Kevin in the chair. The first Webster victory came at an Auto 66 Club meeting at Elvington, East Yorkshire in 1980.

Kevin Leaves the Scene

In 1982, the season when he became British Clubman's Champion (his first title), Steve, with Kevin in the chair, was at another Auto 66 meeting, this time at Carnaby, and when negotiating the circuit's chicane Kevin fell out, badly breaking his leg. As sidecar racing is very much about a driver *and* passenger, Steve then had to find another passenger, or quit. And by now firmly hooked on the sport, he decided to find a replacement. And the man he chose was to stay with him for several years, and together the pair would win the first three of Steve's World Championship titles (1987, 1988 and 1989).

Tony Hewitt

That man turned out to be Tony Hewitt. Exactly 10 years older than Steve Webster, Tony had been a Yorkshire rugby union stand-off triallist long before he had even heard of sidecar racing. In fact, he had been persuaded into the motorcycle world by his younger brother John.

With borrowed goggles and a 'puddin basin' helmet, Tony had volunteered to be a passenger for Derek Brown with a six-fifty Triumph outfit. Neither had raced before. And making their debut at Elvington, they were, as *Motor Cycle News* were later to describe: 'A good last.' And Derek Brown ended his one-meeting racing career there and then.

But as for Tony, he most certainly was not packing it in. And so he teamed up with York-based Dave Snape, a partnership which gave Tony not only the thrill, but his apprenticeship in the art of sidecar passengering.

The Carnaby circuit, East Yorkshire, in 1981. Steve is with Tony Hewitt on a Paul Seward of York sponsored Windle Yamaha TZ 750 outfit.

When interviewed by Norrie Whyte after winning his first world title with Steve Webster in 1987, Tony Hewitt described the sensation: 'The feeling you weren't in control was part of the excitement. It was like being on the Big dipper. You've got to be crazy to start passengering.'

After four years – and only a single Cadwell Park club race victory – Dave Snape decided to retire. Next, Tony Hewitt raced with brother John, who by now had a 1000cc Kawasaki and an 850cc BSA.

The Spartan Phoenix

Everything looked rosy and they ordered a Spartan Phoenix engine unit (a square-four two-stroke designed by Barry Hart). But for the Hewitt brothers it was a plan which never reached fruition; Barton Engineering the makers of the Phoenix engine having closed its doors. However, one can see why there was interest in the Phoenix project, Nigel Rollason having gained runner-up spot on a 748cc Phoenix in the 1979 Sidecar TT.

Following this, John Evans, then the man to beat in the South Yorkshire sidecar scene, at the time was advertising for a passenger, so Tony joined him. As a point of interest, Evans had earlier chaired for Tony's brother. Quite a family affair!

A crash with the Scot Roy Shirlaw at Knockhill in which Tony was catapulted over the top ended the Evans-Hewitt relationship. And was to lead directly to an 'out-of-the-blue' telephone call from Steve Webster, who had been put in touch by John Evans.

Later Tony Hewitt was to comment: 'Steve had been trying a few passengers but most went away shaking and unable to cope. We got on OK and I didn't go away shaking, so we had our first-ever race at Snetterton.'

Steve's View

By the time Steve and Tony Hewitt came together, the latter had almost 11 years' experience as a passenger. Steve contacted him after his brother Kevin's accident, saying: 'I needed a stand-in while Kev got better. He sat in for the rest of that year. That became two years, then three. Then we knew we had a good team and we should carry on.'

Later in an interview Tony revealed how the partnership almost never happened, saying: 'I was out and my wife Eileen took the call but didn't get the number right. I couldn't get in touch so I waited for him to phone back. After a month he did but I'd forgotten all abut it.'

Between Kevin's injury and finally getting together, Steve had, as we now know, tried several passengers, most of which came 'highly recommended'.

But that extra spark, that mutual confidence, was simply not there. But when Steve and Tony got together their racing instincts and personalities hit it off, and so the successful pairing was born.

An Ideal Partnership

In many ways the Webster-Hewitt partnership was an ideal one. As Steve revealed when interviewed by John McKenzie for *Road Racer* magazine in its October/November 1987 issue: 'I was a bit wild.' The more experienced Hewitt acted as something of a calming influence. And Steve became notably smoother – and quicker. John McKenzie's view was: 'They learnt a lot from each other, and most importantly they both felt safe and trusted each other implicitly; a state of affairs which it goes without saying is essential in a sidecar.'

The Webster-Hewitt First Season

Their first year together – 1982 – was a pretty successful one, with the pair recording 13 club wins, 12 national restricted victories and the Marlboro British Clubmans Championship title. They also garnered a sixth spot in the British Championship and set new lap records in the Isle of Man Southern 100 (this speed standing for many years) and Cadwell Park's club circuit.

The First Grand Prix

The following year, 1983, saw the pair compete in their first Grand Prix – the British round at Silverstone. And what a debut it turned out to be. Finally finishing the race in fifth place sandwiched between world

May 1982 Mallory Park after a clubman's win with Tony and stepmum Mary.

The 1983 Czech Grand Prix at the old Brno circuit with Tony Hewitt on a Fowler Yamaha.

champions Rolf Biland (fourth) and Werner Schwärzel (sixth). After the race Steve commented: 'I couldn't believe we were there; it's like a village footballer playing at Wembley.'

In fact, Steve and Tony had given Rolf Biland and his LCR outfit a close race, only eventually losing out by a fraction of a second, in the sprint to the flag. The following weekend they went to Sweden and finished 14th after qualifying 10th. It was the first time they had raced abroad, and they obviously suffered from lack of track knowledge of the Anderstorp circuit. Biland won from Alain Michel, Schwärzel and another future champion, Dutchman Egbert Streuer.

By studying their results at the end of that season, the progress being made was clear for everyone to see. As not only had they made a successful first step in Grand Prix racing, but had also gained two club wins, four national wins, one international victory, added to third in the British and 16th in the World Championships.

The 1984 Season

For the 1984 season the pair moved to the Padgetts of Batley squad, and with a 500 LCR outfit (with Yamaha power) racked up three victories and a couple of thirds in domestic national events before moving on to a full season of Grand Prix racing. As Steve commented: 'It's a totally different world. I could never go back now to just weekend racing.' Continuing: 'After a few GPs you get used to setting the bike up and all the practice. We had so much more time to do everything. With scrutineering one day and practice another everything was so stretched out. It took some getting used to.'

The Grand Prix Trail

After qualifying fifth at the opening round of the Grand Prix season, the Austrian GP at the Salzburgring, the pair failed to finish. However, this was soon forgotten, when at the next round, the West German GP at the Nürburgring, Steve and Tony picked up their first Grand Prix rostrum position with a strong third place finish. This came after being forced to borrow an engine from long-time friend and fellow sidecar racer Derek Bailey, after their own had seized in practice.

As Tony Hewitt was to remark later: 'Suddenly I realised – Hell, we're with 'em. After watching Biland, Schwärzel, Streuer and Michel, we were right with them'.

But their lack of experience at this level was to show in that first full GP year, with a number of annoyingly small problems which caused non-finishes at several rounds of the Championship. This was frustrating really, as these usually came after qualifying well during practice. But even so they were to round off the GPs that year seventh in the final round in Sweden, thus giving them sufficient points to be placed eighth in the Championship rankings. Meanwhile, in domestic events, lap records were broken at several circuits.

The Sponsors

In racing, by the beginning of the 1980s sponsorship was becoming a vital factor in reaching the upper branches of any form of motor sport – sidecar

The 1984 French Grand Prix at the Paul Ricard circuit with Tony Hewitt. This LCR outfit was one of only two built for Rolf Biland, he agreed to sell one to Steve.

racing included. And so it was with Steve Webster's climb to the top. Besides his family, his first sponsor was York businessman Paul Seward, who Steve was to tell the press on many occasions: 'Has been with me since the beginning.' He had first noticed Steve and brother Kevin at Croft back in 1980 – because their outfit was painted in International Harvesters colours, one of the products sold by his agricultural machinery business. He had followed this up by offering the pair a lift to Thruxton in his converted bus, and from this his initial purchase of an engine for them followed.

In 1982, Paul Seward supplied them with another new engine, a 750cc Yamaha, and with this they won the Marlboro Clubmans title. Later still, he spent some £13,000 on an LCR chassis for the 1987 season. There is no doubt that Paul Seward played a vital role in Steve Webster's rise to the very top.

Next came Dennis Trollope. This was in the aftermath of Jock Taylor's fatal accident at the Finnish Grand Prix at Imatra on 15 August 1982. Steve commenting: 'Dennis packed up sponsoring anyone on sidecars for a while, but then decided to help out not an established rider, but someone he could bring through the ranks. It was a toss-up between myself and Darren Dixon [the latter to become World Sidecar Champion in 1995 and 1996 – featured in Chapter 25].' Steve continued: 'Darren was a very good sidecar racer, and we were both doing well in the Clubmans Championship. It was just luck that we got the sponsorship.'

As for Silkoline, as Steve revealed in 1987: 'the deal with Silkoline was firstly through Dennis, but now we deal directly with them. They have been with us three or four years now, bar the one year we were with Padgetts. Dennis supplies the Krauser engine and all the Yamaha engine internals.'

A superb portrait with Tony Hewitt taken by Henk Kaulemans for the ERF lorry company.

For the 1985 season the pair reformed their association with Dennis Trollope and Silkoline. And these two sponsors were to play a major role in the Webster/Hewitt progress in future years.

After finishing second and third in the first two rounds of the title race their entire profile was being raised at a rapid rate. And even being talked about as possible Championship contenders.

The Big Crash

Then came the big crash mid-season at Assen, home of the Dutch TT. Traditionally run on a Saturday and in front of a 100,000 plus crowd, Steve and Tony raced to the front of the field; the first time they had led a Grand Prix. In wet conditions they were pulling away from the other competitors after qualifying on pole, and also setting a new lap record. Quite simply, nobody could stay with them, and their first victory at this level looked only a formality. That was until the rear wheel of their outfit touched a white line. Steve was to comment afterwards: 'It just caught the back. I tried to correct it but it spun and we finished up in the ditch.'

Although it meant they were out of the race, this incident certainly had a positive effect on publicity. The race was being televised all over Europe and the footage was shown time and again on TV. However, the crash did have a downside, with a broken arm for Steve and a cracked vertebra for Tony; effectively ending their hopes of Grand Prix glory for that year. But they were able to return for the final race, again in Sweden, where another third place not only lifted them to fourth place in the World Championship series, but reminded everyone of their future potential.

Even with the Assen crash, 1985 can still be judged a pretty successful year. Not only had they also broken no less than 15 lap records, but also gained the British Championship for the first time.

The First GP Victory

In 1986 Steve and Tony scored their first Grand Prix victory. This came in torrential rain at one of the most difficult venues in the GP calendar, the Belgian at Spa Francorchamps. As the author knows only too well, situated in the heavily wooded area of the east of the country, only a few miles from the German border, Spa has its own weather system. And it can be very hot and sunny or just the reverse, cold and wet. In 1986 it was the latter...Even so, the combination of Webster and Hewitt mastered the conditions and, unlike the previous year at Assen, they remained on the track to take a well-earned debut GP victory.

And by the penultimate round in Sweden, the Yorkshire lads were clearly in line for the Championship title. However, it was not to be, a broken gear selector ruining their chances. As Steve later recalled: 'That must have been the worst race of my life.' While Tony Hewitt said: 'I could've just sat down and cried afterwards, Steve kept going hoping a few would drop out and we'd get some points, but we could only manage 15th.'

Then at the final round at Hockenheim, Germany, the pair were chasing Biland and Streuer until they were baulked by a couple of tail-enders and lost ground. Streuer (who had been world champion in 1984 and 1985) took the 1986 crown, thanks to what one commentator called: 'A bumper car routine', from Biland. While the unfortunate Alain Michel, who many felt had a moral claim to the title, finished way down the field thanks to of all things a broken helmet safety strap catch.

World Champions

And so to the 1987 season, the year that Steve and Tony gained the World Championship title for the first time, with three victories from the eight-round series.

The year began with the Spanish GP at Jerez, an all-new circuit for the sidecar competitors, so everyone was on equal footing. This is what Steve told *Motor Cycle News* after they had won, with Alain Michel second: 'After practice I knew I could go for the same speed throughout the race. Others had been running special qualifying tyres. We knew we had the better of them.'

The next round was the West German at Hockenheim. After a battle with Egbert Streuer, Steve won with the Dutchman second and Michel third.

Next came Austria. Although Rolf Biland had failed to qualify at Hockenheim, the Swiss star stormed back to win at the Salzburgring with Streuer second, Michel third and Webster 'struggling' (*Motor Cycle News*) fourth. The problem centred around carburation, following a practice seizure. At the time Steve commented: 'We adjusted too many things instead of sitting down and working things out.' He continued: 'We stuck with carburation, put in bigger jets and slowed everything down. We even put the bigger jets in all four carbs. Below 10,000rpm it wouldn't pull. Early on it was OK, but it ran richer and richer and slower. In the end we were lucky to get fourth.'

Next came the Dutch TT at Assen. In truly awful conditions, the Webster-Hewitt pairing came home runners-up to local hero Streuer and his passenger Bernhard Schneiders, Steve commenting: 'A good start was essential to get out of the spray. And we knew Egbert [Streuer] was going for it. He got the start, and in the end, we were pleased to finish second.'

In France, at Le Mans, victory again went to Biland with Streuer second and Webster third. Practice went well until the final session, when a front brake disc warped. So the team then had only the 10-minute race day morning warm-up to bed in the disc – which wasn't long enough. This meant that in the race Steve had to adjust the knob which altered the brake bias between the front and rear. As Steve said after the race: 'It took three goes before I got the setting correct.'

Fantastic Scenes At Donington

For 1987 the British GP had been transferred from Silverstone to Donington Park. And as Steve was to admit: 'It gave a big advantage to the Brits, even though we hadn't experienced the new half-mile [0.8km] Melbourne Loop section.'

The race developed into a tussle between Webster and Biland. Steve was faster from Redgate to Coppice, but Rolf was quicker through the new section. As Steve was to recall the same year: 'Everything was set for a British win. It was a shame when Rolf retired, but I'm sure I could have beaten him.' And even though the sidecar race was late in the day Steve recalled: 'It was an experience I'll never forget; all those people lining the track as Tony and I did our lap of honour.'

Taken in 1987 before the Swedish Grand Prix. All were in with a chance of winning the world title. The photograph was titled 'fishing for the world title'. Standing, from left to right: Tony Hewitt, Bernard Schnieders and Jean Marc Fresc. Kneeling: Steve Webster, Egbert Streuer and Alain Michel.

Crunch Time In Sweden

The final round of the 1987 Championship series was in Sweden. And it was here that Steve was to realise the importance of race tactics and reading the race. It was more important to him to stay ahead of Egbert Streuer (his main Championship rival at the time). But when Egbert slowed Steve thought: 'It would be nice to clinch the crown with a win.' However, Rolf Biland had other ideas. He, too, wanted to win. And Rolf held it very tight into the penultimate corner, so Steve went wide to pass him on the exit. However,

Celebrating in 1987 after winning at the Swedish Grand Prix at Anderstorp. This gave Steve and Tony Hewitt their first world title. There is a tradition in Sweden of jumping into a swimming pool. Steve and Tony are already in the pool and Steve's dad Mick is diving in. This was then followed by other sidecar competitors.

wily campaigner as he was, Biland saw what Steve was attempting to do, and as Steve was to recall: 'He just came across and banged into us. It sure took the edge of what should have been a memorable day.' Even so, Steve and Tony were the new world champions.

A Trio Of Titles

1987 was followed by two more consecutive word titles in 1988 and 1989, for the Webster/Hewitt pairing. But then Tony retired, to be replaced by Gavin Simmons. Between 1983 and 1989, Steve and Tony had taken part in 43 races counting towards World Championship points, winning 10 of them.

The ratio was to improve with Gavin, even though in their first full season together in 1990 the pair finished third in the title chase (won that year by Alain Michel and Simon Birchall).

Also on 25 July 1990 Steve Webster received the MBE from Her Majesty Queen Elizabeth at Buckingham Palace, London.

At Rolf Steinhausen's retirement party in Germany in 1989. Steve is being a passenger for a change. Rolf is sat on the BMW outfit. Kneeling to Steve's left is Rolf Biland, stood directly above Steve is Max Deubel and to Max's right is Bernard Schnieders.

Champion Again

In 1991 Steve regained his world crown with five victories; in the US, Spain, Italy, Austria and the European GP (at Jarama in Spain).

Then came three years – 1992, 1993 and 1994 – when Steve finished runner-up. In the final year he had Adolf Hänni as passenger, to replace the departed Gavin Simmons. In 42 races together Steve and Gavin had won 13 races.

During the season with Adolf Häinni in 1994, Steve did not have any victories in the World Championship series.

David James

Then in 1995 he only entered a single race, the last GP of the season (in Spain) and finished fifth with new passenger David James. Actually David had worked for the author after leaving school in the mid-late 1970s before joining the Tony Smith Race School and later having his own tuning business in Wisbech, Cambridgeshire. David currently runs the Ducati website and lives in Italy.

The 1996 Spanish Grand Prix at Jerez with passenger David James (David now works for Ducati in Italy). They were on a Bosiger-sponsored outfit.

Certainly, his time with Steve Webster was to be a successful one, the pair winning three world titles (1997, 1998 and 1999). Although it should be pointed out that during this period the Championship series was referred to as the FIM World Cup.

In their first full season together, 1996, Steve finished third in the world title rankings.

Also the ratio of wins to races was to prove the best of any passenger (at world level) when Steve had David James in the chair – 29 races, 16 victories.

This LCR chassis, in Steve's opinion, is the best outfit he has ridden; he used it from 2002 to 2005. It is fitted with a Suzuki GSXR 1000cc K4 engine and has many titanium parts.

Paul Woodhead

Steve's final passenger was Paul Woodhead, whom he had from 2000 to 2004. In the five years the pairing won 21 races from 43 starts. And they gained three world titles together (2000, 2003 and 2004), were runners-up in 2001 and fourth in 2002.

Together, in 2004, the pair also won the UEM European Championship and the Eastern Airways British Sidecar Championship title.

In Retrospect

Looking back, Steve Webster can be truly proud of what he had achieved – not only his fantastic race record, but the way he had achieved these successes. He has been, and still is, an ambassador for the sport of sidecar racing. And is still very much involved in several ways as *Sidecar Champions Since 1923* was being written in 2010; even appearing in television interviews to provide an experts view in race reports. Long may this state of affairs continue.

Lodge Corner at Oulton Park, Cheshire, 25 June 2010. Steve is on a demonstration ride with passenger Steve Day, the Thundersport commentator. The LCR Suzuki outfit he is using is normally ridden by Scott Lawrie and James Neave, the 2010 Scottish champions.

CHAPTER 24

ALAIN MICHEL

Frenchman Alain Michel, the 1990 world champion (with Englishman Simon Birchall as his passenger), was the first and only one of his countrymen to have so far won the world sidecar crown.

This came after a decade-and-a-half of trying. He had already taken second place in the Championship on three occasions, in 1978 and 1981 to Rolf Biland and in 1976 to Egbert Streuer; Alain had also had four third places and four fourth places to his credit. He was nothing if not determined and had shown real staying power. However, his dream of the title had eluded him until 1990 – and the previous year he had been third. In the author's mind having the highly experienced Simon Birchall as his passenger proved to be the final piece in the Frenchman's bid to take the crown.

18 Grand Prix Victories
The eventual winner of 18 Grand Prix' (one more than four-times champion Eric Oliver), Alain Michel was born in the French town of Montelimar on 23 February 1953 and began racing in 1975, at the age of 22.

His Grand Prix debut came the following year at the French GP at Le Mans, the first round of the 1976 Championship series. And what a sensational debut it was too – when Alain passengered by Bernard Garcia finished runner-up to no lesser man than Rolf Biland. Driving a Yamaha-powered GEP outfit, the Frenchman put in what is probably the most sensational debut at Grand Prix level in recent history.

But although Alain was to finish sixth in the next round, at the Salzburgring, Austria, his real charge for World Championship points did not begin until 1977, when passengered by Gerard Lecorre the pair were placed fifth in the points ranking – behind George O'Dell (champion), Rolf Biland, Werner Schwärzel and Rolf Steinhausen.

The 1978 Season
It was during the 1978 season when Alain Michel really began to make his mark on a regular basis in the GPs. This year there were eight rounds to the Championship.

The first of these came in Austria, at the Salzburgring circuit. Here Rolf Biland ran out the winner, with Britain's Mac Hobson runner-up. Next came

Alain Michel, with yet another passenger, Stuart Collins. Fourth was the previous year's world champion, George O'Dell, with Bruno Holzer fifth.

As for machinery, the GEP chassis had been ditched in favour of the Swiss-made Seymaz, pioneered by Rolf Biland.

Runner-up in France

On home soil Alain Michel and passenger Stuart Collins finished runners-up to Biland at Nogaro, with Hobson third and O'Dell fourth. Sadly, shortly afterward while competing in the Isle of Man TT (now a non-Championship round) Mac Hobson suffered a fatal accident.

At the third round, in Italy (Mugello), Alain did not score any points and this run of bad luck continued in the next race, the Dutch TT at Assen.

However, in round five, the Belgian GP at Spa Francorchamps, Alain Michel and Stuart Collins came home runners-up to Bruno Holzer, with Biland third and Steinhausen fourth.

The First Grand Prix Victory

The British Grand Prix at Silverstone was the setting for Alain Michel's GP debut victory, achieved at an average speed of 96.57mph (155.413km/h). This was achieved against world-class opposition including Rolf Biland (runner-up), Jock Taylor (third), George O'Dell (fifth) and Siegfried Schauzu (ninth).

The Silverstone success was followed by a second (to Werner Schwärzel) at the Nürburgring in Germany.

A Second GP Victory

At the final round of the 1978 season Alain and Stuart scored their second GP victory, beating Rolf Biland once more, with Dick Greasley third and Jock Taylor fourth.

This meant that the Franco/British pairing were to finish that year runners-up in the Championship, which had been won by Rolf Biland and his passenger Kenny Williams, driving the controversial Yamaha-engined BEO outfit, which made considerable use of F1 car technology.

1979 – The Year Of Two Championships

1979 was unique, as it saw the running of *two* World Sidecar Championships – B–2–A and B–2–B. This had really come about due to the technology introduced to the sport via Rolf Biland (see Chapter 19). Like several other drivers Alain Michel (still passengered by Stuart Collins) actually took part in both series, however in Alain's case although he competed season long in the 'A' category, he only took part in one 'B' race, this being the Dutch TT round which was staged as a 750cc event, which he (passengered by Michael Burckhart) won, averaging 89.167mph (143.495km/h).

The New Era

For the 1980 season the FIM reverted to a single Championship, but one which essentially embraced the 'A' category for the previous year – involving the new technology. Something which was to be retained in future years. These new machines were henceforth referred to as 'worms' and were much longer and more fully streamlined than the previous generation of outfits. And from then on there were the F1 'worms' and F2 conventional designs. At lower levels of the sport F1s and F2s often competed at the same meetings. But at GP level only the former were competitive enough to win. Also, again non-Championship level sidecar racing saw either a 350cc two-stroke or 600cc engines allowed for F2, whereas bigger 1000cc or even 1200cc engines were allowed in the F1 class. However, for a considerable number of years the World Championship outfits were restricted to 500cc, which effectively meant two-stroke engines (usually either Yamaha or Krauser).

As far as the Championship was concerned, in 1980, Alain finished third overall in the ratings. Of the eight races that year four were won by Jock Taylor (that year's champion), three by Rolf Biland (second overall) and one by Derek Jones.

As for Alain and passenger Michael Burckhart, they finished runners-up on no fewer that five occasions (Yugoslavia, Holland, Belgium,

Frenchman Alain Michel and passenger Michael Burckhart (500cc Seymaz) during the 1981 British Grand Prix at Silverstone in August that year.

A year later at Silverstone, with a Sonauto Yamaha, they finished third.

Czechoslovakia and Germany); they also came eighth at the opening round, the French GP at Le Castellet.

Runners-up in 1981

In 1981 the Championship was extended to a total of 10 rounds – Austria (Salzburgring), Germany (Hockenheim), France (Le Castellet), Spain (Jarama), Holland (Assen), Belgium (Spa Francorchamps), Britain (Silverstone), Finland (Imatra), Sweden (Anderstorp) and Czechoslovakia (Brno).

With two victories (Hockenheim and Assen), three seconds (Brno, Jarama and Anderstorp) plus a quartet of third positions (Salzburgring, Le Castellet, Spa Francorchamps and Silverstone), Alain and Michael had a consistent and successful season. And Alain had matched his previous best GP season, 1978, by finishing runner-up.

By 1983 Alain Michel (now with Claude Monchaud as passenger) had yet another outfit.

Silverstone 1983. Alain Michel (3) and Derek Jones (5) battle it out for second spot, which Michel ultimately won, with Jones third.

The Remainder of the 1980s

For the remainder of the 1980s Alain Michel tried, with varying degrees of success, to secure his dream of becoming World Sidecar Champion, but the closest he got was another third in 1989.

But the situation was to change rapidly after teaming up with Yorkshireman Simon Birchall (see separate boxed section within this chapter). Simon was already highly experienced having already passengered the likes of Steve Webster, Dave Saville, Derek Jones, Egbert Streuer and Rolf Steinhausen, to name but a few.

World Champion At Last

And so to the 1990 season when Alain was at last to live the dream – and become world champion.

The first round of the Championship series was across the Atlantic at Leguna Seca in the US on 8 April. And what a start, with Alain and Simon powering to an impressive victory, some 20 seconds ahead of the field, led by the pairing of Steve Webster and Gavin Simmons. Yet it had been much closer in the early stages of the race, with no fewer than five crews bidding for glory – Michel/Birchall and Webster/Simmons plus Biland/Waltisperg, Streuer/Haas and the Egloff brothers.

Round two was the Spanish Grand Prix at Jerez, here Webster and Simmons put in a faultless performance including breaking the lap record before being slowed towards the end by a niggling brake issue. Alain and Simon were able

The Elf team in 1990, the year Alain won the title (with passenger Simon Birchall). The pair are on the front row (Simon second left, Alain fourth left).

to close as a result but were never in a position to make a serious challenge; this after the pair had worked hard to overcome the difficult Streuer/Haas.

Round three was in Italy, at Misano. Webster had crashed in practice, and it was Michel who set the pace in the race, but was then to strike mechanical gremlins. But when Webster went past, Alain hit back, holding the initiative till three laps from the end, when the Frenchman lost fifth gear and was forced to quit.

Round four was not any better as far as Alain and Simon were concerned, as during the German GP at the Nürburgring they were forced out with engine problems.

Next came the Austrian round at the Salzburgring. Here the race was run in a track streaming from torrential rain. It was very much a case of whoever got in front at the start had a clear vision, and amid clouds of spray the remaining crews were at a disadvantage, including Alain Michel and Simon Birchall.

Steve Webster attempted to close on Egbert Streuer, but was forced back. Then Alain Michel attempted to pass Webster, but he too was blinded by the vast amount of water being thrown up and in the end took a 'solid' (*Motor Cycle News*) third place ahead of a despondent Rolf Biland who had struggled to combat a series of engine problems experienced during practice and in the race.

Victory Number Two

Victory number two in 1990 came at round six, the Yugoslavian GP at Rijeka on 17 June. Streuer led early on, but Alain overtook the Dutchman

A Passenger View

Simon Birchall, who was the 1990 World Sidecar Passenger to Alain Michel, was born in Goole, East Yorkshire on 5 June 1958. His father Dennis was a shopkeeper and snooker club owner at Rawcliffe, some four miles from Goole, and knew many of that sport's top names including Alex 'Hurricane' Higgins and Steve Davis. As Simon admits himself, he was: 'always interested in bikes.'

His first motorcycle was an old five-hundred BSA side-valve single, which was followed when 16 years of age by a Garelli sports moped. Simon was bitten by the sidecar racing bug during the early 1970s and began his career as a passenger with local man Mick Harvey who had been competing for some 40 years. The first race together being a club event at Cadwell Park, Lincolnshire, in 1974 – illegally – as in reality Simon was not old enough for a racing licence!

Before his spell with Alain Michel, Simon had also been a passenger with Mick Barton, Derek Jones, Dave Saville, Barry Bridley, Derek Brindley, Theo van Kempen (Egbert Streuer Team), Martin Zurbrügg and Steve Webster. In fact, it was the latter who had recommended Simon to Alain Michel. And racing journalist Alan Cathcart was later to remark: 'Bet he wondered why he bothered, seeing as Alain Michel gives a lot of the credit for his Championship to his passenger.'

The following is what Alain Michel himself had to say in 1991: 'I don't want to take anything away from my previous passengers, who all did their very best for me when we rode together.' Continuing: 'But Simon is the first passenger I have ever raced with who I can completely forget about when we're on the track. He is so amazingly strong and fit, as well as skilled, that I know I can depend on him not only to do the right thing in the chair, but keep on doing it even up to the end of a gruelling race on

Simon Birchall passengered for many of the world's top sidecar drivers over almost two decades. He is seen here in the 1970s with a few of his awards.

a physically tiring track like Jerez or Hungaroring. This allows one to drive as hard as I can just thinking about my own race, rather like riding a solo, without having to make allowances for the passenger. Simon's also very helpful technically, which since we do all our own preparations and don't employ a mechanic, is very important. And we get on well together personally, even if we have the odd stand-up argument from time to time when we know the other's wrong about something.'

When interviewed for *MCN Eurosport* after winning the world title, Simon attempted to explain what it was like as a passenger: 'you don't have to be crazy, but a bit…well it's hard to explain. It's not a job for the nervous. You've got to feel what the tyres and chassis are doing all the time. You can make the bike move up to 1.5 metres in a corner just by shifting your weight. In the rain things are more difficult. It's slower but you've got to be more positive and accurate. And when it's wet, it's bloody cold too.'

A deep understanding of mechanical details is also vitally important. And here Simon was an undoubted star. An example of this came in July 1990 during practice at Le Mans for the French Grand Prix. Simon noticed a small change in gearbox noise, even above the scream of the Krauser engine. He listened, counted the gear changes to identify which gear was playing up and told Alain Michel second gear was on its way out, but initially the Frenchman thought it was alright and wanted to continue. They finished the session, stripped the gearbox and found a tooth had broken off second gear…

Techniques among the top passengers vary. When Simon was asked by journalist John McKenzie to explain his skill, he struggled. In the end McKenzie said: 'He just does it – its second nature.'

During the period in which he raced at the top level Simon feels the four drivers were Steve Webster, Egbert Streuer, Alain Michel and Rolf Biland. And of experience with the sidecar racing fraternity, he simply says: 'Fantastic people, ones you can class as true friends.'

When Alain Michel decided to quit, Simon followed suit, and their last season was 1991. As a highlight after this date, Simon recalls a visit to Buckingham Palace in 1993, the 40th anniversary to the Queen's ascension to the throne back in 1953. As Simon recalls: 'There was every world champion – some 1,700 of them – every sport, there were jockeys, Formula 1 drivers, you name it they were there, including me.'

Today he runs his own engineering company and a small property development in Hook, a couple of miles outside Goole.

on the third lap, then was taken by Webster, only to regain the advantage and secure victory ahead of Streuer who had fought his way past third place Webster.

However, as one press report said at the time: 'Michel's success owed much to passenger Birchall pushing himself through the pain barrier to hang on in. He had aggravated a shoulder injury in a spill during untimed warm-up but bravely battled on.'

The pair also had the satisfaction of setting the fastest lap at 98.65mph (158.72km/h).

Victory Number Three

Next came the Dutch TT at Assen on Saturday 30 June and Michel's third Championship victory of the year. While the Championship series leader Steve Webster retired with mechanical woes (the first time this had happened in 40 GPs), Alain Michel's winning performance was achieved in a stylish fashion after he had reeled in the early leader Rolf Biland. But it was not always as easy as it might sound, an overheating engine in the latter stages slowing him down.

At round eight, the Belgian GP at Spa, mechanical problems hit Webster, a shaft breaking to wreak the transmission but he managed to coast home into sixth and salvage some points. The race was run in wet conditions. Michel, battling through the spray, took second place to dramatically close the gap in the table stakes, with Streuer taking victory.

Round nine, the French GP at Le Mans, saw a reversal of fortunes, with Webster putting his troubles behind him with a confidence-boosting victory

Alain Michel (with Avon cap) and Simon Birchall at the Dutch TT in 1990.

Alain and Simon leading
Steve Webster during
1990.

which re-asserted his position at the head of the points table, especially as arch-rival Michel hit his own mechanical problems.

At the start of the race, the Frenchman, despite the sweltering heat, was determined to grab a home victory, and led briefly before engine trouble forced him into an early retirement. And as Webster went on to win and thus gain maximum points, Alain Michel was back in third position in the points table with 111, compared to Streuer (who had finished runner-up in France) on 115 and Webster leading on 136.

The pair racing in the
British Grand Prix at
Donington Park in 1990.

Alain Michel and Simon
Birchall (Krauser LCR)
looking happy after
winning in their
Championship season.
Photo W. Gruber/Archiv

Next came the British GP at Donington Park, which was won by Streuer. Michel, battling throughout the race, finally saw Streuer nipping through on the last corner. Simon Birchall told the author: 'This was the one race I really wanted to win – my home Grand Prix'.

Two More Victories And The Title

Then came the final two rounds of the 1990 season; the Swedish GP at Anderstorp followed by the Czech GP at Bruno. And with victories in both events Alain Michel and his passenger Simon Birchall were crowned World Sidecar Champions, with 178 points compared to runner-up Egbert Streuer on 167 and Steve Webster with 160.

For Alain Michel it had been a long, expensive and often frustrating journey to the summit. Even he was beginning to doubt it would be achievable. However, in partnership with Simon Birchall the dream had become a reality. Entered as Team ELF LCR-Krauser, the Michel/Birchall title was the first ever won by the French petroleum giant as a primary sponsor.

The Final GP Victory

Keen to defend his hard-earned title Alain Michel (still partnered by Simon Birchall) contested the GPs in 1991; however, this time he could only win a solitary race, the San Marino Grand Prix at Mugello. This was largely due to problems with Czech-made gearboxes that year. And so, after a decade and a half of racing at the very top level, and having achieved his ambition, Alain Michel retired.

The 1990 world champions found the going much harder the following year, when in 1991 they suffered a series of problems with Czech-made gearboxes, winning a solitary Grand Prix, the San Marino round at Mugello.

So what sort of man was Alain Michel? Well, this is what Simon Birchall told the author recently: 'Alain was very confident, very positive and hungry for the World Championship title.' Simon also pointed out that Alain: 'Used to do all his own engine work.' And that his wife, Dominique, played a vital role in the Michel team: 'A fantastic cook, did everything, even recording lap times and kept everything in order; Dominique was a very important factor in Alain's success.' In fact, Dominique acted as everything from team manager to chef to accountant, as one journalist of the day described.

In Retrospect

As Alan Cathcart said in the July 1991 issue of *Motor Cycle International*: 'Michel's world crown was undoubtedly the most popular and best-deserved title of recent years.'

And when one looks back at the Frenchman's career it is easy to understand Alan Cathcart's view. As in the 15 years since he finished second in his home GP in his first season at that level, Alain Michel had raced in over 120 GPs, won 18 of them, finished second 26 times and had been third on 16 occasions. That's 60 times on the podium, averaging once every two races. He had finished second in the World Championship three times: 1978, 1981 and 1985 – third three times and fourth four times – until 1990 when justice was finally done. At the rip old age of 39.

Alain Michel's ultimate success was not only a tribute to his skill as a driver, but also as an engineer.

He not only built his own engines but carried out an extensive development programme which resulted in his Krauser engine putting out an impressive 175bhp at 12,500rpm at the gearbox sprocket. Conversely, this benefited not only Alain but ironically his greatest rival – and friend – Steve Webster, a customer of Alain Michel's tuning firm AM Energie! This also tells you much about sidecar racing itself – not just the rivalry, but the undoubted comradeship of the three-wheel brigade.

CHAPTER 25

DARREN DIXON

Darren Dixon, born 9 August 1960 in Kent, is the only man in British motorcycling road racing history to win National Solo together with European and World Sidecar Championships. His natural ability on a motorcycle together with his mastering the art of transition from two to three wheels surpassed the accomplishments of past masters Eric Oliver and Freddie Dixon. With competitive parents Ray and Eileen Dixon, he had the base support and drive together with the experience and ambition to fulfil his dreams. Ray Dixon had a wealth of motorcycle experience from post office delivery boy to solo road racing before moving over to sidecars and pioneering the use of Saab rally works car engine in his outfit. Ray's wife Eileen, mother to Kim born in 1958, Darren 1960, Karen 1962 and Sean 1964, on an occasion passengered the Saab outfit, on which they had a memorable win at the nearby Lydden circuit, not far from the family home.

Competitive by Nature

Always competitive by nature, Darren's early motorcycle experience was riding a little auto scooter round the family garden at about the age of 10. Later this progressed to riding with other lads on local land together with Trevor Banks who would go on to become a grasstrack star. Despite working in the family motorcycle business after leaving school, Darren did not show any interest in racing motorcycles until the age of 20 when he announced he fancied having a go at sidecar racing. Father Ray's reaction was that if Darren was to be given the best possible chance of success they should purchase the best outfit available, within their budget. This was none other than the ex-Jock Taylor Yamaha TZ750 engine Windle outfit. With Terry McGann as passenger, Darren took to three wheels like a natural. Success came immediately when they won the 1981 BMCRC Sidecar Championship that year. In 1982 the Marlboro British Clubmans Sidecar Championship was contested by Darren and Terry, and they finished second to none other than Steve Webster, this despite a broken wire robbing them of an overall win. The outfit was sold at the end of the season and the winter spent contemplating future direction within their financial budget and looking for sponsorship. Unable to secure anything substantial, Darren took a year out.

Ray Dixon

Born in 1936, Ray Dixon's early motorcycling was spent as a post office delivery boy on a BSA Bantam in the Orpington, Kent area. Often racing other delivery boys on their rounds gave Ray early competitiveness. Called up for National Service, he joined the REME as a mechanic from 1954–57. The training and experience of all types of vehicles was a good grounding for later years. During service in the Far East at Kuala Lumpur, he organised the army motorcycle trials section using an endless supply of WD machines. Bend or damage one, another was soon requisitioned. On leaving the forces, he found work as a car mechanic, often visiting Brands Hatch and Crystal Palace on his days off. His everyday transport was a Velocette MAC 350cc, and he soon developed the urge to go racing himself. A seven-year-old Velocette KTT Mark VIII took his eye, and he purchased it from Roy Mayhew, as Roy was upgrading to a Manx Norton. Ray's first race meeting was in 1957 at Brands Hatch, and in his first race he finished a commendable third behind none other than Derek Minter. Riding in mainly Bemsee meetings, he took top-five places at Silverstone, Crystal Palace and Castle Coombe, plus a win at Brands Hatch beating Des Craig (Joe's son) riding the works Norton. By the end of the year he had gained enough points for an international licence.

Ray's racing career was spent mainly riding in BMCRC events. For 1958 he purchased a BSA 500 Gold Star, the highlights of the year being a fourth place at Crystal Palace and being picked by BMCRC to ride in the Clubman's, held that year at Oulton Park.

The Gold Star was replaced by a Matchless G45 twin but, as Ray put it, it was 'not the most competitive machine' and results were nothing to write home about. He did, however, compete in one of three meetings ever held at the Biggin Hill aerodrome. Ray had met Eileen and decided to get married, so the G45 was sold and the £200 raised used as a deposit on

Darren Dixon's father Ray was a successful sidecar racer in his own right. Ray is seen here in 1971 with passenger Chris Philpott and their Saab 3-cylinder two-stroke outfit.

a house at Wingham, near Canterbury, Kent. The move to Wingham coincided with a job at Arter Brothers, the Barham Agricultural Engineers. Tom and Edgerton Arter were the legendary sponsors of TT riders Mike Duff and Peter Williams, among others. To enable Ray to get to work as a storeman, the Arter brothers supplied him with a Francis Barnett trials bike. Any thoughts of racing were now put aside as the Dixon family blossomed; Ray and Eileen became parents to Kim in 1958, Darren in 1960, Karen in 1962 and Sean in 1962. The job with Arters gave way to Ray seeking other horizons to keep the expanding family. He became Southern England representative for Bill Hannah, the notorious Liverpool-based entrepreneur who had purchased a massive stock of Ducatis originally bound for the American importers, Berliner.

Then in 1967 the urge to go racing returned, and as solo machines were expensive to buy and maintain on one's own he looked at sidecars. With prospective passenger and financial contributor Pip Howard, Ray purchased a Triumph T110-engined outfit. They soon got to grips with this new sport, despite having to replace the front wheel many times because of broken spokes caused by their exuberant riding twisting the rim. They won several races at Brands Hatch and Lydden but found the Triumph engine underpowered and expensive to tune. Ray looked around for an alternative power unit and a lightweight three-cylinder Saab two-stroke car engine from a damaged vehicle was purchased and grafted into the existing chassis. This was raced throughout 1968–69 with new passenger Bob Simpson; occasionally winning at Brands Hatch and Lydden. A major accident at Castle Coombe put both rider and passenger in hospital, with Ray sustaining a broken back.

1970, following a win at Brands Hatch, brought Ray's efforts to the attentions of the Saab importers, who invited him to their headquarters. They offered Ray a works rally engine as used by their factory drivers, and he came away with the said unit. Armed with this potent motor, Ray commissioned a new mini-wheeled chassis built by Derek Bailey and Eric Parkinson. With this new outfit Ray was able to beat his nemesis at Lydden, Ron Waters and Graham Croucher, who had dominated many races.

During this period often passengered by Bob Simpson, Ray's wife Eileen thought she would like a go in the chair, and on a Brands Hatch practice day she gave it a go. The early laps were quite hairy as she got used to what to do, and on entering Surtees bend she wrongly positioned herself and Ray had to take to the grass, almost collecting other outfits as they rounded Clearways. Undeterred, the Dixons entered a meeting at Lydden and during one of the qualifying heats Eileen knocked the distributor cap clip off the Saab engine and the rotor flew out, never to be seen again. Ray set off to nearby Canterbury and managed to buy a replacement, returned, fitted it and the couple went on to win the final, a truly memorable occasion.

The Saab carried Ray to a fourth place behind Siegfried Schauzu at Brands Hatch International meeting in 1971. The following year he claimed second place in the Isle of Man Southern 100, together with wins at Brands Hatch and Lydden.

By now Ray, together with business partner Pete Denman, had formed Golden Valley Motorcycles in Cheriton, Folkestone, with Yamaha and Honda agencies. The partners ran this business successfully until 1979, when Ray decided to branch out on his own, purchasing the former Co-op grocery store at Coombe Valley, Dover. Coombe Valley Motorcycles was launched and soon had a Kawasaki main agency, plus adding Morini and MZ.

With sons Darren and Sean taking up sidecar racing with the initial purchase of the ex-Jock Taylor Windle outfit and help and guidance from Ray, the family was well and truly into the motorcycle trade. Darren would take a leading role running the workshop side, with Ray turning the sales side over to Dave Williams in 1989 when he decided to take a back seat. Dave Williams prematurely passed away, and Darren took over the entire running of the business, made easier when he retired from racing. Now, with Darren's daughter Kelly joining him, the family business looks forward to the future.

Ray, from his beautifully sited bungalow within sight of his beloved Lydden circuit (he has written a book on Lydden's history), keeps his hand in maintaining his latest acquisition, a 1934 Velocette KTT Mark IV which at one time held a Brands Hatch grass track record. At times Ray can be seen circulating Lydden on the Velo during track days, mixing it with the guys on modern 1000cc machines. Once a racer, always a racer. He has the added interest following his grandson Jake, Darren's son, who is competing in the Aprillia Superteen series on an RS125, and shows talent to be developed and what a chance with guidance from Ray and Darren, who both know what it takes to make a champion.

Reminiscing to when money was tight with a growing family and finding cash to go racing, Ray and Eileen turned to manufacturing garden gnomes in their spare time, from moulds available at that time. Family and any visitors were coerced into painting the little fellows. Once a number had been made, Eileen would set off to hawk them around the countryside to garden centres etc.

Pip Howard

Pip Howard, successful business man and former passenger to Darren's dad Ray, purchased an ex-Gary Lingham Suzuki RG500 to ride himself, but on test practice day at Brands Hatch offered Darren the chance to do a few laps on it. He was blown away by Darren's sheer speed and lap times which were well below his own, and he offered Darren the chance to race it for the future.

Darren's first season on the Suzuki saw him win the Lord of Lydden title and a round of the Marlboro Clubman's Championship.

For 1985 Pip Howard bought a Honda RS250 and Darren clinched the nine-round Marlboro 250cc British Clubmans Championship. And at the final, televised round at Silverstone Darren finished second in an epic dual with Carl Fogarty, with the duo lapping in excess of 106mph (170.5km/h).

For 1986 Darren moved to the British Open 250cc class, again on the Honda RS250, finishing the year in third place behind works Armstrong riders Niall McKenzie and Donnie McLeod. However he did manage to win the final round at Brands Hatch in the wet.

Solo rider Darren Dixon (1) leading Carl Fogarty to the 250cc British Championship at Silverstone in 1985.

1987

In 1987 the versatility of Darren's ability to ride almost anything began to show when he took a production Yamaha TZR250, sponsored by local Kent dealer Colwins of Sittingbourne, to second place in the World TZR series. He also rode in limited rounds of the Shell Oils Superstock Championship on a Kawasaki GPX750 in Duckhams Oils colours to finish eighth overall.

His performances to date had now attracted the attention of long-time successful sponsors Padgetts of Batley. Brothers Peter and Don Padgett, who were legendary in their approach to road racing, now had Peter's son Clive, an ex-rider himself, running things and Darren was a natural enhancement to the team for 1988.

In his first year for Padgetts, Darren, riding a Suzuki RG500, won the British Formula 1 Championship, the forerunner of what turned into the British Superbike Championship. He also rode on a Suzuki GSXR750. And despite only taking part in six rounds, he finished 10th in the British Superstocks. He also competed in four rounds of the European 500 Championships on the RG, finishing ninth overall.

All this time Darren still managed to hold down his job in the workshop of the family business!

An Irish Debut

The next year, 1989, saw Darren's career stall a bit. He joined the Irish Francis Neal team for a period, riding a Honda NSR500 in the North West 200. Darren's first time on the circuit, he amazingly led the race until the final lap when the engine seized. A one-off outing on a Yamaha FZR750 in the prestigious Japanese Suzuki eight-hour race with co-rider Bob Holden

Darren with his Padgetts-backed outfit, 1990.

saw the pair lapping on the pace until machine reliability let them down and they failed to finish. A somewhat frustrating year of mechanical misfortunes ended with a sixth place at Brands Hatch in the Powerbike International, back on a Padgetts Yamaha OWO1.

Sidecars once again attracted Darren's attention, and after talks with the Padgetts he decided to have another crack at it for 1990. This time he had younger brother Sean in the chair, and, despite Sean having never been passenger before, they gelled straight away. In their first year they won the European Sidecar Championship on an LCR 500cc JPX engined outfit, with wins in Hungary, Holland and Sweden, runners-up in Great Britain and the Czech Republic, and fourth in Germany.

The World Championships Beckon

The World Championships beckoned in 1991, and, with a Padgetts supplied LCR Krauser outfit, the brothers set out. The highlight of the year was a third place podium finish at Laguna Seca in the USA, with both brothers describing the plunge down the corkscrew section of the circuit as: 'The experience of a lifetime.' Taking in 12 rounds of the Championship, they finished 11th overall.

Darren Dixon was a major success on both three and two wheels. Here he is seen with both his Padgett sidecar machine and 500cc solo Grand Prix bike.

Having got married and with work commitments, Sean stepped down as passenger, and for 1992 Andy Hetherington from Yorkshire took over as Darren's passenger. Andy had previous experience with Eddie Wright. Podium finishes in Germany, Great Britain and Holland took the pair to fifth overall in the World Championships.

1993 saw Darren and Andy have a mixed year, with several non-finishes with minor problems. But they still managed to take 10th overall in the Championship rankings.

This improved in 1994 with a win at Catalyuna and A1 Ring and a second at Assen, leaving them in seventh place overall at the end of the season.

One unique event of the year took place at the German Grand Prix, when Darren competed in both the 500cc race on a Yamaha YZF500 V4 and also the Sidecar event. Unfortunately punted onto the grass on the solo ended in retirement, and the sidecar suffered a puncture and also retired.

A Windle Chassis

For 1995, in a team with sponsorship out together by Aden Murcott, Darren obtained a Windle chassis built by Terry Windle. With assistance from and the loan of the ADM engine by its creator Alf Du Mur the brilliant Swiss engineer who would accompany them to the world series, the team set out in the most determined fashion to date.

Such was the reliability of the ADM engine, matched to the skill of Darren Dixon and Andy Hetherington, that they dominated the Championship for the next two years, becoming world champions in 1995 and 1996. This ended the run of success for Rolf Biland and Kurt Waltisperg.

Two World Championship Titles

1995 also saw the English pair take victories in the German and Dutch Grand Prix, together with podium finishes at Mugello, Le Mans and Catalyuna. At the season's end, with determined driving and reliable equipment, Darren and Andy had amassed a substantial points margin over the Swiss driver Rolf Biland.

1996 was more of the same with victories at the Dutch and German Grand Prix, but this time adding the prestige of a home win at the British round at Donington, heading Rolf Biland/Kurt Waltisperg and Steve Webster/David James. Podium finishes at Mugello and the A1 Ring once again gave Darren and Andy the World Championship.

The 1995 and 1996 World Sidecar Champion Darren Dixon and passenger Andy Hetherington. The outfit, using a Windle chassis, was powered by an ADM engine, created by the brilliant Swiss engineer, Alf Du Mur.

Retiring from three-wheels

Having fulfilled his dream, Darren retired from three wheels at the height of his career, but made an abortive effort at returning to solo machines after testing a 250cc ADM machine and then the possible use of a 500cc unit floundered when sponsorship failed to materialise to run in Grand Prixs. A somewhat bemused and disillusioned Darren then channelled his expertise into the family business in Dover, and Andy Hetherington took up hang gliding at extreme levels. For a time in 1997–98 Darren managed a team for former sponsor Aden Murcott with riders Dave Wood and Dave Heal on solo machines.

Darren's talent on a solo was never fully developed and glimpses of what might have been surfaced in recent years with him riding an ex-works Cagiva 500 owned by Chris Wilson at the Spa Francorchamps Bikers Classic meeting; with Darren well on the pace among the array of world champions and top Grand Prix riders of yesteryear.

Recalling his 18 Year Racing Career

Darren appreciated the help and assistance from family and sponsors and local businessmen such as Don Taylor who chipped in when the going got tough.

Darren's only injury was a broken collarbone sustained on a 250cc solo machine at Cadwell Park on the approach to the Mountain section.

His favourite circuit was Assen because of the technical approach needed in setting up an outfit and the need to be precise with racing lines. He also enjoyed Mugello for similar reasons, including the atmosphere.

The hardest man to ride against he considered to be Englishman Steve Abbott. He was the last man you would want in a last lap situation, never knowing which side he would attempt a passing manoeuvre, but you knew he would make one even of it meant ending up in the gravel trap.

The Dixon family pictured at the beginning of the 1990s.

The Family Business

As *Sidecar Champions Since 1923* was being written, Darren was fully in charge of the family business Coombe Valley Motorcycles, and when many of his customers tell stories of their own exploits they are blissfully unaware of just what he achieved on two and three wheels. Such is the nature of the man, he will not enlighten them. Darren's daughter Kelly works in the business, son Kieran had a brief spell at Supermoto, and son Jake is showing promise at solo road racing on an Aprillia RS125 in the Superteen Series.

CHAPTER 26

THE MODERN ERA

Introduction

Prior to 1977, racing sidecars were similar to road-going machines. A traditional racing outfit was essentially a road-going motorcycle outfit without road equipment, lowered suspension and streamlining, plus of course more specialised, highly tuned engine and racing equipment such as tyres, suspension and the like. Both the battery and fuel tank would be positioned either between the motorcycle and the sidecar, or on the sidecar platform. Over time the sub-frame, clamps, struts, sidecar chassis etc would merge with the motorcycle main-frame and form a single unit. But essentially the racing outfit was still a variant of the road-going outfit in principle.

In 1977, that year's champion George O'Dell used a hub-centre steering sidecar, the Seymaz, for at least part of the season; and a conventional Windle design for other races counting towards the Championship.

Then in 1978 Rolf Biland won the Championship using a sidecar called the BEO – which was essentially a rear-engined trike. Next, for 1979 to keep up with technical developments the FIM split the Championship into two: one for conventional sidecars B–2–A, another for prototypes, B–2–B. The latter Championship was won by Bruno Holzer using a LCR (Louis Christian Racing) which made the switch from riding into the act of driving (as in a car), including sitting on a drivers seat and using foot pedals and a steering wheel. Neither the BEO nor the LCR required participation from the passenger. The former required the 'passenger' to sit on a seat, whereas the latter only needed the passenger to lay flat down on the passenger platform.

Due to the huge cost of this technology, the non-active participation of the passenger, and the fact that sidecars would eventually become entirely divorced from motorcycles, the FIM was prompted to take action in 1980 and ban the use of prototypes.

Then in 1981 the sport's governing body reversed its decision due to protests from certain competitors, and allowed prototypes back in. However, the FIM and competitors eventually reached a compromise. The rules now stating: 'A sidecar must be a vehicle that is driven only by a single rear wheel, the "rider" must use a motorcycle handlebar, not a steering wheel, to steer, and there must be an active participation from the

Dave Molyneux

A John Mushet photograph of Dave Molyneux and passenger Patrick Farrance at Oliver's Mount, Scarborough, 18 April 2010.

Dave Molyneux was born on 21 November 1963 in Douglas, Isle of Man. And as this book was being written in spring 2010, had racked up 14 Isle of Man TT victories, more than any other Sidecar TT competitor. He was also joint-third on the all-time list, with legendary solo racer Mike Hailwood. His first race was at Jurby, Isle of Man in 1980.

Moly, as he is generally known, set the fastest Sidecar race time for the 37.73-mile (60.70km) Snaefell Mountain course in the 2005 TT, in a time of 19 minutes 6.39 seconds, an average speed of 114.91mph (184.89km/h) for the three-lap distance.

Up to the beginning of 2010, Moly had contested 24 TT races (1985–2000, 2002–). And his first TT victory came in the 1989 Sidecar TT Race A. His most serious accident in the event came when Dave and passenger Craig Hallum crashed during Thursday afternoon practice session for the 2006 Isle of Man TT races at Rhencullen, after their outfit experienced what was described by the internet website Wikipedia as: 'A 145 mph [233 km/h] Donald Campbell bluebird-style flip.'

In the ensuing crash, the racing sidecar outfit was destroyed after fire broke out from the wreckage. Dave was thus unable to compete in the 2006 TT due to injuries sustained. He is also a builder of road-racing sidecars under the label DMR (Dave Molyneux Racing), and has supplied outfits to several other TT winners, including 10-time winner Rob Fisher and 2006 double-winner Nick Crowe.

In 2007 Dave competed in Superside, the World Championship series for sidecars, on a Suzuki-powered Windle and at the Isle of Man TT on a Honda-engined DMR. In both cases the passenger was Rick Long. Moly won both the 2007 Sidecar TT events, races A and B. this made him the equal third-most-successful Isle of Man TT competitor of all time, the others being all solo stars: John McGuiness, Joey Dunlop and Mike Hailwood.

Dave Molyneux with his
HM Plant Honda outfit,
Isle of Man TT, 2007.

During 2008 Dave Molyneux again competed in the Superside series using Suzuki GSXR 1000 power, but mounted in an LCR chassis with passenger Dan Sayle (this chassis was first raced by Dave for the initial rounds of the 2007 season). In the 2008 TT he raced a Suzuki GSXR 600 powered DMR F2 outfit with experienced TT passenger Andy Smith, thus moving away from a Honda engine at this event for the first time in many years. Then, in 2009, Moly won the TT Sidecar Race A, with the 600 DMR Suzuki, at an average speed of 115.132 mph (185.247 km/h).

passenger.' The only ban still existing today is that the use of trikes or cyclecars is strictly out.

The 1981 rules remain largely unchanged to the present day, with the exception that during the late 1990s the FIM finally allowed the use of car-type suspension for the front wheel, such as the wishbone type. Sidecars that are outside the technical rules can still compete in racing events, but are not able to score points counting towards the Championship or record their positions officially.

Superside

Today, the sidecars raced in the World Superside series (launched in 2001) are extremely sophisticated, modern hi-tech pieces of engineering, related to motorcycles only by the engines they use. The chassis is purpose-built and owe more to an open-wheel racing car technology and the tyres are wide and have a flat profile. These are sometimes referred to as 'worms' or 'Formula 1'. The basic design has remained largely unchanged since 1981.

Klaus Klaffenböck

The 2001 World Sidecar Champion was the Austrian Klaus Klaffenböck, partnered by fellow countryman Christian Parzer, driving an LCR-Suzuki GSX-R 1000 outfit. Klaus was born on 26 July 1968 at Peuerback; Christian on 22 August 1962 in Wels.

'Klaffi', as he is widely known, began racing in 1988 in the German National Championship and road racing in upper Austria.

The following year, 1989, Klaus and Christian made their debut in the European Sidecar Championship series at Most in Czechoslovakia.

In 1990 the pair became German National Champions and once again contested the European series.

1992 A Year of Promise
1992 was the year of promise. Not only did they gain their first podium finish in the World Championship series, in the Dutch TT at Assen, but also came third in the world rankings. Later that year Klaffi and Christian won the Austrian Sportsmen of the Year Award.

The following year, 1993, the pair repeated their third-place finish in the World Championship series.

A New Sponsor
The year 1994 saw the Austrian team gain a new sponsor in the shape of the KM concern, this was followed by sixth in the world rankings; 1995 they were seventh, followed by sixth in 1996. Then, in 1997, Klaffi and Christian gained third.

A Change Of Passenger
Not only did 1998 see a change of passenger, with the Swiss Adolf Hänni, but a leap in performance with Klaffi piloting his machine to runner-up in the World Championship (to British pairing of Steve Webster and David James).

1999 and 2000 saw Klaffi and Adolf finish second each year – to Webster/James and Webster/Paul Woodhead respectively.

Christian Returns And the Championship Is won
2001 saw not only Christian Parzer return as passenger, but this coincided with the re-united pair winning the World Championship! A great result for the two men who had also been close friends. This success was also to mark

the beginning of Team Klaffenböck as sponsors the following year; not only this, but in the solos rather than sidecars.

The Super Sport Team

Team Klaffenböck riders in the World Super Sport Championship series in 2002 comprised Kevin Curtain and Christian Zaiser; a third member, Robert Ulm, joined the team at Oschersleben. After an impressive debut season which saw the team finish third in the world rankings, Team 'Klaffi' was told that it would get official Honda backing for the 2003 season.

As far as Klaffi's own sidecar racing activities were concerned, he and Christian Parzer again put in a strong performance, finishing the year third in the world rankings.

2003

The Honda-support Super Sport solo team saw Robert Ulm joined by the Italian Scalvini for three races, then he left to be replaced by Frenchman Sebastian Charpentier; the latter finishing seventh in the World Championship.

But the sidecar part of Team Klaffenböck did much better, securing an excellent second place in the World Championship (behind Steve Webster/Paul Woodhead). In 10 races Klaffi and Christian took no fewer than nine podium finishes.

2004 And a TT Debut

Sebastian Charpentier took fourth in the World Super Sport rankings, while newcomer Max Neukirchner was ninth, winning the 'Rookie of the Year Award'.

As for Klaffi and Christian, they had quit the Grand Prix scene at the end of 2003, and taken a different route – the Isle of Man TT. And the TT was something Klaus Klaffenböck was to embrace with real enthusiasm, later saying his most exciting moment was 'each foot of the Isle of Man.' That first year was very much one for learning the ultra-demanding 37.73-mile (60.70km) Mountain course. As a seasoned campaigner, Klaffi respected the demanding and difficult, to say nothing of the dangers, that this venue posed to competitors. Even so, he felt he wanted to compete and eventually conquer this, the most difficult of all racing circuits.

2005 Superbikes

2005 marked the debut for Team 'Klaffi' in the Superbike World Championship series; Italian star Frankie Chilli finishing the year 10th, Max

The 2001 world champion, Austrian Klaus Klaffenböck, pictured here during the 2007 Isle of Man TT with his Honda outfit.

Neukirchner 12th. In the Super Sport series the Finn Tata Lauslehto came home 10th.

In the Isle of Man TT Klaffi and Christian were eighth in the first race, but in race two suffered a retirement thanks to a flat battery.

A First Superbike Victory

Then in 2006 came Team Klaffenböck's first Superbike victory at world level, with new signing Alex Barros taking a victory – plus no fewer than five podiums. This saw the Brazilian ex-Grand Prix star finish sixth in the Championship table.

2006 also marked the team's entry into the ranks of TT solo racing in the shape of Irishman Martin Finnegan who was fourth in the TT Superbike race and was sixth and seventh in the two TT Super Sport races.

Klaffi and Christian on their six-hundred F2 Honda LCR outfit were second fastest in practice, set their best-ever Isle of Man lap times, but were beset by problems in both races and retired in both.

TT Only

2007 marked a switch to TT racing only in both solos and sidecars. Martin Finnegan again finished fourth in the TT Superbike race, but in the Super Sport he broke a footrest and eventually finished 13th.

Klaffi and Christian were second fastest in qualifying at the Centenary TT to mark 100 years from the first event which had been staged back in 1907. Their average speed was 111.83mph (180km/h), but after this highly promising start they were destined to retire in both races.

Klaffenböck again, this time taking part in the 2008 TT with the Manx Gas/Padgetts 600cc Honda machine.

2008 & 2009

In 2008, after coming fifth in the Isle of Man TT, Christian Parzer was banned from racing, following his arrest for allegedly drug trafficking. Klaffi stated that he had distanced himself from the situation and: 'I don't have anything to do with it – privately I have no contact with him' (*Austrian Times*, 1 July 2008).

The following year, 2009, saw Klaffi and new passenger, local Isle of Man boy Darren Hope, return to the Island; unfortunately forced to retire after lying seventh on lap one.

The 2010 TT, 10 June at Ballaugh Bridge. Klaus Klaffenböck and Dan Sayle in the Sidecar race B which they went on to win. (© Courtesy of John Mushet)

2010 TT Success at Last

And so we come to the 2010 Isle of Man TT. During June, just as *Sidecar Champions Since 1923* was being completed, Klaus Klaffenböck at last achieved his dream of a TT victory. But just like buses, it was not just one, but two! With another new passenger, Dan Sayle, in the chair. When interviewed after the races, Klaffi was delighted to have won in the Island. It appeared to the author that it really meant more to him than even his 2001 World Championship!

For their 2010 double TT victories, Klaffi and Dan used their Honda CBR 600RR-engined LCR outfit, with backing from the Padgetts/Manx Gas Racing Team.

Back home in Austria Klaffi and his wife Simone have twins, Victoria and Katharini.

Steve Abbott

The 2002 world champion, Steve Abbott, was born on 16 February 1955, the only child of Les and Marjorie Abbott. Les was a horse and general scrap dealer from Wessington, Derbyshire.

The family moved around quite a lot in Steve's early years due to his father's business commitments. In 1960 Les started a scrap metal business in Pye Bridge, Derbyshire and Steve went to school locally in Somercotes and later in Alfreton. Never a keen student, Steve began working for the family business in 1970 when he left school at the age of 15.

Early Interest

Steve always had a keen interest in motorcycles from an early age and bought his first road bike at the age of 16, a BSA 250 C15, progressing quickly on to a Triumph Bonneville 650, Triumph Trident 750 and 750 Honda. Along with his good friend Shaun Smith he regularly attended road race meetings and travelled to the Isle of Man TT. On weekends when there were no road race meetings to attend Steve and another good friend 'Mad Frank' usually spent Sunday morning at the 'White Post' transport café on the A614 near Mansfield, this was a well known meeting point for the biking fraternity and provided ideal viewing for the impromptu 'Races' that were held between roundabouts on this stretch of road, much to the dismay of the local constabulary. This passion for speed inevitably ended in disaster and a spell in Mansfield General Hospital with a broken shoulder and other more minor injuries.

At this point his father suggested that if he was so good on a motorcycle he should spare his mothers nerves waiting for him to return home every night and prove himself with the big boys on the race track where everyone would at least hopefully be travelling in the same direction. In return for a promise never to ride road bikes again his father offered financial help to begin his racing career. Shaun was also interested and the pair sold their road bikes, pooled their resources and with Les' help a sidecar racing team was born.

Their First Outfit
Their first outfit was a 750 BSA which was bought in pieces, and the winter of 1976–77 was spent rebuilding and preparing for the first race meeting which was at Cadwell Park on 6 March 1977 and resulted in a respectable finish in fifth place. As the pair gained experience their ageing BSA was replaced halfway through the 1977 season with an Imp powered outfit which rewarded them with their first win at Cadwell Park later that year. The outfit was upgraded with a new Shelbourne chassis during the winter of 1977 and was campaigned for the next two years, achieving many wins at Cadwell Park, Mallory Park and Darley Moor. In 1979 the pair won the Cadwell Park 'All Wins' series scoring 18 victories. They also took part in the Southern 100 road races in the Isle of Man.

The Windle Yamaha
1980, with further financial assistance from Les, saw the purchase of a 750 Windle Yamaha outfit. This enabled the pair to step up to National and

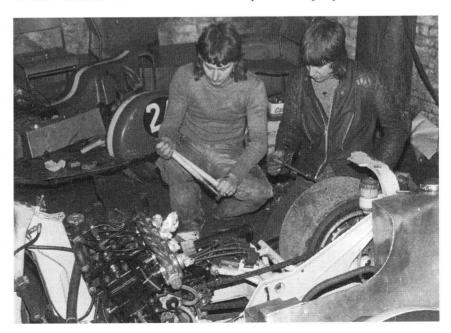

Steve Abbott pictured in 1980 along with his good friend Shaun Smith. In the foreground Windle/Yamaha TZ750, with ancient BSA in the background. As Steve says himself 'Not very professional eh?'.

International races and their success earned them their first Grand Prix entry at the British GP at Silverstone. This was a pivotal year for Steve and Shaun as it placed them firmly at the top level of sidecar racing in the UK and brought their first big sponsorship deal with Rae Hamilton of Hamilton Motorcycles, Team Ham-Yam Racing who had sponsored the late Mac Hobson.

1981 saw their first trip to the Isle of Man TT where they ran out of petrol on the Mountain on the last lap of the first leg. Determined not to give in they 'persuaded' a bemused spectator to 'donate' some fuel and sump oil from his beloved machine and this enabled them to complete the course in 38th place. The second leg was completed in a very respectable seventh place – with an extra gallon of petrol on board!

A European Championship Campaign

1982 was devoted to a full European Championship campaign with wins at Mugello, Italy; Assen, Holland; and Donington Park. A retirement at Hockenheim in Germany allowed Mick Barton and Nick Cutmore to claim the Championship by a few points. The pair also competed in six Grand Prix and scored their first ever GP rostrum at the British GP at Silverstone. The season was sadly overshadowed by the untimely loss of Jock Taylor at Imatra, Finland.

1983 saw the first full GP season with a rear engined Seymaz outfit, with the Ham Yam sponsorship. A crash at the opening GP in Le Mans, France resulted in two broken vertebrae for Steve and several broken bones for Shaun who was sidelined for several meetings and was replaced by Vince Biggs and Donny Williams. The season was generally fruitless apart from meeting the two stand-in passengers who remain Steve and Shaun's firm friends to this day.

A Much Greater Degree of Success

1984 saw a much greater degree of success with a first and third place at the Isle of Man TT resulting in overall first placing on a Windle TZ 700 Yamaha and Steve's first British Championship title using his Grand Prix machine 500cc Seymaz Yamaha.

The following seasons were spent concentrating on World Championship GPs and other International meetings. They witnessed changes in sponsorship support with two years from Padgetts of Batley, and a change in chassis from Seymaz to Windle and then finally to the Swiss built LCR chassis used from 1989–92 provided by local sponsor and friend John Hardwick of Mitregate Steel Fabrications, gaining many podium places and lap records.

Steve and Shaun Smith with the 500cc Seymaz/Yamaha two-stroke in 1985.

Terry Windle

In 1992 a deal was struck with the chassis constructor Terry Windle for the two to work together on the development of a new chassis incorporating Steve's racing experience and ideas with Terry's vast constructors experience and engineering skills. This partnership and development continued until the end of the 2002 season.

The long standing partnership of Steve and Shaun ended on a high in 1992 with a British Championship round race win at Brands Hatch. Shaun retired due to family commitments and the pair still remain best of friends.

In 1993 Julian Tailford joined the team as passenger and the successful pair took the British Championship title for two years in 1994 and 1995. In 1996 Jamie Biggs was recruited and remained with Steve until they both retired in 2003.

A Change of Regulations

The end of the nineties saw a move towards a change in the regulations which would ban the 500cc two-stroke engines from the start of the 2000 season. Many of the leading teams had already moved to the larger 1200cc four-stroke Suzuki and other road based engines. Steve had reservations about the new regulations and had considered retiring from the sport at the end of 1999 when the new regulations came into force, as he perceived it to be a move away from racing in its purer form.

A First GP Victory

Their first, long-awaited GP win came in front of a home crowd at Donington Park in May 1999. The fact that this was his local circuit and was witnessed by his wife (Angie) and two children (Liam and Lauren) and many good friends made the moment very emotional for all, after 19 years of racing at the top level of the sport, but never having stood on the top step of the GP rostrum. This barrier having been broken the pair achieved their second GP win at Brands Hatch later on that year, this was the last race to be won with a 500cc two-stroke machine.

This taste of real success led to some soul searching regarding his decision to retire. The race wins were a result of a whole team effort, with everyone involved playing an equally significant role, everyone was keen to continue, with sponsorship in place from Zlacto Grebensek – (Ringo Innentursysteme) and Maxsym and so the change to the four-stroke engine was made. However, Steve's stubborn streak made him unable to follow the rest of the crowd to a 1200cc machine which he felt was too heavy and cumbersome, so he compromised with the use of a 1000cc FZR Yamaha engine which was upsized to 1080cc by using different pistons and a longer crank shaft. Steve felt that, although this was not as powerful, it was lighter and lower and therefore a better package overall within the Windle chassis.

Securing the 2002 World Title

All doubts were finally dispelled with some good results and rostrum placings over the coming seasons, which culminated in the securing of the 2002 World

Steve (with Jamie Biggs), 2002 world champions, 1080cc Windle/Yamaha, Kylami, South Africa, 7 April 2002.

Steve Abbott with wife Angie and children Liam and Lauren.

Championship crown with five rostrum placings and three wins at Valencia, Spain; Silverstone, UK; and Misano, Italy, and a final total of 151 points.

The Championship was hotly contested with Jorg (son of Rolf) Steinhausen/Trevor Hopkinson who ended the season with the same number of points but fewer wins, giving the title to Steve and Jamie. The determination of 25 years had finally paid off. This determination was best illustrated at the GP held in Lausitzring that year when the pair were leading the race by a few seconds on the final lap; the engine died with a flat battery and coasted to a halt 500m from the finish. The pair quickly jumped off the machine and pushed uphill to the finish line securing 11th place and five vital points which proved crucial in securing the title.

Hanging up His Leathers

At the end of the 2003 season after a long and successful racing career, Steve decided to hang up his leathers and the pair retired from the sport, but after only a year away they were approached to contest the Australian Championship. They achieved 12 wins from 12 starts and broke lap records at Phillip Island, Eastern Creek, Adelaide and Barbagallo (Perth), securing the Australian Championship title.

Achievements

World Champion 2002
British Champion 1984, 1994, 1995
Australian Champion 2005
Isle of Man TT winner 1984
World Championship races 186
World Championship race wins 6
World Championship rostrums 35

Although retired, Steve is still heavily involved in sidecar racing, as a key team member of Birchall Racing with Ben and Tom Birchall, 2009 world champions, and mentor to his son Liam who has also just started racing a 350cc two-stroke sidecar machine with passenger Calum Lawson.

Steve would like to take this opportunity to thank all the helpers and sponsors who have contributed financially and otherwise throughout the years. They are far too numerous to list individually, but you all know who you are, and this success was not just Steve's but everyone who helped along the way.

Tim Reeves

Kentish man Tim (Timothy Michael) Reeves (born 28 August 1972) and so far has claimed the World Championship title on three occasions: 2005, 2006 and 2007, passengered on the first two occasions by his younger brother Tristan and in 2007 by Patrick Farrance.

A Family Affair

Following in his father's footsteps (Brian having been a leading British Championship competitor), Tim started his senior level racing involvement as a passenger in 1990, before moving over to driver position in 1999. His debut victory came at Brands Hatch in that year, with brother Tristan in the chair.

In 2002 the brothers finished runners-up in the British Championship, moving up to the World Championship series the following season. Their

Tim Reeves in 1999 at Brands Hatch with brother Tristan. The machine is the ex-Steve Abbott LCR Krauser 500. This was Tim's first year and first outfit. (© Courtesy of John Mushet)

Sachsenring 2005, having just won the world title. From left to right: Tim, father Brian, Tristan, Sean Ryde and Joel Back.
(© Courtesy of John Mushet)

best achievement during 2003 was at the Imola round of the World Championship where Tim and Tristan came sixth after inclusion as a 'wild card' entry.

After a year with little other success at the highest level, things changed during 2004 with a first GP podium position, a sign of things to come.

As an interesting aside, it is worth commenting that Tim and Tristan's sisters Tanya and Tara are also involved with the sidecar racing world, being part of a cheerleading team providing entertainment for fans before races.

World Superside Champion

As well as dominating the World Superside Championship series and claiming his first title on his LCR Suzuki, in 2005 Tim was voted BBC South East Sports Personality of the Year.

Retaining the Title

2006 proved to be a spectacular year for Tim, still passengered by brother Tristan.

Defence of their title started at Schleiz, Germany, where the duo had mixed success with their LCR Suzuki. A retirement with a broken fairing mounting in the Match race was followed by runner-up spot in the Sprint. However, fortunes changed in the Gold race, when a decision to use wet front and intermediate side and rear tyres for a wet start allowed a sufficient lead to be built up before the conditions became dry and their opposition began to close on, although not catch, the Reeves pairing.

This solid start provided an excellent foundation for the season ahead. Following seven wins, two second places, one third, one fourth and a sixth in the first 12 rounds, a victory at Rijeka, Croatia, would secure the title with three rounds to spare.

Qualifying was 'a bit of a lottery' with both dry and wet sessions, and the Reeves outfit slowed by a blistered tyre failing to take pole position. However, after winning both heat and semi-final races, Tim went on to win the final from the Finn Pekka Päivärinta (his nearest rival in the title chase) by some three seconds.

The Sprint race came next, which the Kent-based team won. This left Tim and Tristan needing only a third place behind Päivärinta to take enough points to claim the title. As the race unfolded, Tim was content to sit back in second place, conserving his tyres for a last lap challenge as he: 'Could see that Päivärinta was having tyre problems and I decided to go for the win.' Continuing: 'I wanted to clinch the title on a winning note and it worked out just fine. We are over the moon with the result and are looking forward to racing in the final rounds with no pressure, we can just go out there and enjoy our racing.'

Donington Day of Champions

Not all sidecar activity involved racing. For example, as he had done for several years, Tim took his outfit to the annual Day of Champions charity fundraiser held at Donington Park prior to the British Grand Prix. The World Championship-winning outfit was available for taxi rides at a £30 donation for a two-lap trip around the 2.5-mile Midlands circuit – sidecar rides making a total of £4,000 towards the Riders for Health charity. Tim commenting: 'We have taken part in this fund-raising event for a few years now…we are only permitted to be on circuit for 1½ hours, which is a shame, we had to turn people away…maybe they will give us an extra half hour next year!'

The brothers then rounded off their successful year by winning the Sidecar Burn Up Trophy for the fourth time at a wet and windy Lydden Hill at the end of October 2006.

2007

The 2007 title defence saw a new passenger in the chair of the LCR Suzuki outfit: Patrick Farrance replacing Tristan.

The pair achieved five World Superside wins to claim the title once more. In addition Tim became British F1 champion, and was voted BBC South East Sports Personality of the Year for the second time.

Knockhill circuit in Fife, Scotland, 14 August 2010. Tim Reeves and Gregory Cluze on their way to winning one of the three legs in the Jock Taylor Memorial Trophy. They went on to win all three legs and the trophy.
(© Courtesy of John Mushet)

Moving on

Having conquered the world on three occasions, Tim took up a new challenge in 2008: the Isle of Man TT. His debut race saw him follow in the footsteps of Jock Taylor by becoming the first newcomer in 30 years to gain a podium place (third in the opening three-lap race of the 37.73-mile/60.70km Mountain circuit). The second race proved slightly less successful, although still an excellent debut with sixth place and a lap time of 112.031mph (194.73km/h).

Three-times world champion (2005, 2006 and 2007) Tim Reeves with new for 2010 passenger Frenchman Gregory Cluze.
(© Courtesy of John Mushet)

The same year Tim started the World Superside Championship with maximum points at Donington, he also scored a further three victories in subsequent in World Superside rounds (giving him second place overall).

2009

Returning to the Isle of Man, 2009 saw Tim achieve fourth place in the solitary Sidecar TT race, in the process setting a new personal best lap of 112.896mph (181.64km/h). In addition, the pairing of Reeves and Farrance claimed three victories in the British F2 Championship.

2010

This TT result was followed up in 2010 by a lowly 16th position with new partner Dipash Chauhan, and partnered in the World Championship series by Gregory Cluze; the pairing losing the Championship by only six points.

Pekka Päivärinta

The 2008 and 2010 world champion, Finnish star Pekka Päivärinta won his homeland's Sidecar Championship in 1994, 1998, 1999 and 2003. And from these early successes began his drive to World Championship status when he finished fourth in the overall Championship standings in 2005, and at the same time racked up three race victories.

Runner-up in 2006

But the big breakthrough was to come in 2006, when together with fellow-countryman Aki Aalto (and later Timo Karttiala), Pekka claimed runner-up spot behind Englishman Tim Reeves, the Finnish team scoring three victories.

A repeat performance (again to Tim Reeves) was secured in 2007, but this time with Timo Karttiala exclusively as passenger.

World Champions

Then in 2008 came the big year for Pekka and Timo, when they not only became world champions, but were also the first to achieve this honour for their country.

Pekka Päivärinta and Timo Karttiala (Team Suzuki Finland) secured the title with a trio of victories, the first of these coming on Sunday 25 May at Donington Park, near Derby, the scene of the British round of the FIM Superside World Championship.

The 2008 and 2010 world champion, Finnish star Pekka Päväirinta at the British Grand Prix at Donington Park in 2008, which he won in appalling conditions.

(© Courtesy of John Mushet)

Donington Park Sets the Scene

The Team Suzuki Finland pairing of Pekka and Timo, by now nicknamed the 'sliding Finns', impressed at Donington in the 20-lap race in what can only be described as difficult weather conditions of rain and wind. We all know how good Finnish drivers have been over the years in the World Rally Car Championships. And the same could be said of how Pekka and Timo coped at Donington that day in May 2008.

Making a decent start from their third grid position on the front row, the Finnish pairing were fourth into the first corner. The pole setters, Sebastien Delannoy and Gregory Cluze suffered a second corner collision with the outfit of the three-time champion Tim Reeves with passenger Patrick Farrance; this saw Cluze tumble out of their machine; leaving Reeves in front and another British team (Richard Gatt and Paul Randell) in second and the Finns third. However, very soon Pekka and Timo were up to second and chasing the Reeves machine.

As Pekka was later to recall: 'It was difficult to reach Reeves as the visibility of the driver was almost zero due to the water jets from Reeves' wheels spraying on the visor of my helmet.' And this same spray prevented passenger Timo Karttiala's visibility even more so. So much, in fact, that Timo's ability to anticipate his driver's actions was making things exceedingly difficult.

First Päivärinta and Karttiala attempted to overtake Reeves and Ferrance side by side a couple of times; however, eventually the Finns were successful on the 16th lap. After that they managed to pull out a six-second lead in the remaining four laps. Just for the record, Pekka put in his best lap time (the fastest in the race) on the final circuit.

The Donington Park result not only got Pekka Päivärinta's 2008 Championship-winning year under way, but also goes a long way in explaining why he has been such a serious contender in the world sidecar Championship series over the last few years. However difficult the conditions, Pekka has shown he is more than capable of matching the best drivers around.

Runner-up in 2009

For the 2009 season Pekka switched passengers, his new one being the highly experienced Swiss Adolf Hänni, who had previously passengered for Steve Webster, Klaus Klaffenböck and Markus Schlosser among others.

With Pekka, Adolf Hänni was to add a second in the standings during 2009 (to the Birchall brothers) to add to second in 1994 (Steve Webster), runner-up 1998–2000 (Klaus Klaffenböck), third 2003 (Mike Roscher), third 2007 (Markus Schlosser) and fifth 2008 (Markus Schlosser).

Added to these results, Adolf Hänni had also been German IDM Champion in 2007 with Schlosser.

2010

Pekka Päivärinta and Adolf Hänni won the first round of the FIM Sidecar World Championship held on Saturday 17 April 2010 at Le Mans in France, with the 2009 Champions the Birchall brothers some 3.3 seconds behind.

The machine they used was, as in the case with so many others over the years, designed and built by LCR (Louis Christian Racing). The material of the monocoque chassis being aircraft aluminium glued and riveted. The fairings being manufactured from carbon-Kevlar. A GSX-R1000 Suzuki four cylinder engine put out some 210bhp, with maximum speed quoted by the Päivärinta team as 187mph (300km/h).

There seemed little doubt that the name Pekka Päivärinta would grace the very pinnacle of the sidecar world with another Championship title in the very near future; and he did just that taking the 2010 title.

Ben Birchall

Hailing from Mansfield, Nottinghamshire, the 2009 world champion Ben Birchall was born on 21 January 1977. His passenger was his younger brother Tom (born 23 December 1986). And in fact, at the time of writing *Sidecar Champions Since 1923* Tom was the youngest-ever passenger in the history, at 22 years and 257 days, to be crowned champion.

Shortly after winning the world title, the following is how Ben summed up his younger brother's involvement: 'That really put the icing on the cake, and Tom is simply brilliant, the best in the world. His attitude is superb on and off the bike. He is my brother and my best mate – the job works perfectly between us.'

Team Work

After winning the title Dave Fern of *Bike Sport News* got things absolutely spot-on when he said: 'Part of the secret of success for this homely team is that it cuts its cloth according to its means and enjoys the business of racing to the full, and rightly they are being feted back home in the East Midlands with celebratory parties, meetings and television.' Ben commenting: 'Everywhere we have been people have made a big fuss of us.'

Bike Sport News again, replying to Ben said: 'So it should be, it is several years now since Ben took the brave step of re-mortgaging his house to buy a new outfit to further his racing ambitions.'

Early Days

Ben and Tom came from a motorcycling family, their great grandfather having had a Norton 16H five-hundred with Swallow sidecar, grandfather had a Panther model 100 (a 600cc twin-port single); while their father (a friend of the author's) had a Honda CB 750 and Squire sidecar.

From a young age both Ben and Tom (the oldest and youngest of four brothers) were encouraged to become involved with motorcycles. Their father told the author: 'I bought Ben his first motorcycle – a Honda Z50 – when he was five years old, we still have that Honda today, all four of the boys rode it at various times.' And he continued: 'Tom rode miles on that Z50. In addition he would travel in the Squire sidecar – he used to lean out on left-hand bends and over the pillion seat of the Honda 750 for right-handers – right from being a small boy of about 10 or 11 years old. We always went to race meetings and the Isle of Man TT for our annual holidays. I don't think Tom has missed a TT since being about four months old.'

Birchall senior continued: 'We always camped as a family at the TT, I made a point of taking them down to the paddock, even leaving Ben with a sidecar crew for the day (aged 10). He loved it, and it wasn't long before he became friends to a lot of the sidecar teams and their families; they are a very friendly and family oriented bunch.'

Other Pursuits

At school Ben was a good cross country runner, but had no interest in any other sport except motorcycle racing. Tom was also an excellent cross country runner, but also played rugby while at school.

As Ben told *Bike Sport News* after winning the title on 2009: 'Dad was always interested, a keen fan of racing and he took us along. I became involved, helping doing a bit of spannering for riders. I couldn't afford a bike, but then I was asked to be a passenger to Dave Holden, and that was how my racing began.'

The Track Debut

Ben's track debut came in 1998, but it was to be another five years before he became a driver in 2003. It should also be pointed out that from 1999–2002, as a passenger, he had consecutive top three finishes in overall standings of the F1 British Sidecar Championship.

Then in his first season, in 2003, as a driver took the 'Rookie of the Year Award' and was also joint fourth overall in the MRO British Sidecar Championship. At first he was passengered by Jamie Winn and sponsored by his employer, Richards Garage of Sutton-in-Ashfield.

Having gained earlier entry than normal into the British Championship series because of the previous record as a passenger, Ben was fortunate enough to receive help from the 2002 world champion Steve Abbott. And Steve is still involved with Ben in 2011.

As for Tom, in 2003, then aged 16, he started the season racing in the British Formula 2 series with a 350cc Yamaha-engined outfit, gaining a first place at Darley Moor. Later he joined Ben as passenger in that year's Formula 1 series.

2004 saw Ben and Tom contest the Eastern Airways Sidecar Championship, gaining a fourth place at the Dutch round at Assen.

F1 British Championship 2005

In the 2005 F1 British Championship Ben and Tom finished second overall, with two wins, 12 podiums and two lap records. They also won the prestigious Bill Boddice Challenge Trophy.

As a wild-card entry they also gained a ninth place at Assen in the FIM World Superside Championship. Finally, the Mansfield brothers were awarded the Ewan Chambers Award for Contribution to Sidecar Racing for that year.

2006 saw Ben and Tom finish 13th overall in the FIM World Superside Championship.

2007 – The Year of the Breakthrough

2007 was the year of the brothers' breakthrough into the top flight, finishing fifth in the World Championships, including second at Salzburgring, second at Rijeka and another second and new lap record at Le Mans. They also won the Jock Taylor Memorial Trophy, Jim Silver Memorial Trophy, Sunflower Trophy (Bishopscourt, Northern Ireland) and Marty Murphy Memorial Trophy (also at Bishopscourt).

2008 And A First Grand Prix Victory

2008 not only saw Ben and Tom Birchall finish third in the World Championship series, but perhaps even more noteworthy was the brother's first Grand Prix victory, at Rijeka, Croatia on 17 August that year. Besides this they had a third in the Sprint race at Rijeka, two third places at Sachsenring, fourth Assen, fourth Le Mans and fourth Donington Park. Besides their GP successes, they also had four wins and set a new outright lap record at the Derby Phoenix Club races at Cadwell Park.

The World Championship Year

And so to 2009 and the FIM World Superside Championship title. This was gained as follows:

Round 1	8–10 May	Schleiz, Germany	2nd
Round 2	22–24 July	Abacete, Spain	3rd, fastest lap
Round 3	17–19 July	Sachsenring, Germany	1st, fastest lap
Round 4	21–23 August	Rijeka, Croatia	1st
Round 5	4–6 September	Le Mans	2nd

Ben and Tom Birchall, the 2009 world champions.
(© Courtesy of John Mushet)

Ben and Tom (1) at
Pembrey, South Wales in
the first round of the 2010
British Formula 1
Championship Series.
(© Courtesy of John Mushet)

The Championship points table read as follows:

Birchall brothers, 151

Pekka Päivärinta/Adolf Hänni, 142

Tim Reeves/Tristan Reeves, 102

The Birchall's 2009 winning machine (main sponsor Mitchells of Mansfield), tuned by JEBS Performance Engineering, was a fuel-injected Suzuki 1000-powered LCR with a monocoque aircraft aluminium chassis and carbon-fibre bodywork.

In 2010 the Birchall brothers defended their Championship, but could only finish third behind the winner Pekka Päivärinta and runner-up Tim Reeves. However, they were leading the title hunt in the early stages, only to suffer a major accident.

SUMMARY

Since 2005, officials have created a new format in which there are now three types of races. A Championship round can have all three types of races; however, sometimes there can be only one type of race (the Gold Race) in one round, usually when a round is a supporting event to a major meeting, such as Moto GP.

Match Race

Teams are divided into groups and race in very short heat races. Winners are the better placed teams in these heats and will advance to the next round (referred to as semi-finals), until only the best six teams are left for the final heat race. A typical heat race distance is three laps.

Sprint Race

All teams participate in a short race. A typical race distance is 12 laps.

Gold Race

All teams participate in a long race, usually at least twice the distance of the sprint event.

So what of the future? After over six decades of World Championship Sidecar action, one is left wondering just exactly what the future may hold. Perhaps the answer will lie in if and when a major sponsor or commercial body comes forward to project world-class sidecar racing at the same level as say Moto GP, or even Formula 1 car racing.

APPENDICES

World Sidecar Champions

	Driver	Nat	Passenger	Nat
1949	Eric Oliver	GB	Denis Jenkinson	GB
1950	Eric Oliver	GB	Lorenzo Dobelli	IT
1951	Eric Oliver	GB	Lorenzo Dobelli	IT
1952	Cyril Smith	GB	Robert Clements	GB
1953	Eric Oliver	GB	Stanley Dibben	GB
1954	Wilhelm Noll	GER	Fritz Cron	GER
1955	Willi Faust	GER	Karl Remmert	GER
1956	Wilhelm Noll	GER	Fritz Cron	GER
1957	Fritz Hillebrand	GER	Manfred Grünewald	GER
1958	Walter Schneider	GER	Hans Straub	GER
1959	Walter Schneider	GER	Hans Straub	GER
1960	Helmut Fath	GER	Alfred Wohlgemuth	GER
1961	Max Deubel	GER	Emil Hörner	GER
1962	Max Deubel	GER	Emil Hörner	GER
1963	Max Deubel	GER	Emil Hörner	GER
1964	Max Deubel	GER	Emil Hörner	GER
1965	Fritz Scheidegger	CH	John Robinson	GB
1966	Fritz Scheidegger	CH	John Robinson	GB
1967	Klaus Enders	GER	Ralf Engelhart	GER
1968	Helmut Fath	GER	Wolfgang Kalauch	GER
1969	Klaus Enders	GER	Ralf Engelhart	GER
1970	Klaus Enders	GER	Wolfgang Kalauch	GER
1971	Horst Owesle	GER	Peter Rutherford	GB
1972	Klaus Enders	GER	Ralf Engelhart	GER
1973	Klaus Enders	GER	Ralf Engelhart	GER
1974	Klaus Enders	GER	Ralf Engelhart	GER
1975	Rolf Steinhausen	GER	Josef Huber	GER
1976	Rolf Steinhausen	GER	Josef Huber	GER
1977	George O'Dell	GB	Kenny Arthur	GB
1978	Rolf Biland	CH	Kenny Williams	GB
1979 B-2-A	Rolf Biland	CH	Kurt Waltisburg	CH

	Driver	Nat	Passenger	Nat
1979 B-2-B	Bruno Holzer	CH	Charly Meierhans	CH
1980	Jock Taylor	GB	Benji Johansson	SWE
1981	Rolf Biland	CH	Kurt Waltisperg	CH
1982	Werner Schwärzel	GER	Andreas Huber	GER
1983	Rolf Biland	CH	Kurt Waltisperg	CH
1984	Egbert Streuer	NL	Bernard Schneiders	NL
1985	Egbert Streuer	NL	Bernard Schneiders	NL
1986	Egbert Streuer	NL	Bernard Schneiders	NL
1987	Steve Webster	GB	Tony Hewitt	GB
1988	Steve Webster	GB	Tony Hewitt	GB
1989	Steve Webster	GB	Tony Hewitt	GB
1990	Alain Michel	FR	Simon Birchall	GB
1991	Steve Webster	GB	Gavin Simmons	GB
1992	Rolf Biland	CH	Kurt Waltisperg	CH
1993	Rolf Biland	CH	Kurt Waltisperg	CH
1994	Rolf Biland	CH	Kurt Waltisperg	CH
1995	Darren Dixon	GB	Andy Hetherington	GB
1996	Darren Dixon	GB	Andy Hetherington	GB
1997	Steve Webster	GB	David James	GB
1998	Steve Webster	GB	David James	GB
1999	Steve Webster	GB	David James	GB
2000	Steve Webster	GB	Paul Woodhead	GB
2001	Klaus Klaffenböck	AU	Christian Parzer	AU
2002	Steve Abbott	GB	Jamie Biggs	GB
2003	Steve Webster	GB	Paul Woodhead	GB
2004	Steve Webster	GB	Paul Woodhead	GB
2005	Tim Reeves	GB	Tristan Reeves	GB
2006	Tim Reeves	GB	Tristan Reeves	GB
2007	Tim Reeves	GB	Tristan Reeves	GB
2008	Pekka Päivärinta	FIN	Timo Karttiala	FIN
2009	Ben Birchall	GB	Tom Birchall	GB
2010	Pekka Päivärinta	FIN	Adolf Hänni	CH

GB – Great Britain   NL – Holland
IT   – Italy   AU – Austria
GER – Germany   FIN – Finland
CH – Switzerland   FR   – France
SWE – Sweden

Printed in Great Britain
by Amazon